perfection

a memoir of

betrayal and renewal

JULIE METZ

SCRIBE
Melbourne

A NOTE TO MY READERS

I have changed the names (except my own), and other details of persons in this book. I have not changed the name of a certain dog, which suited the animal and my story perfectly. Sometimes real life surprises fiction even in the details. I have, on a few occasions, changed the order of events, where those changes benefit narrative flow without altering a factual telling of the story. Otherwise, all dialogue and events took place as I remember and recount them in these pages.

Scribe Publications Pty Ltd
PO Box 523
Carlton North, Victoria, Australia 3054
Email: info@scribepub.com.au

Published in Australia and New Zealand by Scribe 2009
This edition published by arrangement with Hyperion, USA

My Mother's Wedding Dress by Justine Picardie, copyright 2006 by Justine Picardie. Permission to reprint granted by Bloomsbury USA.

'The Summer Day,' from *New and Selected Poems* by Mary Oliver, copyright 1992 by Mary Oliver. Reproduced with permission of Beacon Press, Boston, MA.

Text design by Susan Walsh
Tulip photo © Susan Walsh 2008
Printed and bound in Australia by Griffin Press. Only wood grown from sustainable regrowth forests is used in the manufacture of paper found in this book.

National Library of Australia
Catalogue-in-Publication data

Metz, Julie, 1959-
Perfection: a memoir of betrayal and renewal

9781921372797 (pbk.)

Marriage; Husband and wife; Adultery; Wives–Biography; Forgiveness.

306.736092

www.scribepublications.com.au

For my Chimwemwe,
I hope this book will give you answers when you are ready to
ask the questions.

And for Clark,
For being loving and kind, just as you promised.

In memory of my mother, who was brave, right to the end.

MY WIFE
From Henry, Valentine's Day, 2002

Your name
A groaning table for my ears' hunger

Your face
A palette of joys for my eyes' old master

A life with you
Enough for my mind's forever

part one

fog

Explaining is where we all get into trouble.

—RICHARD FORD,
The Sportswriter

one
———

January 8–12, 2003

It happened like this: Henry's footsteps on the old wooden floorboards. The toilet flushing. More footsteps, perhaps on the stairs. Silence. Then the thud.

I was working downstairs in my office on a bitterly cold Wednesday afternoon. My work space was an enclosed sunporch off our living room, the small-paned windows on three sides framing a view of the snowy hills across the road. Wrapped in a shawl, wearing fuzzy socks on my chilled feet, I continued studying the project on my computer screen. At forty-three, I had been a graphic designer for nearly twenty years, a freelancer, specializing in cover designs for book publishers. Today's project was a novel about hard-luck cowboys, due yesterday, as always. I stopped fiddling with type design possibilities as I glanced at the computer clock— in an hour I would have to make a dash out to the car to pick up our six-and-a-half-year-old daughter, Liza, just before school let out at 3:10. Henry had been sick in bed all morning. There would be the freezing cold wait and the daily social milling with the other mothers on the school playground, then the quick drive home to finish my work. I'd wear my new sheepskin coat today and feel guilty about its expense on a warmer day. On second thought, the distressed sans serif type worked better with the moody image of a cowboy leaning against a split-rail fence.

Suddenly my brain rewound sharply.

It wasn't a package dropped outside by the UPS guy.

My office phone rang. Instinctively, I answered. The photographer on the line asked me how I liked the images he had e-mailed.

It wasn't the cats knocking groceries off the kitchen counter.

"I can't talk now—something bad is happening." I ended the call abruptly.

The rooms were silent as I ran up the stairs, calling for Henry. Two of our four cats skittered out of my way, their nails clawing the wooden treads. The bedroom was empty. I raced back down the stairs.

I found Henry on his back, spread-eagled on the kitchen floor, his head a few inches from the oven broiler. He was still breathing. His body was silhouetted against the sea blue of the painted floorboards. I imagined a police chalk drawing of the outline of the victim at a crime scene. I was overcome with the feeling that I was in the scene and watching a scene on television—an opening sequence of an episode of *Six Feet Under,* our favorite show that year. Usually some minor character dies in the first five minutes. Henry inhaled with a shallow breath; small dribbles of saliva on his curved lips, the skin on his face now sallow and ashen. He exhaled with a feeble sigh. His eyes flickered half open. I spoke to him to let him know that I was there with him, but for once in our life together he could not speak back.

A long, elastic minute stretched out and snapped: *Is this when people call 911? Or is Henry going to sit up and tell me to stop fussing, like he did yesterday after he passed out? This must be the same thing.*

He came in after taking out the garbage and fell down flat on the floor. The doctor said all the tests were normal—

I called 911. I sat down on the floor next to him, stroking his forehead, watching him breathe. A hissing sound, as spittle pulsed between his lips.

I wish I had a notepad and pencil. Henry would want me to take notes. The EMS guys will come. They'll check him out. He'll be fine. He'll be telling people about his near death at our next dinner party. "The report of my death was an exaggeration" is what he'll say. Everyone will laugh, and I'll feel pathetic for having worried so much. I'm happy to feel pathetic if everything will just please, please turn out okay.

I called 911 again, just to be sure. I called Emily, who lived five minutes away and was usually home at two in the afternoon. Anna was more reliable—I knew she wouldn't freak out, no matter what happened today—but she lived twelve minutes away. Then I called Matthew, Henry's best friend, who lived with his wife in a nearby town.

Every minute will make a difference. The EMS guys will come; they will bring oxygen tanks, defibrillators, and IV bags. All will be well. Emily will help me find a babysitter for Liza, then she will go with me to the hospital, and we'll get there and Henry will be awake, smiling and joking as usual.

I sat back down next to him on the blue floor, stroking the familiar wrinkles, the scar over one eyelid, the small mole at the crest of one cheek.

Inhale. Exhale. A blue gauze curtain passed over him. His skin turned to wax.

"Breathe!" I screamed at him. "Start breathing now!" I pounded him on the chest. He wasn't listening to me. I placed my mouth on his and blew my breath into him; the blue briefly faded into rose like a watercolor wash. But the flush faded back to blue. He was still. The man who for sixteen years had loved me, driven me crazy, fought with me, fed me, made love with me, made a baby with me, exhaled one last breath, the air I had blown into his lungs.

I looked up, distracted by the sound of the sliding porch door, followed by a blast of cold air. The EMS guys had arrived with a gurney and gear and gently hustled me out of the kitchen. Emily followed right after them.

————

You'll know it's bad when they take you to the little waiting room. Emily held my left arm. Her face was pale, her lips still rosy from the cold, her dark bobbed hair peeking from under a familiar blue cloche hat. Matthew sat on my right. Matthew was tall, built like a tree. The sad-eyed young doctor told us it was a pulmonary embolism. A blood clot, formed in the leg, had moved upward and lodged in the lung, causing cardiac arrest. They had tried everything they could to revive him. But.

Everything moved in slow motion as I processed his words. This couldn't be right. He was only forty-four. Whenever we'd watched *Six Feet Under* together, the main characters had made it safely to the next episode. I slid off my chair to the floor and screamed.

"You can lie next to him if you want," Emily said. She was calm, amazingly, looking at Henry's lifeless body on the gurney. "Go ahead, it won't bother me at all."

I climbed up onto the narrow gurney and lay down next to him. He would have wanted me to note every detail for him—the way his chest was still warm, while his arms were already stiff and cold and his fingers were curled and blue. He had a bruise on the left side of his face. It was comforting to rest there with my arm around him, touching him in a familiar way, relieved still to have a companion, even a quiet one.

He had beautiful feet, elegantly articulated toes, like the feet on a Greek statue. I peeled back his shirt to look at the distinctive scar on his chest. A bit of cornhusk had punctured his skin while he was working on a farm as a teenager. The healing wound had formed an inch-long raised keloid that I loved to touch in the dark. I touched the large dark mole on his left shoulder. I felt the scar over his right eye, received when he was a child in a hotel in Honolulu (designed by Frank Lloyd Wright, Henry always added when telling the story), when a window had fallen suddenly out of its molding as he passed under it with his family. All his scars and moles, so well known to me, like stepping-stones marking the way home through a dark wood.

Two nurses came in. "You should go home now and get some rest," one said. She put her hand on my shoulder and squeezed me gently.

Emily took my arm, and we walked down the fluorescent-lit corridors and stepped out into the twilight, inky blue with low-hanging clouds. A flock of black birds rushed up into the sky, their wings moving in unison, a tragic banner.

"I feel like I've been hit by a truck," Henry had joked two weeks before he died. We were on our Christmas vacation, visiting Henry's college friend and his family on Bainbridge Island, off the coast of Seattle. During the short daylight hours under the

continuous gray blanket of northwest cloud cover, the kids played and drank hot chocolate, while we adults planned meals, decorated the holiday tree, and prepared for the arrival of Santa Claus. Henry, who loved all parties but disliked Christmas, watched from the couch.

His quip was familiar to me. When he was sixteen, he had taken a spin on a friend's new motorcycle straight into an oncoming white pickup truck as he came around a tight curve. He loved telling this story, with a new embellishment every time.

"I'm lying there bleeding, with my right leg broken in seven places, the guy is weeping and begging me not to die. I had to calm the guy down so he'd go get help from the neighbor." Henry's leg had been repaired, but he always had some pain and swallowed daily doses of Advil. He predicted that he would need a knee replacement by the time he was fifty, a wheelchair at sixty.

Jokes aside, I worried as I watched Henry—dozing, reading a magazine, tapping away on his laptop, dozing some more. During these vacation days, he had barely gotten off the couch. When I asked him about how he was feeling, he said that he was just tired from all the traveling of the last year, that he couldn't wait to get home, to begin writing his book.

The subject of his book was *umami*, a Japanese word that translates as "perfection," usually as it relates to food. *Umami* also translates as "the fifth taste," best described for Westerners as "savory." The other tastes are sweet, sour, salty, and bitter. *Umami* is the feeling of mouthwatering deliciousness during, and complete satiety after, a good meal. *Umami* is the taste of protein, caressed by fat—the pleasurable viscous taste of a meat stew, a rich sauce, or a morsel of creamy cheese. There is *umami* in a piece of sun-ripened fruit, or a glass of complex wine. More crassly, Big Food corporations hire food scientists to add chemically enhanced *umami* to otherwise tasteless food—Big Macs, snack chips, and those frozen dinners in your freezer. *Umami* is also the taste of the demonized flavor-enhancer monosodium glutamate (MSG), favored by Chinese restaurants.

But Henry's mission was to hunt down the real thing. He had gravitated to the West Coast, where the freshness of food, produce particularly, embodied the idea of perfection more than did the off-season shipments of unripe tomatoes and mealy peaches typically available on the East Coast. Under contract from a publisher, with half his advance paid, he traveled up and down the coast during 2002, sampling farm-ripened fruit, exotic varieties of seafood and seaweed, and regional wines.

He spent most of the year back and forth, making at least eight trips out West, some as long as three weeks. He ate meals at food temples such as The French Laundry in the Napa Valley and The Herb Farm in Woodinville, Washington. He tasted freshly harvested oysters and wild mushrooms in Oregon. He visited wine producers and experts up and down the coast. He wrote me a long e-mail about the now rare Marshall strawberries he tasted at one of the small family-owned farms in the San Juan Islands of Washington State on a trip with David Karp, a well-known fruit expert.

Henry returned from his trips with jars of Meyer lemon preserve, homemade salsas, and a nifty gadget called a Brix refractometer, which measures the sugar content of fruit. The produce manager of our local grocery store was impressed as Henry jabbed his pocketknife into nectarines and oranges to release juice for testing. FedEx surprised us with another treasure—a box of organic peaches from Frog Hollow Farm in Brentwood, California. Each drenching bite sent my salivary glands into almost painful overdrive.

Liza and I had joined him once during this long travel year, in May. We stayed at the Sooke Harbour House, a hotel-restaurant on Vancouver Island, British Columbia. Liza, who already showed signs of having inherited the culinary gene, loved the seafood and the special tour of the kitchen. She and I spent our days enjoying walks and outdoor play while Henry and the proprietor went deep-sea diving for underwater creatures. They returned one afternoon with a story of a nearly exhausted oxygen tank, a large octopus, and several purple-hinged rock scallops. The octopus and scallops ended up as soup ingredients later that evening. The intense and complex perfume of the broth, like nothing I had ever tasted, was the essence of *umami*.

Liza, not quite six years old, finished that meal and announced her career goal of opening her own hotel-restaurant. Her hotel would have yoga classes for me and room service for her cats.

December 31. We had returned home from our Christmas vacation on Bainbridge Island. Henry stood in the center of our kitchen, chewing his right pointer fingernail while he considered the last preparations for our annual New Year's Eve party.

His rounded belly wrapped in a stained apron, Henry picked up a wine goblet and took a generous swig, reinforcement for the task ahead, then gnawed the nails of his left hand. Sometimes when we were driving up the highway toward the dreary miles of strip malls, Henry would roll down the window and spit out the bits of skin and nail he had torn off with his teeth, like stray bones in a piece of fish. With similar energy, he joyfully crunched the cartilage of chicken bones and stripped his steak ribs down to bare white, displaying his sharp canine teeth with the gusto of a ravenous dog.

Henry set the wineglass down on the table and fretted over the crust on the roasted leg of lamb resting on a platter, peeling off and eating a morsel to satisfy himself that his guests would be pleased. He walked to the refrigerator and took out a platter with a side of home-cured salmon. His slicing knife flashed, and his greasy fingers offered me the thin slice of the gravlax, coral and translucent like amber. The fish slid down my throat. It was delicious. It would be even better eaten on toast with capers and chopped red onions, when our guests arrived in an hour. He sliced another piece and popped it into my mouth.

Henry had fed me our wedding cake thirteen years earlier with this same careless and childlike enthusiasm—pressing a big wad of chocolate cake into my widened mouth. I was startled and embarrassed at the time. But his irreverence was a secret promise that we would create together an unconventional and passionate life. He licked the remains of the cake from his fingers and flashed me one of his wide Cheshire Cat grins. He looked so devastating in his midnight blue vintage tuxedo, his dark skin, almond eyes, and curly hair set off by a crisp white shirt. As he seized me by the waist, and whispered in my ear how much he loved me, I creamed the lacy panties I had bought for the occasion.

After replacing the salmon in the refrigerator, Henry took out a small plastic container of veal stock saved from a prior cooking adventure—many bones, many hours. He emptied the contents into a small pot, coaxing a sauce from the veal stock, the drippings from the roasting pan, and port wine.

I watched him work and tried to clean up the mess. Wrapped in a white apron, sponge and paper towels in hand, I mopped up the stray grains of rice, turkey giblets, and vegetable parings that had rained down from the counter onto the blue-painted wood floor. I had chosen a color that would reveal everything in sharp contrast—not hide or camouflage. Now I could see bits of salmon in the cracks between the narrow floorboards, I just couldn't get them out.

As I brushed by him, attacking the mess, his face grimaced. "Get out of my way, goddammit, can't you see I'm busy here?"

Despite the togetherness we presented at our New Year's Eve parties, Henry and I could barely get through a week without yelling at each other. In our early days, we'd argued about politics, but now we fought the domestic battles of child rearing and housekeeping. Once, during one of our more heated battles, he threw volume one of *The Oxford English Dictionary* at me. It missed, but I still felt wounded by the weight of a book with so many words I didn't know, words I hadn't been able to summon up as a clever retort to his insult. Later he had apologized, as he did now, quickly and tenderly.

I rushed to the cellar to hunt down the plastic champagne glasses. Although alcohol inspired carelessness in our guests that made me fear for our beautiful Venetian glass champagne flutes, Henry always insisted on releasing them from their glass case for the early birds. Delighted by their flamboyance, Henry liked showing them off to guests, even if there was a risk of breakage, while I treasured them as objects and would rather have saved them for more intimate gatherings. They were a wedding gift from a generous friend, too expensive to replace. Returning upstairs with the plastic glasses, I placed them and the paper plates, napkins, and cutlery on one side of the dining room table, soon to be heaped with a mighty spread. A large cooler waited with ice and several dozen chilling oysters, ready to be shucked. I didn't dare ask Henry what those oysters had cost. Urging restraint seemed pointless. When he took my debit card to go food shopping for our dinner parties, I made a point of barely glancing at the receipts. Living with Henry meant embracing the necessity of a $150-an-ounce white truffle.

When I reentered the kitchen, he smiled and offered me a taste of his potion. The sauce was velvety and impenetrable, the tastes of dinners past mingled with the present drippings and port, a bay leaf sailing on the surface of the dark liquid. I gazed around at the mess in the kitchen—my mopping and tidying had done nothing to calm the hurricane.

"What does it need?" he asked.

"Nothing." I watched him stir with tenderness. For him a sauce was such a serious business. Too bad he hadn't become a professional chef, with a staff of minions to admire him and clean up after him.

He fussed some more, stirring and tasting. "I think it needs more salt."

"It's excellent," I said. "Perfect. Really." But I suspected that his sauce just needed a larger, more appreciative audience.

Liza galloped down the stairs, looking for her friends. At six and a half, her face had the look of children from another time and place, with an eclectic combination of traits from the available gene pool—Henry's Asian-Anglo background and my mishmash of Eastern European Jewry. She had inherited Henry's olive skin, and the bowed lips that reminded me of a pink rosebud. Dark honey-colored hair fell in perfect corkscrew ringlets to her shoulders, framing large almond-shaped eyes the color of seawater cupped in gray granite. She had my firm chin and my square-tipped fingers, purposeful and charming in diminutive size, especially when painted with robin's egg blue nail polish, as they were that evening.

Our first guests arrived, bringing an icy blast of snow and the musty scent of dead leaves from the wintry backyard. They carried cold bottles of champagne, and the bakers of the group brought homemade Swedish chocolate cookies and almond torte.

Emily and her husband, Justin, arrived early. I could always rely on Emily to provide a bit of bohemian glamour, a taste of the urban life I had left behind. I had sought her out after spotting her with her family at a local restaurant. The cute haircut, the red lips, the cloche hat. *That woman, she could be my friend*. Like many women in our town, she wasn't working and spent the time while our kids were in school on her personal writing and artwork. My life was all about deadlines, but since I was a freelancer we talked daily about books and art, often while I worked at my computer. In the afternoons after school, I often took Liza to her house. Her younger daughter Zoe had become one of Liza's good friends. While the kids played, Emily and I continued our talks over cups of tea. She could be the most exuberant fun, and a breath of fresh air in my otherwise quiet life, but sometimes, in contrast to her confident-looking appearance, she was as fragile as a needy child. Now her party persona—an all-smiles starlet on the red carpet—was on full view as she burst into the kitchen to admire the preparations.

"My God! Look at this feast!"

Henry put an arm around her shoulder, embraced her affectionately, and kissed her rosy cheek with enthusiasm.

"You are the *best*, Henry, the absolute *best!*" She received the wedding champagne glass Henry offered in her honor, giggling and flushing happily as bubbles drifted upward in her fluted glass.

. . .

Anna, a more recent friend, her husband, John, and son, Leo, stomped into the hallway. Leo kicked off his snowy boots and dashed upstairs, happy to charm the girls.

Lively, with bright blue eyes and long, curly, unnaturally dyed red hair (a "correction" is what she called her color choice), Anna dressed like a real New York girl. I was surprised when she told me that she had grown up in Ohio. She had left Ohio immediately after college graduation and headed to New York, where she worked at Betsey Johnson's retail shop in SoHo and partied at night in the East Village. Looking at her bright red hair, I could believe anything she told me about her wild days in the 1980s.

After we were introduced through a colleague, our friendship developed as we struggled to shed our lingering pregnancy weight. We signed up for a brutal calisthenics class at a local health club. Jumping jacks, push-ups, jogging in place. Every class was like a bad day in high school gym class, but we each lost five pounds. The deep muscle pain after each class was a true bonding experience. After eight weeks of boot camp, we decided we deserved something more soothing.

We became devoted yoginis over the next two years. I looked forward to our weekly outings. She drove down from her house, honking her horn in front of my driveway. In the car we had time to commiserate about work, fret about our kids' education, and listen to our favorite Lucinda Williams CD.

We appreciated each other's pragmatism. We both worked as graphic designers. We even shared an assistant. We mothered our same-age kids. She grumbled if I was late for our exercise outings. I was annoyed if she forgot about lunch plans. We understood each other. We were busy, our lives slotted into half-hour segments. There was nothing extra, no padding, no time to waste.

. . .

Our small group of younger, unmarried, and childless friends included Tomas and his housemate, Nick, my assistant. Tomas seemed restrained, holding a beer in his lanky hand. I smiled at him in a friendly way as I rushed around playing hostess. The party was alive at last, people in motion, mingling, talking, laughing. Tomas smiled at me as I moved toward the living room to change the music.

We'd become friends over the course of a few years, growing closer after we took a trip with him; his then girlfriend, Lindsay; and a group of friends to Costa Rica the prior winter. Tomas had lived in our attic for two months while he renovated his new house in the town north of ours. He was a very good-looking young man, over six feet tall with sandy brown hair. He changed his hairstyle frequently, so I was not surprised by his periodic transformations. Sometimes he cropped his hair short, like a boy from the 1950s; a few weeks later he might be sporting a short beard and "I've just returned from three weeks in the wilderness" shaggy curls; or he might try bangs that brought to mind an early sixties pop star or a monk about to take holy orders. His personality showed those extremes—by night he was happy to throw back a few beers with friends, but by day he worked on large figurative sculptures alone in a studio up the hill behind his house.

Tomas had made a good addition to our household. Henry liked cooking for an extra, very appreciative male pal, and I often found them together in the kitchen, drinking a beer, deep in conversation. When I entered, I became an intruder. Talk stopped, and I always left quickly with the feeling of having interrupted a confidential moment. Tomas had well-known girlfriend problems, the subject of small-town gossip. He was at our house the night his girlfriend broke up with him on the phone. He came into our bedroom, sat down on the bed, and cried. We, the long-married couple, were quietly supportive and comforting.

Liza loved riding up the stairs high on Tomas's shoulders and wrestling with him on the living room rug. She giggled when he tickled her. He listened generously to the stories she told about her school day—who was mean, who got in trouble, who she played with at recess. She loved drawing pictures with him at our kitchen table.

And having an outsider around kept Henry and me from squabbling.

While I was folding laundry one evening, Tomas looked at me in a strange way, and said I was beautiful. I thanked him—while my stomach turned somersaults—and kept folding laundry. Most of my life was spent at home, working and mothering. I felt invisible to other men, especially young, handsome men.

Once his new house had plumbing and electricity, Tomas moved out of our attic. I was surprised how much I missed his company. The next time I folded laundry I smiled, remembering his compliment, happy for the safety of his absence.

Henry envied Tomas's new bachelor life. One evening, as we cleaned up the kitchen, he remarked, "How would you feel if I moved in with Tomas and just visited you and Liza on weekends? Then it would be more like you were my girlfriend."

I looked up from the sink of dirty pots and pans and forced a laugh to show him I knew he wasn't serious. "No, I wouldn't really like that."

"And you should have an affair with Tomas," he continued, clearly enjoying this game. "Don't you think he's attractive? I wouldn't mind at all."

"Tomas is very good looking, but right now I'm married to you. Why do you even say things like that to me?"

Henry never gave up. He was like a cheerful dog, playing with a bone. "Would you mind if I went out on a date with his hot new Mafia Princess girlfriend?"

"You definitely don't get to go out on a date with the Mafia Princess."

I scrubbed at a dirty saucepot with extra effort. Sometimes Henry really was just maddening, though there was always something exhilarating about his willingness to push the limits.

Back in full New Year's Eve party hostess mode, I brushed by Tomas again on my way back to the kitchen to find more plastic cups. He took a swig of his beer and smiled shyly again. Tomas and I were similar—we both preferred solitude and quiet and were perhaps a bit out of our element at this large gathering.

Cathy, her husband, Steve, and their daughter, Amy, arrived with some of their friends from church. Steve was tall and handsome in an American, square-jawed way. Wineglass in hand, he took up his prearranged position as oyster server. A crowd gathered immediately around him, and he beamed from the center of his small theater in the round. Amy bolted upstairs to find Liza.

My friendship with Cathy was the common result of exurban parenthood. You move to a new place with your not-quite-two-year-old. After the Tuesday run up to the shopping center to buy cleaning spray, laundry detergent, and diapers in bulk, you head to the local playground. Your kid sees another kid the same age. They bond while building sand castles and riding on the seesaw. You check out the parents. Maybe they aren't exactly the people you would choose for friends, but they seem responsible, educated, not ax murderers. Though different in personality, Cathy and Henry were both writers and had seemed to bond quickly over their work.

Until this past summer, Cathy and I had been inside each other's houses almost every day. We picked up each other's kids from school. We provided each other with emergency child care. We took each other's kids for sleepovers. The four of us ate meals together. Our houses were almost interchangeable. I had spent many hours with the mother of my child's best friend, but in reality, I knew very little about her.

Cathy and Steve were a bit old-fashioned in their parenting, and their politics were more conservative than mine. Though she could at times take on the role of beer-drinking party girl, Cathy had grown up in a wealthy New York suburb. Cathy and Steve insisted on proper table manners that I found excessive for finicky three- and four-year-olds, who were still learning to wield a fork (I was more interested in my daughter actually eating food). At Christmastime I smiled at the propriety of the outfits Cathy's mother sent for Amy to wear—stiff, formal dresses with plaid taffeta skirts, patent leather Mary Janes—uncomfortable clothing I would never have presented to Liza but similar to outfits I wore in the 1960s.

Henry frequently made caustic remarks about Cathy's appearance, which seemed unkind to me. Petite, an inch or so taller than I, she had dark hair, small light eyes, pale skin. She was slim and fit from daily race-walking, an enviable victory over postpregnancy flab. Henry said that she was haglike and gaunt from overexercise. I envied her wiry legs.

The women of my circle of friends were undecided about her, and I found myself lobbying on her behalf. "She's shy," I'd say, when people complained about her manner. One-on-one we shared engaging conversation about books and films we loved, but she was withdrawn at parties, tucked in a corner holding a beer, looking ill at ease, waiting for the alcohol to melt her chilliness. And after a beer or two, she was unpredictable.

The year before, Cathy had arrived at our party and, while shedding her coat, announced quietly, "I'm going to get shitfaced." She made good on her promise, downing beer after beer for the remainder of the evening, laughing too loudly. She spent the first hour of 2002 vomiting violently in the bathroom while our daughters slept entwined on the living room rug.

I sincerely hoped that we would not witness a repeat performance this year. Her appearance suggested the opposite. She was dressed in a simply cut, knee-length purple dress with a high, round collar, black pumps, and stockings. She looked ready for a Sunday church service.

I wondered if the recent trend of weekly church attendance was more of a plea for social acceptance than a genuine attempt to connect to a higher power. Henry told me about a car trip with the girls during which Amy cheerfully sang "He's Got the Whole World in His Hands" complete with too-cute hand gestures. An agnostic girl of vaguely Jewish upbringing, I had sung that song too, at my Episcopalian summer camp.

I wanted to raise Liza differently. Cathy and Steve often invited Liza to attend Sunday services with them. But our daughter was turning out to be a skeptic just like her parents. If you couldn't see, smell, or hear Him, then how could God exist? And why was God a He anyway?

Henry told me abruptly in June that he no longer wanted to spend time with Cathy and Steve. "She is narrow-minded and the most conventional person I know," he announced. I was surprised—but relieved—and didn't press him further.

But in September, on the school playground, Cathy started

crying, upset that we had pulled away. Amy missed seeing Liza for playdates, she said. I didn't miss spending time with Cathy, but it seemed unkind to cut her off in such a brutal way, unkinder still to hurt her daughter. I arranged a playdate for the girls, and as the holiday season drew near, I urged Henry to invite Cathy to our annual party. I secretly hoped that Liza would make other friends.

The New Year's Eve banquet continued noisily. Henry, ever the eager host, roamed through the rooms, carrying champagne bottles, refilling glasses. At last he seemed to be reviving his bon vivant self.

One family had brought a telescope. While Henry entertained our guests, I escaped for a peaceful moment outside with father and stargazing son to peer through the lens at the full moon. The son eagerly explained to me that there was an unusual alignment of the moon and planets. It was a clear night, the lunar craters brilliant in the cold air.

After the midnight toasting, parents gathered up their children. While I helped them search for hats, gloves, and snow boots, we made vague plans for the last vacation days before school began again and declared the party a complete success.

The energetic promise of New Year's Eve was short-lived. Over the next few days, Henry slumped into lethargy, slept frequently, and began to complain of breathing problems, possibly related to his asthma. His inhaler, though, didn't help. He told me he had scheduled a doctor's appointment. I was surprised— I usually had to force him to see a doctor.

January 6. With my workload light and Liza back at school, Henry encouraged me to take a break with him that afternoon. We wandered upstairs to make love. I had always loved the light in our bedroom. The walls were painted a gentle mushroom gray. Low winter light filtered through the layer of dust on the windows onto the rumpled sheets and the carved headboard, a family heirloom. As we moved into our bed, the moment felt tender, calm, and familiar. I knew when I would come; I could count down the final seconds before liftoff in my head. We lay quietly in bed.

"You are a beautiful woman and I love you very much," Henry told me. Lying next to him, my head buzzing, I believed him.

The next morning was Tuesday, January 7, garbage day. As I prepared Liza's Cream of Wheat, Henry's boots crunched in the snow and gravel outside, and the garbage cans scraped along the asphalt driveway. He reappeared on the back porch and struggled with the sliding door with an effort that seemed odd. He lurched into the house, hunched over, took a few stumbling steps, and fell forward flat onto the wooden floor.

He came to as I reached him. Ignoring his protests, I hustled Henry and Liza to the car. I dropped Liza off at school and drove straight to the doctor's office, earlier than his scheduled appointment. His EKG and blood pressure were normal. His doctor arranged an appointment with a cardiologist for the following Monday, six days away.

I wanted the appointment to be sooner.

"Oh, Julie, stop fussing," Henry said, brushing off my concern. I tried not to worry. But worrying is in my nature.

The shock of the morning kicked Henry into action. He spent the evening cleaning out his office while I read a work manuscript in bed. By midnight he'd set three bags of trash outside his office door alongside filing boxes filled with neatly organized papers. He looked tired but satisfied. "Tomorrow, I will be ready to begin my book," he said, with a weary grin.

I recalled this exhaustion as Emily drove me home from the hospital, leaving Henry behind on the gurney. Matthew, who had been close to Henry's family for twenty-five years, and my friend for sixteen, decided it would be best to tell the news to Henry's family in person. He offered to drive up that evening and left straight from the hospital. I feared my own task ahead. Liza was still at a friend's house, completely unaware of what had happened that afternoon.

It was now dark. Anna had arrived at my house. I had called her from the car on the way to the hospital, but she had heard the news from the bookkeeper we shared, whose son was, coincidentally, one of the paramedics who came to our house.

Irena, a close friend from Brooklyn, my parents, brother, and sister-in-law had driven up from the city. A small group of local friends who had heard the news had come over as well. Anna and Irena greeted me at the door. I was grateful that Irena had managed to extract herself so quickly from her busy city office. Her normally exuberant dark curls were tamed in a hair tie without her trademark feather accents. A head taller than I, she had always been sisterly with me, and I suddenly realized how badly I needed someone who would tell me that everything would be all right. Irena walked me over to one of the couches, where I collapsed. Everyone had gathered on the other couch and the chairs in front of the fireplace, creating an odd preparty atmosphere. Even with my sheepskin coat on, I was shivering. I grabbed a blanket from the back of the sofa and draped it over my shaking legs.

Just after 8:00 P.M., Liza returned home from the playdate Emily had hastily arranged that afternoon, when we still hoped that everything would turn out okay. Liza looked around, smiling awkwardly, looking for Henry, wondering why her grandparents and so many others were visiting. It was a party, she thought. But where was the food? Where were the other kids? She joined me on the couch, hopping onto my lap.

"Mama, why are you still wearing your coat?" The room was quiet; everyone waited.

"Lizzie, do you remember how Daddy wasn't feeling well—how he fell down in the hall the other day? Well, he fell again today, in the afternoon, while you were at school. I called an ambulance right away and they took him to the hospital—the doctors tried to do everything they could to save him. But he died."

Liza listened to me—a few seconds of complete silence—then she wept while I held her in my arms. She cried for a long time, deep, brokenhearted sobbing. I was too drained to cry.

When she stopped crying, Liza sat quietly on my lap for several minutes and looked around at the adults, many of whom were quietly weeping. I could see her thinking, her eyes scanning the room—now she understood why everyone was in our house.

With a sudden sense of purpose, Liza jumped off my lap and walked to the shelf where we kept the ashes of Chester, our dear dead cat. She took down the small metal box, opened it, and walked around the room showing everyone the ashes.

"Chester, our tabby kitty, was very sick. We got up one day and he was just lying on the porch and he wouldn't eat or drink or get up, so we had to take him to the doctor right away, but the doctor told us that Chester was too sick to live. So he said he would have to give him a shot to make him sleep forever, but it wouldn't hurt him at all."

Chester's death a year earlier had served a most poetic and instructive purpose.

Irena stayed overnight. We slept next to each other like school-girls.

Matthew, Anna, Emily, and Tomas appeared early the follow-ing morning to make arrangements for a memorial. I lay in bed while Irena and the others busied themselves in Henry's office, across the hall from our bedroom. I heard distressing sounds, bursts of heated conversation and a woman's muffled scream. I got to my feet and stumbled into the office. Something was wrong. Anna led me back to my bed and quietly tucked me in. I was grateful to lie down again.

Later, I heard Cathy's voice calling for Matthew as she climbed up the stairs. She disappeared behind Henry's office door. More muffled voices, but I could not understand the words. Henry's door opened again. I sat up in bed and looked into the hallway. Cathy rushed quickly down the stairs. *Why didn't she stop in to see me?* I lay down again, drifting in and out, my first widowed day dreamlike, foggy, unreal.

We arrived early at the funeral home for the viewing so that Liza could spend time alone with Henry. She boldly walked up to the open coffin, positioned for adult view on a platform.

"Mama, can I have a tall chair?"

We found a high stool.

"Mama, look, you can't move his fingers. Daddy's lips are chapped. Can we put some stuff on his lips?" I rummaged in my bag and found a tube of lip balm, which Liza applied with care. Cathy's daughter, Amy, came over, and we found another tall stool for her. The two girls sat near each other and talked and gestured at Henry. The ease of their friendship comforted me as I watched from across the room, greeting guests. Henry's family arrived and sat quiet and stunned in the seats near the front. Townspeople arrived, some just acquaintances, many complete strangers. Henry's high school friends came together in a pack to greet me. One of Henry's former girlfriends sadly shook my hand.

I glanced over, searching for Liza near the coffin. I saw Cathy in her place. She was weeping hysterically, her head and arms draped over Henry's lifeless torso. Steve stood next to her, stoic, uncomfortable. When she lifted her head, her face was red and wet with tears. Not even I, the widow, had allowed myself such public emotion. A woman from our wider circle of acquaintances, her face set with concern, walked over quickly to speak with Steve while Cathy wept on. Finally, Steve gently drew Cathy away from the coffin. The awkward moment passed. I watched with relief as everyone returned to handshaking and quiet conversation.

I lay in bed the morning after the wake, my mind still soft and dreaming, in a tangle of sweaty sheets, light filtering through the dusty windows, obscuring the mountains and fog-draped river. Henry was dead; I was a widow. Irena lay sleeping next to me, her steady breath a small comfort. But soon she would have to go back to the city and I would be left here with Liza. Henry was gone.

A cloud gathered above my body, vaporous fingers extending and reaching around my torso and into my secret internal spaces. My mouth was pried open tenderly but insistently. He was invisible but present, an essence that seemed to hold me firmly on the bed. I allowed him to wash over me, enter me, enfold me.

He wanted something from me—to tell me something important, to be with my body. But he had no body; maybe he didn't understand that yet. Irena stirred and opened her eyes. Now my arms were reaching up to hold him.

"Are you okay? What's happening?" Irena murmured.

"It's Henry, he's here."

Why was Henry here? What did he want to tell me? He needed a body, but he was floating now without one. I felt anguished for him that he didn't understand what had happened to his body, that I couldn't speak to him and explain. Suddenly, I was floating too.

My body felt light and airy in the bed while he visited me each morning after that first time, the intensity of the visits gradually softening. I floated through my days. People spoke to me, and I realized I wasn't really present. I floated in the icy wind, wishing I could pass into his world, though I was unwilling to leave my child. I was in some in-between place, a dreamlike landscape where the horizon line vanished in a whiteout snowstorm.

———

The memorial service took place on January 12. I stood before an overflowing crowd at the lectern of a local church that had kindly offered their space for the ceremony.

"Henry was the love of my life," I told the crowd, "but also a completely impossible person." Nervous laughter. I had assumed the audience would be intimate with Henry's love of excess, his trademark lack of restraint. Surely some of the hundreds of friends, family, and local acquaintances packing this local church knew what I meant. Henry never liked to do anything small. Everything—from his romantic marriage proposal to his dinner party menus—was executed in grand gestures. A reserved twenty-seven-year-old when I met him, I had been drawn to that exuberance and to his forceful love. I had never before received such unabashed love from any man, and I'd welcomed it eagerly.

Snapshots came to mind: our meeting sixteen years earlier at a winter party; a day during our first spring together when he positioned me under a blooming cherry tree to take a photo; Henry cooking one of many amazing dinners for me on the humble stove in our apartment; Henry handing me a ruby ring over a warmly lit restaurant table where we celebrated our third wedding anniversary; a meal in a Paris restaurant where I tasted blinis for the first time; Henry sighing over the delights of a rabbit stew he prepared on a trip to Italy and the afternoon siestas we enjoyed on the warm afternoons in that Tuscan farmhouse we'd rented with friends. More images: Henry squeezing my hand as I pushed Liza into the fluorescent glare of the hospital delivery room; Henry and I as we walked through Prospect Park with our new baby. And recent images: Henry outdoing himself with a three-course lunch for ten women in honor of my fortieth birthday—grilled figs wrapped in pancetta, fresh pea soup with truffle oil, braised quails with pomegranate sauce. One of Liza's birthday parties, as twenty families and their children gathered around our swimming pool while Henry, in his favorite apron, presiding over the grill, beamed proudly. Henry throwing Liza and other delighted children into the water and swimming after them, as happy as a golden retriever playing with a litter of eager, squealing puppies. Yet another image as Henry showed Liza how to stir a sauce at the stove.

He had often been childlike in his pursuits, so eager to try anything new. In our best times together, I had felt loved and cherished with a similar enthusiasm. As I stood at the lectern, I saw clearly what he had brought to me, a naturally cautious and quiet person: a room full of hundreds of people whom he had delighted, who cared about him, and me. I thanked all the guests for coming and returned to my seat between Liza and Irena, passing the lectern to other speakers, who read poems and letters, and other tributes to their deep love for Henry. Person after person spoke about his loyal friendship, his insatiable curiosity about life, and his devotion to Liza and me. I held Liza's hand tightly.

Now composed in a dark knee-length dress, Cathy read a familiar Dylan Thomas poem in a restrained voice, her face tired and pale. No more coffin for her to weep over. Henry's body had already been cremated.

A rosy-cheeked man, his head topped with a cloud of blazing red curls, walked up to the lectern. It took me a moment to place him as a salesman at the local wine shop Henry frequented. In a voice choked with genuine grief, he spoke about their long afternoon conversations, Henry's impeccable taste, his wicked sense of humor. He read a poem he had written the morning before. I was startled to realize that Henry had a real relationship with this man, someone almost unknown to me. He had never sat at our dinner table or come to our parties. I had never exchanged more than a few words of polite greeting on the rare occasions when I ran into the shop to buy a bottle of wine. How could Henry have had such a meaningful, ongoing friendship with this near stranger, a friendship strong enough to inspire this heartfelt attempt at poetry?

There would not be four hundred, or even one hundred people at my funeral, I thought to myself, gazing over the crowd. Henry's gift was making everyone feel special—with a joke, a story, a dish of food. I recalled the ecstasy on people's faces when he served them a beautifully arranged plate. He had won me over that way, even with a humble dish of pasta, presented as if I were royalty. This memorial ceremony was a farewell not only to Henry but to the me who had shared his life of culinary and intellectual adventure, one that had been frequently exhausting but also thrilling.

I returned with Liza to a house filled with bouquets of pink carnations, white lilies, and dip-dyed daisies housed in plain glass vases. A far cry from the extravagant arrangements Henry used to bring home for Valentine's Day or after our worst arguments. After the carnations wilted, I washed out the vases and stowed them beneath the china cabinet in the dining room, a part of the house I was quite sure would never be used again.

two
_____

January–February 2003

Friends and family returned to their lives, the house was quiet.

My new loneliness frightened me. Living alone with my child was not what I had planned.

A small group of friends, family, and Helen, a caring therapist whom Henry and I had been seeing for several years as a couples counselor, graciously surrounded Liza and me in the blurred weeks following the funeral. My friends tended to my daughter when I could not. They brought food into my house, filled and emptied my dishwasher, hauled my garbage cans to the curb, as Henry used to do. They listened to me cry and held me.

Within two weeks I felt able to take Liza to school again and do some work, run a load of laundry. I wanted to feel like a competent human being again, in charge of my new life.

My brother, David, began the process of reorganizing my financial life and wading through Henry's will. His wife, Susan, helped me tidy and organize my house during their weekend visits. My parents called daily.

Other friends invited Liza and me to join their families for meals to blunt the loneliness of too many evenings on our own. But sometimes visiting friends was unbearable. As we departed, offering thanks, they stood in the warm incandescent light of their doorways, waving good-bye. It didn't matter that I knew how complicated family life was, that their lives weren't perfect. They had the illusion of perfection, a warm family feeling. Whatever illusion we had was gone, and I knew they pitied me. My life was a mess, but I didn't want pity.

Our house had become too large. I found myself getting lost. My prior roles of sous-chef and weekend hostess were over. Liza and I lived quietly in just a few rooms. I dropped Liza off to play with her friends at Cathy's or Emily's house more than their children came to ours. The door to Henry's office stayed closed except when my brother visited. The dining room was unused, passed through weekly by my housekeeper, who dutifully dusted the tables and the serving platters, stacked in the same concentric ovals I had arranged after the New Year's Eve party.

———

Liza and I sat in our kitchen one evening. I twirled a spoon in my soup bowl. Liza ate more enthusiastically, then put her spoon down on the table.

"How do we know that we are not people in a movie?" she asked.

I looked at her, not sure how to reply.

"Mama," she continued, reframing her question, "how do we know that things are real?"

Great. Now we have a junior existentialist in the house.

"Well," I said, "we don't know. We just have to hope that what we think is real is real."

"But how do we know?" she asked, insistently.

Ah, a scientist, who wants empirical evidence.

"We don't know," I said. "We just have to hope."

"Mama," Liza said, "how do we know that things aren't a dream? You know, how sometimes life feels like a dream? Do you ever feel that way?"

"Yes, sweetie, I feel that way all the time."

I forgot to drink water unless a glass was placed before me. My face became gaunt, my lips, parched and peeling. Neighbors and friends brought food—casseroles wrapped in foil, roast chickens from a nearby gourmet shop, containers of homemade lasagna. I placed all the offerings in my refrigerator.

Liza needed to eat, of course. I warmed up the food, placed dishes in front of us on the table in the blue-floored kitchen, and watched her eat. I dished a small amount of food onto my plate, took a few bites, and pushed the remainder around with my fork, hoping to look purposeful.

Liza was not fooled. "We aren't really a family anymore," she declared thoughtfully one evening as she spooned up yet another bowl of Annie's boxed macaroni and cheese. I murmured something about reinventing family with just us two, but it felt false. Dinnertime had been a time when we were together, the three of us, eating Henry's carefully prepared food. Food was family. Now she ate, I watched, then mechanically collected and scraped the dishes.

I had always eaten. I was born into a Jewish family, where food was love. I was raised on stews with boiled potatoes smothered with butter and dill, schnitzel with cucumber salad, and roast chicken scented with tarragon and lemon, my adolescence padded with cookies snitched furtively one at a time from the kitchen cupboard after school. Never in my adult life had I been skinny. Widowhood was turning out to be the diet of the century.

I hadn't seen much of my friend Anna, though she lived in the town just north of mine. After the funeral, we had both retreated into our graphic design work, exchanging frequent e-mails and phone calls. In late January she called me up to see if she could stop by for tea. Her face was tight and tired looking, and her long, extravagant red hair was woven into a restrained braid. I could see dark roots peeking out at the base of her scalp, a sure sign that life was in disarray. Of course, my own graying roots were showing.

"John and I are separating," she said.

I had hoped that the rest of the world would stand still while I got myself together again, but Chaos and Tragedy had marched along into other lives close to mine as well. Anna and I had lived our lives around work deadlines, homework, laundry, the restocking of the pantry, and the scheduling of our children's social lives. Now the careful working of things had tipped into disorder.

Henry had always told me I was too careful, not spontaneous or fun enough. He loved arriving out of breath with a minute to spare before the train pulled out of the station. But I felt wistful about that time when I had the illusion of control over my life. I hated feeling like I was hanging out of a small, rickety plane, its engine failing, gazing down at a checkerboard of suburban sprawl below, praying like hell that my parachute would open when I was brave enough to let go of the hatch door.

"When did this happen?" I asked, dumbfounded. How could Anna and John separate? They couldn't separate—she had just finished a beautiful renovation of her glorious, sunny kitchen with views of the sunset over the river.

"John was behaving really weirdly during Christmas vacation, taking the cell phone out of the room to make calls. I hit redial, and it's a woman's voice. I recognized the name on the caller ID."

Her agitated fingers fiddled with the frayed ends of her braid.

"Julie, it's one of his students! Can you fucking believe it? She came to our house for dinner, that night a few months ago."

I did remember her vaguely. A dark-haired young woman. I had assumed she was one of the young guys' girlfriends. The small group of John's students and I had all milled around admiring the new, crisp white cabinets with slate countertops—nibbling snacks, pouring drinks. I had watched the sun set, sipping a glass of red wine, enjoying the contrast of the rich, warm colors outside the window with the newly painted walls, a delicious shade of fresh olive green.

"Anna, I can't believe this. What a horrible way to end a marriage." We hugged quietly and both started crying.

At least I don't have to deal with that. At least I can cherish the good memories of my relationship.

"Looks like we are fellow travelers now," Anna said.

"We'll look after each other." I couldn't recall ever offering her this kind of comfort before. Now our relationship felt balanced. I hoped I could be useful to her as we muddled forward.

One afternoon a week later, I visited Tomas. We walked up the path to his sculpture studio, a small brick structure behind his house. The river rushed below us, the torrent muted by a layer of ice. As we trudged up the snowy path, I strained to hear his voice above the din. He pulled open the heavy door, and we stepped into the dark, frigid studio. He turned on a light and a heater as I tried to distract myself by blowing warm air from my mouth, watching it pass upward like drifting fog. I wished our friendship would allow him to enfold me in a warm hug. He didn't seem to mind the cold very much, though I noticed his hands were parched and chapped.

Tomas had been kind and attentive, calling me and receiving my phone calls or e-mails every day since Henry's death. I appreciated that with him I was able to speak about something other than my loss. I felt hopeful for myself as I listened to him talk about his life and his ambitious plans for the future.

His skills were formidable. A man in a reclining, twisting pose that recalled a deposed Christ figure. An entwined couple, the bodies stretched out long and lanky like his, unlike mine, almost androgynous. They wrapped around each other in a way that defied the realities of the human body, but the result was arresting, elegant, and arousing. I stood quietly for a while, admiring the sculptures. Though I enjoyed looking at the male bodies, I felt shy, simultaneously wondering if Tomas's penis was the size of those of his sculpted alter egos and embarrassed by my crass speculation.

"Here, I want you to have this," he said, breaking the awkward silence as he offered me a small sculpture of a female figure in a seated yoga pose. The cold cast metal warmed in my hands and then warmed me.

We left the studio and walked down the narrow path to his small meadow, where he proudly showed me a new tree he had planted in the fall. Other large sculptures were installed nearby.

Two back-to-back standing male figures looked at home in the unmown grass, dusted with snow. One of the figures crouched slightly, with arms bent behind his head; the other stood proud and exultant, with extended chest and arms raised up above his head.

The new tree Tomas had planted seemed lonely in the overgrown grass.

"I could give you some cuttings from my garden in the spring," I said. I was proud of my own garden and loved giving plants to friends. He didn't answer, and I regretted offering him a gift, though I was still holding his small sculpture in my gloved hand. "I'd like to cook you dinner sometime. I need to start cooking."

This offer he accepted.

Timidly, I tried out the pots and pans in the kitchen, once entirely Henry's dominion, with Julia Child and Nigella Lawson propped open for moral support. Lacking Henry's experience and confidence, I applied effort and study to the problem, reading recipes, making the same dish several times until I felt I had achieved some mastery. Lamb stew and coq au vin. I could still hear Julia Child's cheerful, high-pitched voice from the television shows I had watched as a child with my mother. Roasted chicken and minestrone soup. Nigella's carefree "whatever you have in the fridge" attitude comforted and reassured me.

Tomas played Attack with Liza in the living room while I worked at the stove. Attack was a game with simple rules, one that Liza and Henry had invented. Scary stories delighted Liza, as long as everything turned out well in the end. Henry had to say something like "I am a terrible, scary ogre and I am coming to get you . . . and when I find you I will suck out your brains with a bendy straw!" Then Liza and sometimes other friends would race around the house screaming, trying to elude the growling ogre. In the end, the ogre found his quarry, but the tide turned at the last minute, giving the children the upper hand. This was a game that truly illustrated kid philosophy—if it's fun once, it's fun a hundred times.

After a rousing game of Attack, Tomas happily devoured everything, and it was relaxing to have him in the kitchen, leaning back in a chair drinking a beer as I stirred and sautéed. He didn't mind helping out with some household chores, such as changing ceiling lightbulbs. At six foot three, he could do this without wobbling on the top tread of a stepladder.

On one of these evenings, as I prepared a steak for the broiler, I sensed Henry's presence in the kitchen. His voice echoed in my head: "Don't forget to salt the meat!"

By February, as my skills improved, I felt ready to throw a modest dinner party for Tomas and a few friends. I decided to offer them the homemade Korean dumplings Henry used to make, floating in a simple broth. This was a meal I could serve in front of the fireplace. The friends gathered, I added another log to the fire, and we all found seating. I sat next to Tomas on the couch. My long, unbrushed hair was bundled in one of Liza's hair ties. I was comfortable in my woolly socks and jeans, wrapped in a favorite pilled and frayed gray sweater.

The bone of his kneecap stretched the canvas cloth of his pants, revealing the indentation where the bone meets the muscle. I sat as close to him as I dared, a few discreet, magnetically charged inches between our seated thighs. I cast my eyes down at that narrow separating space, wondering about the meaning of the electrified feeling in my chest and a sudden hyperawareness of the effort of my lungs' expansion and contraction. My small hand reached into the charged space between us and found his large, warm hand. His long, elegant fingers took mine in a gentle squeeze. A painful pulse shot up the center of my body, a long-ago sensation.

I remembered the smell and glaring hot colors of New York City in July 1976, my clammy T-shirt, and an ineffectual, rattling fan blowing hot air in my face. A boy with half-closed eyes and tawny hair leans over awkwardly to kiss me as we entwine on my childhood bed, his parted lips steamy with the aromas of pot and liquefied chocolate chip cookies.

That sensation of desperate wanting.

Henry had been dead for a month. I was horny. I was horrified.

"Mama," Liza said one evening as we walked upstairs to bed, "I want to tell you something. I feel bad about something, but you might be mad at me if I tell you."

I sat on the stairs, and Liza joined me. The stairs had become a favorite place for us to talk, a neutral place. As she started to cry, I held her close to me, this warm, lovely creature, all I had left now of my marriage. I missed Henry, and I was furious. Why had he left us so suddenly?

"No, Lizzie, I won't be mad. Tell me anything you want."

"Are you sure you won't be mad?"

"I'm sure."

"Well, sometimes Daddy was mean to me," she said tentatively.

Liza had expressed so little of her feelings about her loss that I was grateful for any opening, though I hadn't expected this. "Sometimes I was playing in his office and he would yell at me to get out for no reason," she continued. "I feel sad about that and angry that he got mad at me." She began crying, and I reached over to comfort her. "I wasn't doing anything wrong, and he yelled at me for no reason."

I knew what she was talking about. I had done my share of yelling. Parenting young children is hard, and I was ashamed to admit how many times I'd snapped at her after tripping on toys she'd left on the kitchen floor, even for spilling cups of milk at the kitchen table. But I did recall the times Henry had abruptly made her leave his office, and the fury I'd felt at the time rushed back. Liza loved drawing pictures, snipping colored paper into confetti, or molding Sculpey figures of kitties on the floor of my sunporch office while I worked in the late afternoons or evenings. But Henry frequently shooed her out of his office, shutting the door behind her. He insisted on a kind of privacy I had been able to give up.

"You weren't doing anything wrong," I replied. "I don't know why he was like that, but I remember that sometimes he would yell at you. I know how much he loved you, though, even if he was mean sometimes."

He didn't love her enough to stay here.

Another flash of anger, as if his death was something he could have prevented. Then sorrow. He couldn't possibly have wanted his life to end as it did. In spite of our conflicts and his impatient nature, Henry had been a proud and devoted father.

"I think we have to try to forgive him. Now, it's just the two of us, so please always tell me how you're feeling," I said to Liza.

We sat together quietly on the stairs and hugged each other.

Then it was time for bed, where we huddled under the quilt, holding hands tightly till I felt the muscles of her hand relax in sleep.

––––––––

My social status had flipped a switch. I was no longer a married woman; I was not sure yet exactly of my new place. But I welcomed a new comfort in a group of women around whom I had formerly only circled at the town and school playgrounds: the single mothers. We were precious few in this place. One woman I had always liked—the mother of another one of Liza's school friends. After the girls met in class, Tanya and I began arranging playdates. Tanya was quiet, her voice almost a whisper. She wore wristfuls of jingly bangles, dangly earrings, a bear-claw pendant on a leather lace around her neck, airy shawls. In the warm months, she liked to walk through town barefoot, her toenails painted scarlet. Some people thought the barefoot thing was weird, but I secretly liked that Tanya did just as she pleased.

Her home was just another quaint cream-colored clapboard house on a short, tree-lined street, but the interior was like the magical world of a Gustav Klimt painting. Gold Egyptian eyes shimmered on the living room walls; the bathroom walls featured a decoupage of a thousand and one photos of women, clipped from magazines; while pieces of colored glass arranged as a kitchen backsplash mosaic depicted dancing mermaids. Tables and shelves brimmed with bowls and baskets of colored pebbles and shells; free-form weavings of yarn and more shells hung from the ceiling. Two cats roamed the house and yard, a cuddly gray bunny hopped about, colorful fish slowly circled in a fish tank in the kitchen.

Snuggled on her slouchy couch, I drank the large, steaming cups of tea she offered me. My own home felt staid and traditional by comparison. How had I found myself in that beautiful house with a housekeeper and neatly arranged furniture? I felt like I belonged in this house, Tanya's house.

I could feel myself withdrawing from my familiar social world. But the friends who did see me as I moved through my days— taking Liza to school, picking her up in the afternoons, shopping at the grocery store—had sounded the alarm. One morning Emily, Cathy, and two other friends, Louise and Diane, arranged themselves at my kitchen table in a kind of gentle intervention.

Cathy told me I was too thin. I needed to eat. She had brought a can of powdered protein drink and a bottle of calcium tablets. I tried to focus my attention on her well-intended appeal concerning the importance of maintaining weight and bone density during a stressful time, thinking that Henry would have offered a more caustic assessment: "Julie, you look like shit."

I started crying. I knew she was right. I had to eat. I just couldn't seem to get anything down. My lack of appetite frightened me.

From her sturdy canvas bag, Diane presented a homemade raspberry pie, the beautiful, flaky brown crust oozing ripe, red fruit. The aromas of buttery pastry and warm berries were suddenly tempting. I cut a small sliver and ate.

Cathy said that she wanted to arrange a private talk for me with her minister.

"Fine, that sounds okay," I heard myself saying between small, exploratory bites, though I had no idea how I would talk to a minister. I wasn't interested in ministers. The only thing that interested me was the pie.

My stomach revolted from the shock. Once the cramping and subsequent nausea passed, I cut another slice. Later in the afternoon, I ate another slice, and I ate a piece of pie for dinner and another for breakfast the next morning. When the pie was gone, I called Diane and asked her if she would make me another pie, and she did.

Cathy called a few days later to arrange a time for her minister to visit. I'd forgotten about her offer but agreed to see him. A cup of coffee seemed harmless enough.

He arrived, and I led him to the kitchen table. He was burly, with an open, friendly face, clear, light eyes. I had seen him several times in town and once at the church, when Cathy had invited us to the winter holiday concert and Christmas pageant. Amy was in the pageant, so of course Liza had been anxious to attend.

This meeting seemed to be something Cathy wanted to offer me so particularly, though I remained deeply uncomfortable with the idea of ministers generally and told him so. But it seemed rude to refuse what was intended as a gift.

If I let him do the talking, this will be over sooner.

He spoke to me earnestly and thoughtfully about the Christian view of death. The eternal life of the spirit, how we can accept loss. I realized that I wasn't retaining his words—it was all becoming a kind of white noise. For some reason, his kind message made me feel angry, even outraged that this thing had happened to me. It wasn't fair. I couldn't listen, though I wished that my mind would open cheerfully, like fingers in the hand game children play ("Here is the church, here is the steeple, open the doors and see all the people!"), and suddenly find that this all made perfect sense. Then I too could show up at church services and feel welcome somewhere.

What would this man think of Henry's morning visitations?

Tweed jacket, light blue button-down shirt, khaki trousers, sensible and sturdy brown, laced walking shoes. I decided to keep my sexual encounters with the afterlife to myself.

———

More successfully than her minister, Cathy herself offered me comfort in her e-mail letters, telling me not to despair, that things would get easier with time, that she believed me to be a strong person capable of remaking my life. It felt strange to receive comfort from someone who had always remained oddly distant. But I was ready to take the comfort, wherever it came from.

···········

My brother, David, visited on Fridays, shutting himself up in Henry's office and reading through endless files. At the end of each day, he handed me a list of tasks: call the bank and the insurance company, sign and mail these documents with death certificates attached, envelopes already addressed and stamped, so that I could have title to the car, so that accounts and investments could be transferred to my name. I couldn't even look at the documents without glazing over and weeping.

David told me that Henry had left behind quite a bit of debt—credit cards I didn't know about with large balances that would have to be paid off as soon as the estate was settled. Forty

thousand dollars' worth. I didn't ask what the debt was for. It was
too late to be angry, and thinking about the money just made me
worry. I was not surprised that he had debt—he liked buying
things. I figured it was hotel rooms, meals, wine, and rental cars
out West during the research year. And a new travel bag. And a
new laptop. But $40,000? Henry had blasted through the entirety
of his book advance without writing a word. That was a lot of
white truffles, even at $150 an ounce.

In spite of the prospect of Henry's debt, I had a fierce urge
to shop. I bought a pair of boots on Zappos.com: short, brown
suede, high-heeled platform boots with zippers up the slender
hourglass insteps. When the box arrived, I tried them on, briefly
wrestling with guilt about the price, wondering if I'd ever wear
them. What life were these boots part of? Not the reclusive life of
the town's young, grieving widow. These boots were part of the
life of a young single woman, who lived in the city, worked at a
job in a sleek office, and went to parties and downtown restaurants, listened to music in dark nightclubs, tongue-kissing eager
young lovers between sips of colorful cocktails.

My friend Chloe persuaded me to join her for a shopping trip in
the city. She was the only young widow I knew, and she seemed
to be making her way after a few difficult years. She even had a
boyfriend. As we wandered through stores in SoHo, I admired, as
always, her age-defiant face, radiant at forty-eight, her lips
painted the color of wild beach roses. As we stood in front of a
rack of dresses at our first boutique stop, Chloe put her arm
around my shoulders and confessed that she had bought a lot of

clothes right after her husband died. I missed her husband, a last-of-the-true-English-gentlemen, who had died of lymphoma at fifty-five, four years earlier.

I bought a dress I would never wear in my town—made of a foliage-printed, terra-cotta, silky material with a flouncing hemline that hugged my new, thin body. I was now as slender as I had been at sixteen. And for the first time in my adult life I liked my body. My butt looked positively girlish as I twirled around for Chloe.

"You look . . . delicious!" she murmured, smiling with approval.

Two weeks later I took the train back to the city and bought a pair of mule sandals at another store in SoHo. They were expensive, even on sale. They were Italian, of an elasticized woven material that hugged the foot (and would likely give me blisters), in narrow cabana-awning stripes of green, ocher, and gray perched on curvy, sculpted heels.

Back at home I admired the shoes in their fancy box on the floor of my closet, drew them out, slipped my feet inside, and took a turn before the full-view mirror on the bathroom door.

I imagined the tippety-tap patter of the heels on the ancient paved sidewalk of a beloved seaside village in northern Italy. Twenty years earlier I had been in love with that Ligurian town and with a man there. I remembered the silver color of the late afternoon sea, the houses painted in shades of rose pink, sage green, and ocher, the distant mauve mountains flattened in the haze. I remembered the smell of fresh-caught fish displayed in the open-air market, and seaweed, alive with hopping sandmites, exposed at low tide along the pebbled beach. The sun warmed my bare arms and legs, as did the admiration (*"Che bella!"*) of men who passed by me during the evening *passagiatta.*

Henry's ashes were stored in a wooden urn in my office. Liza asked if she could see them. The top of the wooden urn unscrewed easily to reveal inside a thick plastic bag, sealed with a twist tie. I untwisted it. Liza and I sniffed the contents. They smelled like ashes, but not like our fireplace ashes, with their woody, smoky odor. These ashes smelled like bone, the last remains of a charred barbecue. Liza was not repelled or frightened; in fact, she seemed intrigued.

"Mama, we need a spoon!"

I ran to the kitchen and grabbed a teaspoon from the flatware drawer and a small bowl from the dish cupboard. We took turns scooping out some of the ashes into the bowl. We discovered bits of tangled metal, perhaps from fillings, or the metal pins from the repair of his right leg, the one he broke in the motorcycle accident when he was sixteen. We poked at bits of bone that had not been incinerated by the heat of the cremation oven.

"Mama, can I put some ashes on the flowers outside? Can I have some of Chester's ashes too?"

Henry and Chester, the old tabby cat, were carefully mixed in the bowl and carried out to the backyard. The clematis vines, Chinese balloon flowers, and roses, dormant still in the winter cold, all received a nourishing dusting.

Liza asked if she could have some ashes to keep with her. I found a small red silk jewelry bag with a drawstring, and she scooped some of Chester and Henry into the bag. She insisted on wearing the silk bag to school the next day. I wrote a note to her very understanding teacher.

The lonely urn needed companionship on the desk, just as

Henry had needed an audience in life. We placed objects around the urn: a pliant twenty-four-karat gold ring from Korea (a gift from his mother), a plastic snow globe containing a gold plastic Buddha (from Henry's desk), shells and stones from trips to Maine, a note he wrote me on my birthday, a poem of three couplets he wrote for our last Valentine's Day.

For a writer, he was never much of a letter writer. We had rarely been apart for most of our sixteen years together. I had a few e-mails from the year he was out on the West Coast, but even then, he preferred to make phone calls. I regretted that now, wishing I had more pieces of him, more pieces of paper with his words.

Emily called me every day. Since the January afternoon when she had arrived to find Henry on the kitchen floor, she had been attentive in every way. I was grateful for her companionship, though now I had the first worries that I owed her a kind of emotional debt I could never repay, and with those worries the first waves of regret that I hadn't called Anna that day. There had always been a sense of balance between Anna and me that allowed me to ask for something—be it help or sympathy—without worrying about when I would be able to pay her back. My decision to call Emily had seemed so rational then, the extra minutes had seemed so important, but I hadn't anticipated the fallout.

On several occasions, as we sat with cups of tea at her house or mine, Emily looked at me mournfully (or was it impatiently?) and asked, "When do I get my friend back?" I never knew what to tell her. The friend she was missing seemed to have vanished.

I often visited Emily and her family, eating meals with them, grateful that Liza was able to feel happy and play. Emily's home felt warm, energized, and alive, if full of the usual subterranean family conflicts. In contrast, the quiet of my home was oppressive. I had never realized how completely Henry's personality had filled up the rooms.

When the weekends arrived, Liza and I curled up together on the couch, under blankets, the leftovers of our scrambled egg breakfast on the nearby coffee table. We watched SpongeBob's manic adventures in the cheerful blue-green tropical glow of Bikini Bottom or Timmy Turner's adventures with his fairy godparents. *That's what I need, some fairy godparents.* It was comforting to be together. Liza's cheeks smelled of peaches and fresh biscuits.

three

February–May 2003

A few weeks after Henry's death, I received a note from Maya, a local massage therapist, offering me free bodywork. I had never met her, but I called her and made an appointment. The idea of receiving help from a stranger was oddly comforting. The next afternoon I found myself in her twilight-lit treatment room.

I lay quietly on the massage table, listening to the CD of birdsong and gentle waves while her confident fingers, coated with fragrant oil, burrowed into my bony back. She found a place at the center of my back that felt tender when she pressed, like a button wired into my sadness. I wanted desperately to cry, but I was too embarrassed to reveal all of my wretched life to this stranger. After a long silence, just the birds and waves and the swish of her oiled hands on my skin, she volunteered that it was okay to talk during the sessions. I hardly knew where to begin, but fortunately I didn't need to start at the beginning. I was the town's young widow. Almost everyone had heard something of this story.

The next week I went to her again, and I talked. In fact, I couldn't stop talking and crying. What a relief to let myself go and be cared for by someone who was compassionate but did not seem to pity me. My body felt sturdier when I left her office.

By my third visit, I genuinely liked Maya, a small, wiry woman with open, curious eyes in a freckled face, a laughing voice, and strong hands. We had no other social connection, so the darkened treatment room felt safe. I went back the fourth week and asked to become a paying patient. Now the relationship was balanced.

Maya was the first person I spoke to about Tomas. I told her about Henry's visitations, how I felt that Henry wanted a body to be in, because he had lost his body so suddenly, how I wondered if Tomas would be the body. I felt like a crazy person even thinking these thoughts aloud. I told Maya I wanted to ask Tomas if he would do this.

"That seems like a good plan," she said, as calmly as if I were telling her about a job-search strategy. "I don't think you are crazy. In the path of Tibetan Buddhism I follow, there is a great understanding about the place where Henry is now, the in-between place."

Tomas made me a cup of tea in his warm kitchen.

"Henry visits me every morning," I said. "I can feel him when he visits. I know it sounds crazy, but I feel him in a physical way." I couldn't look right at Tomas, so I stared at the ceramic tea mug. The glaze was a lustrous, warm green.

No backing out now.

"I feel like he needs a body to be with me. He liked you so much. He trusted you. And I trust you. So I want to ask you."

I cried, because of the cascading relief of speaking to him at last and also because I was ashamed, sure that Tomas would think I had lost my mind. But Tomas did not push me away. He listened, hugged me, and said, with a strange laugh, that he would think about it.

He was leaving the following day for a two-week visit to see his mother in Costa Rica, where we'd traveled. I wished I were going. I wished Liza and I were going with Tomas to lie on a beach for two weeks to stare at a blue sky and the waves and dip our feet into the warm sea. I drove home, hoping that I wouldn't feel like a complete fool the next day.

Henry always said I was neurotic and moody. I couldn't deny it. I had suffered from depression since the gray autumn following our April marriage in 1989. After struggling with Prozac and Zoloft, I settled on Wellbutrin, which worked well with only moderate side effects. A year before Henry died, my doctor had added an antianxiety drug, Celexa. Henry had insisted I take this medication; he said my anger was "out of control."

I wanted to go off my medications so I could maybe have sex with Tomas and actually feel something. Henry and I had worked our way around the side effects, but Tomas was a young man; he wouldn't understand, or have the patience. The colorful pills in their amber plastic vials pleaded with me like rejected friends from the shelf in my medicine cabinet. They had been loyal companions, it was true, but I needed to feel like a young woman again, with a young woman's nerve endings.

I stopped taking them. The surface of my mind remained calm under a milky, overcast sky. Stunned, I kept waiting for the shattering depression and anxiety to return, but instead there was calm. I was sad but calm. I was pressing forward, one foot in front of the other, taking care of my child, eating a bit, working, and paying bills.

Tomas would return soon. I was excited about that. I was stunned to feel excited about anything. When I read his e-mail notes, I tried to imagine his life in Costa Rica, based on my memories of our own short visit: the warm sea, the breeze under the palm trees, the rain forest, where exotic birds sang and blue morpho butterflies slowly flapped their delicate wings as they sipped nectar from colorful blossoms.

A cold wind rattled my office windows, as if someone were trying to get my attention from outside. Instinctively I glanced over at the wooden urn filled with Henry's ashes, positioned in front of the window, now illuminated with late afternoon winter sunlight. I had loved that man whose ashes were in the urn, though he had been an exhausting companion.

And then my eyes opened wide, as after a long and restorative sleep.

I understand now.

I understood the cause of my anxiety. I understood the nature of my depression. Though I had my fair share of Jewish neurosis, the source of my calm was Henry's absence. Some tightly wound ball of twine inside my body was slowly unraveling. I told no one but my therapist, who nodded thoughtfully.

After Tomas returned from his trip, I drove up to his house. We sat again in his kitchen and tried to talk about whatever it was we might begin. He said he'd had a sense, since Henry's death, that we were being drawn to each other for some purpose, and that he'd been curious about what might happen between us. Leaning toward me, as we sat in our chairs, he kissed me, his way of saying yes to my unusual proposal two weeks earlier.

A few days later, after a breathless e-mail exchange to arrange logistics, Tomas and I sat on my living room rug. Liza had been happy to go to Tanya's house for a sleepover. Tomas and I ate lamb stew I had made following Julia Child's instructions. I imagined Henry nodding approvingly from his corner of the kitchen; I had remembered to salt the meat before browning. We drank glasses of the red wine I'd bought from the redheaded wine merchant in town. I sat close to Tomas. He smiled and reached over to hug me—every cell in my body was thrilled and terrified.

I had to tell him how scared and nervous I was. He told me he was nervous too. I relaxed a bit. I hoped he had remembered to bring a condom. He leaned over again, and this time he kissed me. His soft lips tasted of everything young and fresh. My insides exploded. *I can't do this.*

"Let's look at you," he said as he took off my T-shirt. I silently prayed that my forty-something body would not horrify him. I had a flat belly. But the skin crinkled in a telltale, postpregnancy way if I leaned over. *I will not lean over.*

We kissed again.

Upstairs in my bedroom, I felt Henry's presence, as if he were reclining in the sitting chair watching me. I hoped Henry understood. Tomas said he could feel Henry too as we lay down, undressed, and slid under the covers. My body felt like it was levitating. A new man was touching me in my bed. My body was lying on the bed, but my consciousness was rising out of my body, floating above the bed. I watched this scene from a height above my body, the man making love to the woman that was me.

I felt him come. He sighed. My brain settled back into my head, and into my body on the bed. I felt the warmth of the sheets and Tomas's body next to mine. I cried with relief, sobbing and gasping. He cradled my body kindly. I felt alive.

After our first night together, we corresponded daily in a loving way, letters that someone else might have called love letters, though I hesitated to use such a word because it was clear that Tomas was both available and unavailable. Sensing that too much commitment would scare him away, I tried to reassure him that I would not ask more than he wished to offer. For now, I was stunningly happy to have his company.

A few weeks later, a friend in town threw a big party. Because Tomas and I were trying hard to be discreet about our whatever-it-was-we-were-doing, we arrived at the party in our separate cars—my muddy but still fancy-pants wine red station wagon with leather heated seats and his young dude pickup truck.

After briefly parting the ranks of the beer-drinking, loud-laughing smokers on the porch (wearing my impractical but wonderful new brown suede, high-heel platform boots), I greeted Tomas in what I hoped was a casual way. I poured myself a glass of wine and chose a chair against a wall, where I could slowly sip my wine undisturbed and take some pleasure in watching the rowdy crowd. Tomas stood silently, a short distance away, but when our eyes met we smiled. Our secret was undeniably fun.

A tall young woman walked over on her tall pointy heels to greet Tomas. I wasn't jealous, for I didn't think of Tomas as "mine"; he was more loan than gift. I watched, fascinated, as she smiled and chatted prettily, and swayed her cute, young, jeans-sheathed butt side to side, tipping her pointy toes this way and that, edging ever closer to him. His previous girlfriend had had a bit of this look, I recalled; so would the next one, I felt sure, watching the scene unfold. I would turn out to be the brief experiment, an anomaly.

A part of me wished this thing could work out. We had much in common, similar interests and temperaments. But the age difference was a ridiculous impediment we'd never manage easily. Not to mention that my first obligation was to my child. Tomas was too absorbed in his young man's life to be available in that way. "Your transitional relationship" is how Helen, my polite but no-bullshit therapist described it. Part of me wanted to prove her wrong. The wiser woman in me knew Helen probably had it perfectly pegged.

Tomas looked my way with an awkward, pained expression, and I smiled back at him, hoping to communicate this: "Relax. I am fine. You are beautiful, and everyone wants some of that beauty."

While Tomas had lived in our attic, we'd had many conversations about his future, personal and artistic. In the friendliest way, Tomas and I continued to have such conversations now. He would tell me how he wanted a tall beauty for a girlfriend, a muse for his work, like his previous girlfriend, but he worried about ending up with someone insubstantial and superficial. He believed in the connection between physical and spiritual beauty. I sighed over his naïveté, the innocence of a handsome young man. Though I too had been innocent, thrilled to marry Henry, who also had been such a pretty young man.

"Henry is so handsome," my friends gushed when we married. People said we looked good together, and I felt proud. As a young woman, that had seemed important.

"You are so lucky to have Henry, and he loves you so much." I had felt lucky and loved. Until the dictionary came flying at me.

Physically, Tomas and I were not such a suitable pairing. When we kissed, I had to stand on tiptoe. It made me feel small, though in public situations the height differential offset the age difference, which was sixteen years.

———

Anna called one morning, crying. Since her earlier visit to tell me of her separation from her husband, I'd been doing my best to keep track of her progress, though I felt completely lost in my own fog. For both of us, work was an anchor and a comfort. Sometimes, on the days our shared assistant worked for me, I tentatively asked him how Anna seemed, because I hadn't seen her much since her announcement. Thin, he reported. He too had been one of John's students. He quietly told me how disappointed he was in his mentor. When Anna and I talked on the phone, she always sounded tired and wrung out, sometimes on the edge of tears. This morning, however, there was no pretense of self-control; she was hysterical.

"He's still here," she sobbed. "And all his stuff is here. He's sleeping in the barn and he won't leave, and I can't stand it anymore." The barn was their shared work space, across the lawn from their house.

"So you have to work in the studio with him all day? What's he saying? Does he want to stay married or go off with the girl?" We did not refer to this woman by name.

"He isn't really saying. It's like he's still thinking about it, but I know he's still seeing her. Fuck, I hate my life."

She cried some more, and I cried too, thinking about the inevitable mess of their divorce. There didn't seem to be such a thing as a gentle divorce.

"Anna, I think you have to just march right down to the barn and tell him to leave now. And just get his shit out of the house if it's making you upset. He can't have it both ways. Either he's married to you or he's seeing the girl. He has to choose. I think you should go tell him right now. If you need me to, I'll drive up there and do it myself. But I think you can do it."

Later that day I called her back. She told me she'd dumped John's clothes into some black garbage bags and left them on the snowy lawn. Within days, he cleared out of the barn and rented an apartment in town. She felt better, more in charge, but new battles were just beginning. She was looking for a divorce lawyer. No point waiting any longer now.

Sara came to visit from England for a week in March. A friend from my college days, she had promised to help me sort through Henry's things.

"This will be my gift to you," she told me. I knew she could get this job done. She was a librarian both by profession and by temperament; I could trust her to be ruthless yet compassionate. We had the love of over twenty years behind us. She was so like a sister that I forgot we'd chosen each other as friends.

"Maybe you'll find Henry's wedding ring," I said hopefully as she surveyed his office files. "I've been looking for it everywhere."

Sara and I were brought together by a powerful force—a torrential downpour the first night of freshman year—as we stood on the portico of a stately academic building at Smith College, following the first meeting of the future class of 1981. I peered out into the storm. This rain was not a late summer gardener's gentle tip of a watering can but more like a plumbing disaster, a bottom-

less bucket endlessly dumping its contents. The road to my faraway dorm room was already flooded past my ankles. Just as I
was preparing to roll up my pants, take off my shoes, and walk
home barefoot, I felt a tap on my shoulder, and there was a young
woman with bobbed light brown hair and bee-stung lips wearing
a jingly silver ankle bracelet.

"You look just like someone I know from home," she told me,
perhaps a bit homesick. Despite my initial irritation at not being
noticed for my uniqueness, ultimately I did feel chosen by her. I
switched dorms to be her roommate. After a junior year abroad, I
returned to campus to her co-op house, where Sara had picked a
beautiful, sunny room for me.

Our late seventies and early eighties campus was a hothouse
of radical feminist political disputation. Dinner conversations at
our co-op house devolved into noisy arguments over our school's
divestment policy in South Africa, vegetarianism, lesbianism, and
literary criticism. The debates often carried on upstairs; we
weren't always the best housemates, though we were inventive
cooking partners.

Sara and I discovered our friendship's perfect medium after
college, when we moved away from campus and began writing letters. Two decades of snail mail and now e-mail later, through her
Peace Corps service in Africa, marriage, and children, I knew that
if I needed her she would come, and now she was here with me.

For a week she spent the workday hours in Henry's office,
periodically calling me upstairs to assess piles of papers and peri-
odicals.

"You should throw these out," she announced quietly and
firmly, pointing to a pile of Henry's cherished but moldering magazine clippings. I was ready and relieved to let those piles go.

"You should really consider this situation with Tomas," she

said to me one afternoon during pile assessment. "This seems impulsive and too rushed. You aren't ready for anything serious with anyone." I couldn't argue with that, but I knew that as soon as she left for home I would call Tomas.

During her last day with me, Sara found Henry's missing wedding ring in one of his many travel bags, hidden in an interior pocket. He had told me that he didn't want to wear his ring anymore. I'd tried to be open-minded. Rings had never been that important to me, though I continued to wear my wedding band. But I wondered why he went to the trouble to take the ring with him on his travels.

————————

Emily and I were at a party at Tomas's house. I had recently told Emily about my relationship with Tomas. While not offering criticism, she had made it clear that she didn't want too much information. She'd been happy to come with me to this party, as we were all friends with Tomas. She loved parties, and nights out without our kids were few.

I watched Tomas laugh with his friends. I knew I would never be part of this world. It would be too jarring to spend too much time with people in their twenties—I'd start feeling ancient. And Tomas wouldn't want to be part of my routine-bound life with a child—this would be too much responsibility for a young guy who liked to make few plans and change those at will. Eventually, soon, he would want to be with a young woman again.

He was beautiful, but I often found our intimate encounters rushed, as if the moments together were being squeezed between the heavier metal plates of our other obligations—my child and my work, his art. I loved talking to Tomas about our artistic lives, and our goals for the future. When we spoke about these topics, I felt hopeful, with all my life still ahead of me, full of possibilities. I didn't want to be with him long enough to endure heartbreak or jealousy. What was left of my rational mind understood that nothing about our relationship made sense in any long-term way.

Emily and I, the oldest people at the party, sat together. We lingered for a while; but we had children who needed us to make breakfast in the morning. Near midnight, Tomas's friends set up instruments and began playing music, and people gathered to listen and dance. Emily and I walked to my car, the sounds of laughter, guitars, the smack of the drum set gradually muffled by the rush of the river outside the house.

We sat in my warm car in her driveway.

"I miss Henry," Emily said. "I miss the excitement of his dinner parties, the repartee, the flirting."

I looked at her; she was crying.

I missed so many things about Henry, but not those things.

Tomas and I drove out on slushy roads in his pickup truck, tunes blasting, to a nearby Mexican restaurant. He spoke Spanish to the proprietors, and I was charmed and melted even before the warm soup arrived. His hands were more expressive when he spoke his mother's language. I found that I could enjoy food again in this setting, away from the associations of home, and Henry's kitchen. Between courses, Tomas held my hand and I felt briefly cherished. On other nights we went to restaurants, discreetly out of town, that I knew he could never afford on his own. I felt awkward as I took out my credit card to pay. What were other diners thinking? Did they think I was his older sister? His mother? Or what I was—his too much older lover? I was quite sure that Tomas felt like a "kept man" in those moments. And I felt a discomfort as well. I didn't want him to be burdened by any sense of obligation. I did not want pity. I got plenty of that from my well-meaning friends and neighbors.

One evening, after returning home from dinner, we lay next to each other on our stomachs across the big bed in his tiny bedroom. While we talked, I enjoyed looking at the pieced-together rectangles of moonlit night through his old-fashioned, small-paned window. Tomas gently caressed my back as he spoke. His housemate, Nick, stopped by our open door with his girlfriend to say good night on their way upstairs. Tomas continued to stroke my back, and for a moment everything felt quite normal. Being with this man, in his house, getting ready for bed.

In the morning, he cooked eggs for me, and that felt good. Simple food, jelly-jar glasses, hot tea in eclectic ceramic mugs, mismatched flatware. We were equals then.

I called Tomas on Mondays to arrange a time to get together for the weekend. I needed to make child-care arrangements for our interludes.

"Well, Julie," he often began. "I don't know yet what I want to do. Let me think about it. I'll let you know." It was useless then to remind him that I had a child and that my life was all about organizing, planning, and marking things in my calendar. The irritation I felt would have been justified had I been in a more defined relationship with a man my own age. In that situation, I would have expected some understanding. From Tomas, I expected nothing at all. After these conversations, I hung up, feeling rejected, wishing I could disappear.

Now that our relationship was sexual, I noticed that Tomas spent less time at my house when Liza was around. Perhaps we both felt that some artifice would be required to hide the nature of our connection from Liza, an exceptionally perceptive child. I regretted this change; I felt like I was taking something valuable from her. She began asking for Tomas after several weeks of absence. When he finally came for dinner, she was delighted to see him again, and they returned to their comfortable ways. In one e-mail to me, Tomas wrote that being with Liza and me tempted him to consider being part of a more domestic life. I was thrilled to read this but didn't dare hope for more than what we had. Within days of this e-mail, his mood again changed, and he seemed cautious and distant.

We continued seeing each other in this back-and-forth, frequently confusing way. I had told a few close friends, he had told a few close friends. But in a small town, where everyone knows what car you drive, it is hard to keep a secret.

One morning, Tomas's truck was spotted parked in my driveway. The night before I had remarked to myself that he had chosen to park smack in the middle of the driveway, which faced a main town road. I thought about asking him to be more discreet but then checked myself. He was free to do as he pleased.

Now the news spread quickly beyond the small group of friends who had known of our whatever-it-was these last months. The reaction was not always kind. Some people, who didn't understand that Tomas and I had been friends long before our affair, felt that he was taking advantage of my widowhood to have an adventure with an older woman. Some speculated that our affair had begun before Henry's death. Though Tomas and I knew differently, it was still painful to be the subject of gossip.

In some ways, though, being more in the open was a relief. Perhaps we all want our secrets to be found out at last.

––––––––

My brother, David, had helped me wade through the piles of legal paperwork. Henry had a four-page will, leaving everything to me, yet the matter was crawling along, with his assets still frozen and bills unpaid. The final hurdle was imminent. Probate court required that a court-appointed lawyer, a guardian *ad litem,* interview Liza, alone in a room at the county seat. This was supposed to determine that Liza was being well cared for by me, her sole parent.

For the weeks before the appointment, I descended into a vortex of anxiety, convinced that somehow, inadvertently, Liza or I would say something wrong and she would be taken from me. I called my brother in tears. David calmly reminded me that, while I had no choice in the matter, he was sure all would go well. Nevertheless, I lay awake at night, worrying. I tried to prepare Liza for the event without frightening her, but I could tell she didn't like the idea that I couldn't be in the interview room with her.

The appointment date arrived in early April, and with it a freak snowstorm. As I prepared to drive to school to pick up Liza for the interview, Emily called me from her cell phone, asking if I could pick up her daughter, Zoe, as well—her train from the city was delayed by the weather. At this point, I was always happy to offer Emily help—anything to chip away at the mountain of emotional debt. Zoe was one of Liza's more recent friends, a slightly older child who was easy to have around. Zoe's companionship seemed like a windfall as we headed off for the forty-minute drive to the county courthouse through whirls of sometimes blinding snow.

The attorney was late. We waited in the chilly hallway. Zoe helpfully kept up a friendly conversation, resorting to I Spy and

Twenty Questions to pass the time, while I sat silently, willing the ordeal to be over. At last the lawyer arrived—a woman about fifty, only slightly severe in a trim navy suit and a tight, dark chignon. She escorted us upstairs to a long corridor with many office doors. Outside her door, the attorney directed Zoe and me to a wooden bench and kindly guided Liza into her office. The door closed.

I sat nervously on the bench, trying to listen, but the door was too thick to make out anything. Zoe, who seemed to sense my anxiety, tried her best to make up for my silence by telling me a story about something that had happened at school that day. None of her words penetrated, but I was grateful for her effort.

A few minutes later, I realized a miracle was in progress. I heard laughter, a grown woman's laughter, and I knew that Liza had understood what was required. A frequently reserved child, she had nevertheless pulled off a grand performance.

"What was that lady laughing about?" I asked Liza as we returned to our car.

"Oh, I was just telling her about Daddy, you know, just funny stuff he did."

For this I would receive a bill for twelve hundred bucks. But finally it was over, the will resolved, and the bills paid. And I relaxed a tiny bit, with the knowledge that Liza and I were a solid team. I knew Henry would have been proud.

One evening in late April, as we lay in his bed, Tomas told me he would prefer that we not make love anymore.

"I feel like I am doing something wrong with you."

"You aren't doing anything wrong, but if it's easier for you, yes, let's do that. That will be better." I knew it would be easier for many reasons.

"Thank you, thank you," he murmured, kissing me all over my chest with a heartfelt warmth and intimacy I could trust. Oddly enough, this would remain for me the most erotic experience I shared with him.

So we tried holding each other in bed.

It was better for me too. I wondered if asking him to be Henry's body had been such a smart idea after all. Maybe this transposition had never really happened. Being close to Tomas, even in our tentative way, had helped me reinhabit my own body. I wasn't floating anymore, as I had been after Henry's death. My feet felt more firmly settled on the ground.

Just when I was getting used our new arrangement, Tomas arrived unexpectedly at my house one afternoon. I was always pleased to see him. I stood on the stone steps, and he kissed me with enthusiasm.

"Let's go upstairs," he said. I was confused but thrilled. Men had always confused me; it was only Henry I had ever felt I understood. In bed I felt present with Tomas, happy to enjoy what was, instead of thinking about whatever it all might mean. As we lay in bed, the neighbor's son arrived to mow my lawn. Because it was spring now, a spectacular green and sparkly spring, and the grass was growing an inch a week. From downstairs the young man's voice called out, "Hey, where do you want me to dump the grass clippings?" Like two teenagers caught by a parent who has arrived home earlier than expected, Tomas and I muffled our giggles under the covers.

After that day, I didn't see Tomas for a week or so. I called him with some uneasiness one afternoon, after dropping Liza off for a playdate at Anna's house. I had a few hours to spare, during which I was supposedly running errands. Tomas was working in his studio but invited me over.

I'd dawdled for an extra half hour at his house, and now I was going to pay. I hadn't meant to linger. I was just going to stop by, hang out on the porch with him, and drink a soda, but he'd looked so lovely sitting next to me and I knew Liza was safe at Anna's house. What would another half hour matter if we ducked inside for a quickie? I just wanted to feel like a stupid twenty-year-old girl, who wasn't a mother and didn't always have to be responsible.

Worst of all, I had kind of lied. "Um, I'll be right there," I'd told Anna on the phone while zipping up my skirt. "I'm so sorry, Anna, I'm just five minutes away, I just lost track of the time." She was pissed. And not fooled, I was sure. I knew I couldn't do this again.

Irena visited me from the city in early May. We'd planned a visit to a local museum. She wore her strand of ruby boa feathers in her dark Botticelli curls and jingly gold earrings. She rummaged in her gorgeously impractical handbag for her BlackBerry.

Tomas arrived in his pickup truck. Irena studied him thoughtfully.

"He's very young, isn't he?" There was no judgment in her voice. Her statement was merely an observation.

"Yes," I answered, "too young."

"You know, it's not that he's young that I have a problem with. I just don't want to see you getting involved with another self-absorbed artist."

I admired her honesty. It was true that my married life with

Henry had been organized to further his artistic ambitions, not mine. We had agreed that Henry would stop taking the commercial scriptwriting jobs that had been his bread and butter for many years so that he could write his first book, and then his *umami* book. Meanwhile, I took on as much work as I could manage and the big-ticket financial burdens. It had seemed like a good gamble at the time, and I knew many marriages like ours—wife as support staff.

Spending time with a committed artist like Tomas had reawakened my own urges. He had been enthusiastic about my work, always encouraging me to pursue my painting. He was a man who truly lived for his art and made few compromises. But I knew from experience that, with two such persons in a relationship, the more accommodating partner was bound to make choices to support the other's chances for success. Now, perhaps, was my opportunity to be the self-absorbed artist in the new family that was just Liza and me.

four

Late May–July 2003

Once my affair with Tomas was fully out in the open, the town started to feel even smaller. I longed for some kind of escape from my closed world.

Of the many condolence letters I'd received following Henry's death, one e-mail had inspired hope for just such a way out. It was from a Frenchman who organizes a "food happening" in Paris called The White Dinner. One night a year, several thousand people descend with tables, chairs, and loaded picnic baskets upon a location in Paris, kept secret by the organizers till the final hours before the event, when cell phones spring into action. The participants converge, folding tables are set up, food laid out, and a meal takes place, with all participants dressed in white. The gathering is illegal—no permits are secured—but the spirit of camaraderie and joie de vivre overwhelms the halfhearted complaints of *les flics* (the famously much-maligned Parisian policemen). The photos on the website showed glamorous Parisian women in floaty dresses and flamboyant hats, men in white linen trousers and jackets, everyone waving white napkins exuberantly, laughing and cheering. Henry had planned to attend The White Dinner in June and had mentioned it to me as something we could do together—an excuse to go to Europe, a deductible trip that would provide material for his book. The White Dinner seemed to have *umami* written all over it.

As winter passed into spring, I was desperate to go somewhere away from my town. I hated watching myself rearrange my weekends to see Tomas, but without this companionship to anticipate during the week, my future life stretched out terrifyingly before me, the new monotony of my widowhood. I hated thinking about the future of Me. My mind traveled to frightening places as I paced in my house like a bored zoo animal.

I arranged a meeting with Henry's editor and agent to discuss trying to finish the book he had researched. I proposed completing the book myself, though I wasn't sure how to write a book. I presented the idea of a trip to Paris to attend The White Dinner. I headed home on the train, giddy with the prospect of an adventure to plan.

I booked plane tickets for Liza and myself. A male escort is required for every woman at The White Dinner, so I mailed a letter off to Jean, my decidedly low-tech old flame in France.

I also sent an e-mail to Stefano, a friend in Italy, where, I thought, we might as well go after Paris, as we were traveling so far. Stefano e-mailed back. We would be able to stay in his family's apartment in Florence. I hadn't been to Paris or Florence in years, since before Liza was born. I knew my French was rusty, and I hoped I would still be able to remember some of my neglected Italian, though I was encouraged when I had a dream in which I was attending The White Dinner, speaking fluently *en français*.

June arrived at last. The days had warmed, the flowering trees had leafed out, my blue Siberian iris had unfurled, the roses were in full explosion, and our bags were packed. I said good-bye to Tomas, wondering, uneasily, how things would be when I returned.

I am no fan of plane travel. I have always been too skeptical of the physics of the phenomenon to ever be truly comfortable in an airplane. On the advice of the cheerful flight attendant, I was taking a moment to read the safety card in the seat pocket in front of me. I read every section of the safety card, including the part where we were instructed calmly to take off our shoes and slide out onto the inflatable raft. *We'll be bobbing in the middle of the Atlantic Ocean (if we were lucky enough not to be ripped to bits), amid plane wreckage and dismembered bodies. Sharks circling the carnage. Twenty-foot waves. With my luck, a hurricane.* Undeterred by its futility, the flight attendant continued her demonstration. It sounded somewhat more reassuring in a French accent.

I glanced over at Liza, who adores plane travel. She was nestled cross-legged, a book cracked open on her lap, gazing and pointing as we broke through the clouds. Her immediate neighbor, a promisingly eccentric fellow, was ready to talk after determining that she was a reading—rather than a petulant, noisy, electronic-gadgeting—sort of American child. A colorful red and gold embroidered fez capped his graying, shoulder-length hair. His face was vertically lined, with features that suggested his New England origins, though I could tell he wanted me to think he was French.

After the seat belt signs were turned off, our neighbor (his name was James, and he turned out to be very American) drank red wine and chatted for most of the flight. Since I am unable to sleep in planes, what with the pressurized air, the noise of the engines, and worrying about those life rafts, I was happy for the company. While Liza read, ate, watched a movie, then slept, he told me about his work (he was a translator returning home from a meeting with a New York publisher), his great apartment just near the Rodin Museum, and his girlfriend (younger, French). I figured she smoked as much as he did—his long, twitchy fingers and the clinging aroma of stale tobacco on his clothing betrayed his nicotine habit.

"You must bring your daughter to the museum," he said with patrician inflection, as he gave me his phone number. "There is the most marvelous little café right in the museum gardens." I was entertained by the idea, though I doubted the meeting would come off. I jotted his name and number in the notebook I had begun for this trip. We would go to the museum on our first day, I decided, with or without James.

Outside the baggage claim area, James, cigarette lit, gallantly hailed us a cab. He looked so suave with his cigarette that I wished I still smoked, like everyone in France, except that, like many ex-smokers, I felt immediately suffocated by the fumes. James smoked for the duration of our journey into central Paris, courteously holding his left hand outside the open car window as we cleared the airport and passed through the wretched outer industrial areas of the city. At last the familiar nineteenth-century rooftops appeared through the summer haze and we entered the city limits. James directed the taxi driver down the narrow street to the small hotel my brother had recommended in the seventh arrondissement.

"*Alors, à demain!* We will go to the museum!" He waved earnestly as the taxi pulled away.

In our hotel room, Liza and I undressed, exhausted, climbed into the crisp white sheets of the double bed, and drifted off, lulled by the sounds and smells of a midweek day in Paris: mopeds speeding down the narrow street, snippets of workday conversation, the clickety-click of elegant European shoe heels on ancient stone sidewalk, the faint aromas of baguette, melting butter, and someone's freshly brewed *café*.

"Happy birthday, Mama," Liza murmured sleepily, taking my hand under the sheets. I was now forty-four years old. She was six and three-fourths. We were together and happy, a more than acceptable birthday present.

Liza and I had walked all the way to the Place des Vosges, across the Pont du Carrousel. Along the Seine's right embankment, we passed a large pet shop, where we stopped to look at bunnies and puppies eagerly pawing the windows. We continued down narrow side streets till at last we arrived at the ancient, small square where the grassy lawns around four grand, symmetrically positioned fountains were dotted with a hundred Parisians searching for relief from the heat of this unusually warm summer. We found a spot near one of the fountains, enjoying the gentle, cool mist. Liza took off her sandals and splashed water on her face and then at me. She considered a piece of plastic packaging from our lunch and set about making a small boat. The noise of the fountain and the people chattering drowned out her little voice, but I could tell from watching her lips that she was singing to herself. It was like watching a silent movie. Her self-absorbed contentment gave me a chance to take a relaxed look around.

A Frenchman of my age, not especially good looking, just a regular guy, settled down on a spot of lawn. He had an expectant look, his gaze shifting this way and that along the angled paths.

After a while Liza visited me for a drink and a snack. We both laughed as a toddler stripped her clothes off and climbed into the fountain wearing only her underwear. Then Liza returned with her plastic boat to the fountain and I turned back to the Frenchman on the grass. A woman had arrived, not pretty, but striking, with long dark hair and straight-cut bangs, a look that perhaps only French women can pull off without looking severe and over-determined. They lounged lovingly in the grass. A moment later they were madly making out.

The French! My heart quickened with deep admiration and envy. I stared shamelessly. They were busy and did not notice me. I silently prayed that it would be me one day, lying in the arms of someone who was truly happy to be with me, just as I was—a forty-four-year-old mother with a wrinkled belly.

I needed a real grown-up man who could love me, and my child. Liza and I were now a package deal, a two-for-one special. This man wouldn't have to be pretty (maybe I was over that pretty thing now), but he would have to be kind, with a heart as big as my two-car garage back home.

———

Jean, my old flame, arrived at our hotel riding a rusty bicycle that looked like it had weathered a decade or two of rainy Parisian winters. He was wearing a white shirt and tan trousers. He was too rebellious and frugal to fuss about things like white pants.

We had met when I was twenty years old, on my junior year abroad from Smith. We were both working at a printmaking studio on the ground floor of a building in the fourteenth arrondissement, a neighborhood still inhabited then by artists, now by investment bankers.

He was twenty-eight at the time, tall, underfed, with a mop of strawberry blond curls. There was something nineteenth century about him. When he took breaks from his work, he stood in the building's inner courtyard smoking a pipe. I could not resist this archaic habit in a young man, or the engaging splay of his two front teeth, revealed when he removed the tooth-marked pipe-stem from his lips and smiled. When he wasn't smoking or work-ing, he bit his fingernails, down to the quick. For months I watched him, afraid to speak to him. He had an intimidating dedication to his work; my efforts felt childish by comparison, my French was still crude, and I wasn't sure if he was comfortable speaking English.

Marianne, the owner of the studio, liked assigning chores. She taught me my first new useful French words: *la poubelle* (garbage can) and *balayer* (to sweep). Marianne was an ample woman, with a corresponding voice and personality. I was *la petite Américaine*. She was autocratic, affectionate, insulted when I missed days, al-ways insistent that I should eat more.

"*Tiens, tu dois déjeuner avec nous,*" she urged as she led a group off to the nearby bistro at midday. I had little extra spending money, but one lunch hour, when I saw Jean heading off with the others, I impulsively joined them after discovering that I had twenty francs in my wallet. I ordered an omelet. "*M'enfin, tu manges trop peu, ma petite, ça va pas!*" Marianne harangued. She disapproved of such light midday eating, though for me this was a grand feast. They all tucked in to *steak-frites*. As we drank glasses of red wine, I saw that Jean spoke English fluently, with a soft and musical accent.

From that afternoon on, Jean and I became friends. Unfortu-nately, however, I never felt any special attention from him, certainly nothing like the crush I had. I waited patiently for some sign, often lingering at the studio past my usual hours until he called it quits for the day.

One spring afternoon, my crush at its peak, Jean rose to leave the studio. I waited a moment, put down my work, and walked with what I hoped was a casual gait out the door onto the street. He was twenty paces ahead of me. I broke into a jog to catch him before he reached the Métro stop at the end of the block.

"Jean!"

He stopped, surprised to see me, perhaps thinking he had left something behind. *"Qu'est-ce qu'il y a?"*

"Jean. May I speak to you in English?" I paused, but he did not seem rushed, so I took heart, caught my breath, and continued. "Would you consider a brief affair?"

He laughed affectionately, and his two splayed front teeth winked at me. "What are you asking me? You know, my life is very com-pli-ca-ted." He told me about his girlfriend in Holland and Gabrielle, his other girlfriend in Paris.

"Well, I'll be leaving soon, in May," I replied. "I won't complicate your life for too long."

"Alors"—he laughed—*"on y pense."* He offered me the smile of one willing but wary and we parted. I returned to the studio and pretended to work for another hour. Marianne, no fool, cast a sharp and knowing look across the room.

I was living for that school year in the home of a mysterious Madame de P., an elegant woman of the aristocracy in her sixties, a veteran of a wartime concentration camp, imprisoned for her involvement with the French Underground. She wore cream-colored silk Yves Saint Laurent blouses buttoned up her swanlike neck to the base of her white-haired French twist, slender pencil skirts, and Charles Jourdan high heels. Madame whisked an unseen lover in and out of her vast apartment in the elegant sixteenth arrondissement in the afternoons, while my friend Katie, the other student living in the apartment, had a brief but thrilling affair with Madame's daughter—on other afternoons.

Alors, I joined the grand adventure—sneaking Jean into the apartment, past the all-seeing eyes of Josepha, the Spanish maid, whom I feared and adored, covering the cage of annoying living room parakeets with a blanket so the endless chirping would not disturb our lovemaking. Josepha's raised eyebrow at dinnertime told me she had found us out in spite of my efforts.

After I returned to the States to complete my senior year at college, I looked forward to Jean's large brown envelopes, addressed in an antique Spencerian script, adorned with festive stamps from Mali, Senegal, and Morocco, where he wintered. Two years later, I went back to see him. We made love on the floor of a friend's apartment.

We corresponded on and off over the years—sometimes just a letter a year. The friendship continued after I began my relationship with Henry. A few more visits, now chaste. He had married Gabrielle, the girlfriend in Paris, and now they were parents of a daughter.

Jean was leaner; the curls of his hair had grayed to the color of cinnamon toast. His face was tanned, and deltas of wrinkles fanned out from his hazel eyes. His nose was sharper, his curved lips thinner. The years of pipe smoking had stained his teeth, though not the two front ones, their splay broadened, still charming and familiar to me.

I looked much younger, I concluded, taking a mental inventory of the number of skin potions, tubes of whitening toothpaste, and boxes of hair color I had purchased since turning forty, my part of the American obsession with self-preservation and denial of old age and death.

"Vous êtes tellement chic." Jean admired our white outfits with amused irony. In our white dresses, Liza and I were ready for a Victorian tea party.

My camera captured the scene in the cobbled square in front of the famous Panthéon: women's hats and scarves floating against the twilight sky, a man dressed in a white 1920s suit and spats like Jay Gatsby come to life, the exuberant synchronized waving of white napkins as the meal progressed. The police showed up to cheering and jeering and more waving of white napkins. Amid the festivity, Liza played with a friendly dog under the table. I wondered if all the commotion and new people were overwhelming her, or if she was missing her father, who had often reminded me of a playful terrier and who, in affectionate moments, had sometimes even licked my face. I was glad to have Jean there; it was good to take his hand as the evening concluded and the tables emptied.

At midnight, Jean walked us back to our hotel. We had made plans to meet at the Gare d'Austerlitz in the morning—we would spend our last weekend in France together in the country village where he lived with his daughter.

As our train rushed through the flat countryside, Jean raged about the evils of city life, the Internet, cell phones, computers, and the abject materialism of modern society. I smiled, grateful that I had left my cell phone and laptop at home, amused that, compared with Jean, I was a paragon of modern-age wizardry, whereas at home I engaged in a love-hate relationship with my computer and all things technical. As he continued on and the landscape softened, I considered how completely unhappy we would have made each other if we had ever tried to be together. How much better was this—a twenty-year friendship, still respectful and loving.

His house was a magical cottage, overgrown with ivy and flowering vines. His daughter's room was welcoming, and soon, despite the language barrier, our girls found a way to play together. Jean took me around the back of the house and up a flight of wooden stairs to show me his studio, a perfect artist's garret: a table with neatly arranged papers and notebooks, plant specimens, rocks and shells, a few examples of his work framed on the wall, a saggy but comfortable old sitting chair. A good place to spend life. That's what I would need to find for myself.

Gabrielle, Jean's wife, met us at the train station upon our return to Paris. She had always remained here, in her small city apartment. The French have such interesting solutions to the problems of cohabitation and marriage. Petite with long dark hair and those straight-cut bangs, she was stylish and urban in a crisp white blouse and dark skirt, perched slightly above me on modern black platform sandals. We ate Parisian hot dogs in the nearby Jardin des Plantes, sweating in the stupor of the record heat wave burning all of Europe.

I had never envied Gabrielle, though I understood the choices she had made, having made similar ones myself with Henry. She was alone for half the year, married to a man who placed his art above all other things, except his daughter. Another self-absorbed artist whom I had loved, indeed still loved, because, like Tomas, he had always encouraged me to pursue my creative life.

We parted on the blistering sidewalk, and Liza and I hailed a well-deserved taxi for the trip back to our hotel, where we packed up to leave for Italy the next morning.

Stefano, a friend of many years, drove us from the airport in Pisa to his family's apartment just outside the Porta Romana in Florence, where we would stay for the next week. Waking late in the morning to thick and heavy heat, Liza and I found relief at the local *caffè-gelateria*—homemade ice cream in at least twenty flavors. We couldn't think of a good reason not to eat ice cream at ten in the morning.

We left the hot streets to enter the Brancacci Chapel, site of famous frescoes by Fra Filippo Lippi, Fra Angelico, and Masaccio. In these paintings, one sees familiar faces: the man who just cut you a piece of parmigiano cheese, the friendly shopkeeper who sold you a pair of shoes. The gene pool seems unaltered since the Renaissance.

During a visit years earlier, Henry and I had stepped into a *caffè* and remarked together on the face of the bartender. With his long dark hair, aquiline nose, and large dark eyes, he seemed a Fra Angelico portrait subject come to life. After drinking Campari cocktails in the bar, Henry and I had polished off a huge *bistecca alla fiorentina* and a bottle of red wine in a nearby restaurant, then made a drunken trip to a friend's house on a motorcycle we had rented for the week. I hugged Henry's waist while the engine buzzed and he navigated the cobbled streets. I felt like Claudia Cardinale in *8½*, young and glamorous.

Henry and I had eaten lunch at this particular restaurant ten years earlier, and now Liza and I were here at last. I'd gotten us lost in the narrow streets as I tried to find the place from memory. Liza was complaining, a rarity for a kid who so far had been a trouper. I had dragged her all over Florence to museums and chapels to look at art, plying her with frequent stops for *gelati*.

"Mama, when are we getting there?" she whined wearily.

"It's worth it, Lizzie, I promise, you'll see." I didn't blame her, we were both fading, the promise of a cold drink and a memorable meal the only thing that kept me from ducking into the nearest pizzeria and calling off the search. Finally, the small square I remembered appeared, and Liza and I found shelter from the sun at a little table under the restaurant awning.

On the previous occasion, Henry had ordered *colli di pollo ripieni*. Each stuffed chicken neck was presented in the vertical position, the head and coxcomb centered in a ruffled collar of sautéed vegetables, as if the chicken's head and feathered shoulder had pierced through the white plate. The effect was macabre, and the horror on the faces of our vegetarian lunch companions must have exceeded Henry's expectations. I had laughed heartily, despite feeling repulsed, with wifely pride—Henry had outdone himself. He had great fun moving the heads around on the plate, making squawking noises, while the vegetarian friends recoiled in their seats.

No chicken necks today.

"We'll both have the *pomodoro in gelatina* and then the

polpettone." The tomato gelatin was a specialty of this restaurant. Our white plates arrived with the upturned, flat-ended cones of carmine red gelatin quivering in pools of bright green olive oil. Liza and I had fun jiggling the gelatin with a fork, playing with one's food being just one of the many delights of eating a meal with a six-year-old epicure. White, unsalted Tuscan bread absorbed the tomato and oil; we squished it all between our fingers before popping the sodden sponge into our mouths.

Polpettone, the next course, might be translated as meat loaf. This was not American diner meat loaf (which I love, with a big dollop of mustard). This dish was more like a pâté. We ate the rich slabs silently and reverently.

Fully satiated, Liza made a still life drawing of the remains of her lunch, complete with her glass of Coke, a rare treat, in colored pencils on the paper table covering.

While we forked up mouthfuls of our dessert, a light but intense chocolate cake, a man wearing elegant tan suede, tasseled loafers seduced a woman at the next table. The suede loafers reminded me of a pair Henry had owned.

"We never ate the wild boar sausages!"

As Liza and I left the restaurant, I remembered this line, Henry's frequently quoted favorite, from the Japanese film *Tampopo*. The gangster of several of the film's vignettes utters these dying words to his weeping lover. They are both dressed in white, his jacket stained with the fresh blood of many gunshot wounds.

I felt a sudden pang of sorrow for Henry, who never got to eat this meal, sweep his tasting pointer finger through the sauces, or pick at the leftovers on my plate.

A *week later,* Stefano drove us back to the airport. At the gate we said our good-byes. *"Allora ciao, Giuliettina,"* he said, embracing me forcefully and kissing me on both cheeks. He seized Liza and raised her up high, which she loved. I thanked him for having us and gave him some last-minute girlfriend advice. Any delay in boarding our plane was welcome—I was dreading the return home.

My refrigerator was empty except for a bowl of fruit salad with a note from Cathy, welcoming us home and thanking me for letting her family use the swimming pool during our absence. I filled a small bowl and nibbled at it while reacquainting myself with our house and sifting through piles of mail.

I called Tomas the next day, and we made plans to get together. I felt peaceful, tired from the journey but restored in other ways. Neither Tanya nor Emily could take Liza for a sleepover, so I called Cathy. I figured she owed me one, fruit salad aside, after using the pool for three weeks.

She was reading a book on her porch hammock when I arrived. She came over and embraced me as I walked up the steps to her house carrying Liza's sleepover bag. Cathy's hugs had always made me uncomfortable. At that moment, however, she was a most convenient babysitter. I wasn't interested in lingering long on her porch.

"I'm off to see Tomas. Let's hope that absence makes the heart

grow fonder," I joked. Cathy gave me another hug before I walked
back to my car.

I felt cheerful driving up the road, beside the railroad tracks,
enjoying the view of the mountains and river, listening to the All-
man Brothers. I hummed along to "Stormy Monday," reliving my
adolescence of the mid-1970s, when young Tomas was just a newborn. While listening to Duane's guitar licks, as heartbreaking as
the song lyrics, I reminded myself of the futility of unreasonable
expectations, while there was still time.

Later, we were lying in the dark. An ambulance passed by on the
main road a half mile away, audible but invisible through the trees.
For me, the sound of an ambulance siren immediately brought
back the afternoon of Henry's death.

"I still miss him so much, I can't bear it. How long is this going to go on?"

Tomas replied softly, "Do you miss everything about him?"

I paused. *The man asked me an honest question. I should give him
an honest answer.* "No, I don't, but when I think that way I feel
very guilty."

"You shouldn't feel guilty."

"What do you mean?"

Tomas stared at the ceiling. A crack was forming in my brain.
He had something to tell me.

"Tomas, please, I want you to tell me. Please tell me."

"There was a woman in California," Tomas said. "I thought
you knew. One time I was in the kitchen with Henry, he was telling me about her. You came in, and the expression on your face
made me think that you knew, that it was something you two were
working out. But now I see that you didn't know anything."

. . .

But I knew just who the woman was. Henry had come home from one of his trips out West. While unpacking his suitcase, he told me about meals he had eaten and people he had met.

"I met this woman, you'll love her. She lives in Portland with her two kids. She's petite, just like you. She even likes knitting. Her place is a complete mess. I guess that's what happens when you get divorced."

"Is anything going on between you?" I asked Henry, feeling chilled. Even allowing myself to ask the question felt shocking.

"No, nothing," he replied.

"Is there more I need to know?" I asked Tomas as the darkness of his room gathered about us.

"Yes, there is," he said, "but I think you need to speak to other people. I don't know everything, but there is more."

A few more quiet moments passed. "Tomas, I feel like I'm going to find out some very dark things, is that right?"

"Yes."

Amazingly, we slept.

In the morning, I slipped out of Tomas's bed and retreated with my cell phone to the bathroom. Cool morning light filtered through the outsize green leaves of a tropical potted plant. I sat on the closed toilet seat and called Emily. I sensed now that the tension I'd felt these last months might be related to some burden she'd been carrying, greater even than witnessing Henry's last moments with me. She started crying when I told her what I knew. I had caught her unprepared, but it took little coaxing to get the truth out of her. She must have been feeling like a corked bottle full of secrets.

"It's Cathy," she said, her voice choked. "Cathy and Henry were having an affair, for two years at least. We found all their e-mails on his computer the morning after he died."

I listened as Emily described the panicked decisions made the morning after Henry's death—that morning in his office when I heard a woman cry out. *Whose voice had screamed?* Matthew had hidden the evidence on Henry's computer so that I would not find it during such a vulnerable time. In the midst of everything, Cathy had come over. She wanted to help with funeral arrangements, she said. Matthew confronted her, and she left. Later she was summoned over to delete her correspondence from Henry's e-mail.

I listened; my brain was a wide-open portal; I felt calm. There was me, listening, and the inner caretaker of me thinking about how I should feel about what I was hearing.

My first thought: *I have to go pick up my child.* Liza was in the home of a woman who had been involved in a long affair with my now dead husband, who had used her own daughter to gain daily entry to my home, who had insinuated herself into my life, eaten my food, preened by my swimming pool, pretended to be a friend. A woman who had left a fucking fruit salad in my refrigerator.

A gun was too swift, too merciful. I wanted a sword to slit her end to end and then, with one hundred more cuts, dice her body into small pieces and leave the bloodied, quivering remains of skin, muscle, and soulless guts on her front lawn, arranged in a gruesome scarlet letter.

I couldn't kill Henry anymore, since he was, conveniently enough, dead.

part two

storm

... I can't escape from that unsettling
sense of recognition that accompanies
Jane Eyre (which must be shared by
innumerable other readers)—and I don't mean
that I recognize myself in the novel, but
I recognize something else in it, the secrets and
the madness and the heroine who must
learn to uncover her true self, as well
as several others'.

—JUSTINE PICARDIE,
My Mother's Wedding Dress

five

July 2003

Heat rose in waves from the asphalt road ahead of me.

Jesusfuckingchrist

I gripped the steering wheel so hard that I veered off course.

I want to fucking kill that woman.

The road was arrow straight, alongside the railroad tracks.

slit her from her head to her fucking

Vertigo overtook me as I stared at the perfect receding vanishing point.

A summer day, two years earlier.

I had stopped by to visit Cathy's next-door neighbor, Jenny. I drooped into one of her Adirondack chairs and gratefully accepted a glass of lemonade. Her younger children ran around the yard, supervised by their older brother. I was amazed they had the energy in the stifling heat. The rose petals were wilting on the bushes, and the lawn was turning brown. I wiped sweat from my forehead, though we sat in the shade.

"You know, he's over there all the time," Jenny said, nudging her chin in the direction of Cathy's house, whose gingerbread roof peeked over the dividing fence. She settled into another chair with her lemonade. "You don't think there's anything going on, do you?" She looked at me, as if embarrassed to present such an idea.

Cathy? The woman Henry had called "a gaunt hag, with oversize boobs and sloped shoulders"? These defects were severe aesthetic sins in his beauty standard book, just one level above thick ankles. Not to mention the fact that Cathy could be just plain weird and chilly. My face registered surprise.

Jenny, allegedly Cathy's close friend, answered herself. "Yeah, ewww. Couldn't be, right?"

But then again.

A year ago, six months before his death.

I had passed in and out of Henry's office several times that evening, to find him involved in a lengthy phone discussion. He addressed Cathy by name in a soothing manner that signaled this was an Important Talk. At last he hung up.

"Why do you have to fix all her stupid problems?" I asked with irritation. "You should be spending time with your family, not talking to her."

He and I never had Important Talks anymore. We talked about whether we should call the electrician to fix the ancient exposed wiring in the back hall, whether he or I would be picking Liza up from day camp that day, who was coming to dinner that weekend, what the menu would be, what we would eat that night. Food, our final connection to intimacy.

I paused, glaring at Henry as thoughts coalesced in my brain. Words came out of my mouth that shocked me.

"Are you having an affair with Cathy?"

Henry smiled gently and after a beat replied, "No, I am not."

He was a fucking liar. I was a fucking idiot.

The back of my neck prickled, in spite of the car air-conditioning. I had allowed this ugliness to happen, right under my nose. I hadn't wanted to see it, but it was always there. Now I understood her personality and my feelings of unease around her. Some part of me had never trusted her. Why hadn't I listened?

Her sudden religiosity made sense—some kind of advance penitence. I smiled—darkly—at the twisted logic. Attend church, suck up to well-meaning minister, sing in choir, sign child up for Sunday school now, and perhaps things won't go so wretchedly later, when everyone finds out about your adultery *and what a lying fucking cunt you really are.* Hypocrisy has its own elegant symmetry.

Excruciating—like sunburn searing my brain—to consider the many meals we had shared while their affair went on secretly. Henry proudly presiding over the steak on the barbecue while we four had conversations that felt authentic about our hopes for our daughters, our work, books and music we loved, our plans for the future.

On a few rare occasions Cathy and I had even spent time together away from our husbands. There was the time she had insisted on taking me out for my birthday along with her neighbor, Jenny. I still had the Polaroid in my office taken by the waiter in the Mexican restaurant—the three of us in an embrace, I in the center, wearing an enormous and ridiculous sombrero hat.

Cathy and I had gone clothes shopping together on one idle weekday afternoon, a trip to the Old Navy at the mall, where we bought T-shirts and jeans. It was supposed to be fun, but in the end, I had anguished, noting that she wore a smaller size than I did. It was like a bad day in high school when what you remember most is that you felt fat. I never went shopping with her again.

And all that exercising might have been not for herself but to please Henry, who liked his women slender. How often I had felt fat and full of self-loathing during our marriage—wishing I could perform self-surgery on my offending blobby bits—a feeling in no way softened by my observation of Henry's own slowly inflating midlife paunch.

He was a piece of shit bastard making me feel like a crazy person. Insisting that we invite them over all the time, every goddamned weekend, the way she sat like a queen by the pool and wore those super-low-cut bikini tops with her tits hanging out, like a fucking porn star.

There was that day when I peeked into Henry's office and noticed that the sheets on the twin guest bed looked rumpled. I saw a small damp spot—it looked like middle-aged nap drool. I offered to wash the sheets with that day's laundry. No, Henry insisted, he would wash them. What an idiot. At least it was in his office, not in our bed. I wondered if I had been in the house at the time, working in my office downstairs. Anything was possible.

She has been so fucking nice to me since January.

Cathy and I had shared meals in these last months since Henry's death. I had listened to her book recommendations while eating her serviceable meat loaf, mashed potatoes, and oversteamed broccoli. We had watched movies afterward while sipping cups of tea on her couch. That couch—the silent witness—had undoubtedly seen a lot of action.

I found myself on Cathy's quiet street, parked in front of her house, a sweet, gingerbread-trimmed Victorian. I could see her, relaxed, reading in her hammock on the porch. *He's over there all the time.* With dumbfounded disgust I realized that I must have provided child care for Amy after school, while Steve was at work and Cathy and Henry fucked on her couch, or in her spare bedroom, or wherever they did their fucking.

My car door slammed with a satisfying, German-engineered *thunk*. I walked up to her porch steps. She put her book down, smiled, then the corners of her mouth dropped, her expression changed to concern; my face felt like stone.

"Get over here," I said between gritted teeth. "We are going to talk *now*." She rose from the hammock, and I walked her to the vacant dirt parking lot of a nearby building, where we stood next to each other for a silent moment as I tried to focus my thoughts. She looked at me expectantly.

"I have been told about your affair with Henry."

"Julie, I need to sit down." She slumped onto a rotting tree stump, her already pale face immediately drained of remaining color.

Fuckingcuntbitch. My hand twitched, it wanted to smack her face. But the thought of touching her skin felt toxic. I never wanted to touch her again. Standing so close was more than I wanted, but I would have to endure this, what I hoped would be our last time in such an intimate situation.

"What," I asked, tensed with bewildered anger, "*what* did you think you were doing?"

She murmured her response. She had been weak, Henry had been so persuasive, she was so sorry, so sorry.

Blame the dead guy. That's nice. That's easy.

"That fucking fruit salad you left in my refrigerator. Did you think that if you were really, really nice to me that when I found out I would forgive you?"

She nodded weakly.

"You are a fucking cunt." I had never used that word directly to another woman. My mouth felt ugly, polluted. I had reached into a dark pit inside me and pulled out a slimy swamp creature.

"My love for you was genuine—" she began.

"What do you mean, *genuine?* There is nothing genuine about you. How can you feel love for a woman in friendship and be fucking her husband? What kind of woman does that and thinks she is being a friend? A psycho case, that's who. You disgust me. You're like poison."

She looked down at her feet. "You know, Henry never loved me, he never really cared about me at all. He loved you, he always loved you."

"And what kind of love would that be?"

No wonder I was taking fucking medication for twelve years.

I wonder how many others there were.

There were definitely others. Maybe the woman who screamed was one of them.

"So." I looked at her hard, daring myself to make eye contact. "Here's what's going to happen. You have a week to tell your husband or I am going to do it for you. You weren't going to tell him—were you?"

"I'll do it," Cathy replied quietly, choosing not to answer my question. Her head slumped farther down. She looked at me with the look of a sorrowful child, chastened but still hoping to squirm out of trouble.

"Julie, I'm begging you, for the sake of our children, can they still—"

She doesn't get it, not at all. A sword. Is what I need. Maybe death by one hundred cuts is too kind.

"I do not want my child to ever be in the same room with you or your child ever again if I can help it. Do not blame me for this. You and he did this. This is your fucking fault. Now, I'm going to get my kid."

I turned around and walked back toward her house. She remained seated on the tree stump.

Henry, you are so lucky to be fucking dead.

He had been a clever man, blessed with a great sense of dramatic timing. Seven months earlier, Henry's death had been a random medical catastrophe, a tragedy that had caused so much misery for Liza and me. Hundreds of sad people at his funeral. Now it looked more like the Great Escape.

The inside of Cathy's house, as quaint as the outside, smelled familiar. Coffee, toast, that morning's *New York Times*, the faint ammonia smell of a favored brand of kitchen cleaner.

I called for Liza, who appeared promptly with Amy on the second-floor landing as if she understood my urgency. Liza scurried down the stairs with unusual promptness. Her sleepover bag was neatly packed, slung over the banister post. I grabbed the bag, took Liza's hand firmly, pulling her out the door onto the sidewalk, across the street to our car. Liza climbed in silently. I slammed the car door closed.

Cathy was still sitting on the stump in the empty parking lot across the street.

———————

Insanity followed behind me in a beat-up red pickup. The driver, a beer guzzler, gut busting out of his stained wife beater, slumped behind the wheel of his truck with mismatched chop-shop doors, muffler burnt out, spewing exhaust. Beer Guzzler reached for the can in the cup holder, slugged the last of it, wiped his mouth with the back of his hairy hand, and tossed the empty can onto the road just to piss off my tree-hugger soul. The can clattered away, my brain jangled. *Maybe I really am crazy.*

My hands were shaking on the steering wheel, but the car kept going forward. We approached the town's lone intersection with a traffic light. I registered the red light just in time to apply the brakes.

"Mama, why are you so sad?"

"Something terrible just happened between Cathy and me. Cathy did something horrible. I can't ever trust her again. I'm so sorry, but I don't think we can have any more playdates with Amy."

Liza started crying. She and Amy had been friends since they were two years old. I was crying too—crazy and furious. What was I doing to my child? But what else was there to do? The light turned green.

Drive us home, get us there in one piece, and then set up the barricades. Get us home, close the windows, push heavy furniture against the doors to keep out the crazy guy right behind me.

Was Henry laughing at me? He drove us both mad, Cathyfuckingbitch and me. Maybe he enjoyed it. He did enjoy it. It was a game.

"Mama, what did Cathy do?"

"I can't tell you now, but one day I will. I just can't tell you now."

"If she said she was sorry, would that make it better?"

"No, because what she did is so terrible that I can't ever trust her again. I can't trust her to take care of you."

"Did she take something from you?"

I paused, wondering if Liza knew something.

"Yes. Yes, she did."

When we got inside the house, I could see that it was too late; the craziness had slipped in through the screen doors on the hot July air, and now it floated everywhere, permeating every room.

My marriage was a dead thing. Leaving Liza standing in the kitchen, I walked up the stairs to my bedroom dresser, took off my wedding ring, dropped it into my jewelry box. The world of my marriage seemed to be mostly illusion.

I remembered the many times in recent years when I hadn't wanted to have sex with Henry. I had felt repelled by him, there had been something insincere, almost smarmy that I couldn't place, as if he were a stranger inhabiting the body of the man I'd known for sixteen years. Even kissing him felt like a violation. I had retreated sexually—to preserve myself from the deception my body understood. Now I could be honest. I hated him. I loathed him. And I still loved him.

———

I phoned Cathy on four successive days. It was like talking to a dead line. She said nothing, though I tortured her for a response. I ranted.

"Isn't adultery the big no-no at your church?"

"Isn't it pretty much the big no-no everywhere?"

"So, Henry was some kind of hypnotist?"

"That's your explanation for an affair of almost three years?"

"For two, three years you couldn't say 'No, this is wrong, we must stop'?"

"What is this, the death of free will?"

"A fucking fruit salad was supposed to fix things?"

It was unsatisfying and maddening. My anger was a creature, wounded and flailing. My anger wanted red meat. My anger wanted revenge. It couldn't sink its teeth in anywhere.

I thought of all the times I hadn't been able to say no to Henry. When he wanted to buy a new computer, a new bag for his computer, a new pair of biking shoes, a new bike, when he wanted to throw yet another expensive dinner party.

At last, on the fourth day, she hung up on me, in medias rant.

Good. This has to end. It would be so easy to destroy myself with my anger if she didn't fight back. I need to retain some shred of self-respect.

Steve, Cathy's husband, almost forgotten during the first days, phoned me. "Couldn't we keep things private? For the children's sake?"

This was my raw, weak spot—my child. I agreed. Yes, that made sense, why did everyone have to know? My own sense of shame longed to keep everything quiet.

But then, later, I imagined future scenes.

We lived in a very small town.

Our houses were barely half a mile apart.

There would be functions at school, concerts in town, encounters at the grocery store and the drugstore, the dry cleaner, the little gourmet shop where I bought cookies for Liza in the afternoons, the toy shop on Main Street, where we walked on Saturdays to be fussed over by the shopkeeper, grandma to all the town's kids.

There would be dinner parties. If no one knew, they would continue to invite Cathy and Steve to these dinners, because they were part of our social group. I would find myself sitting at the same table with her, or sitting on lawn chairs at a barbecue, forced to look at her, forced to greet her and make pleasant conversation. How could I keep our girls apart in that scenario?

I will be worn down.

I will lose my mind.

I will have to live a completely false life.

I can't pretend. I don't have the stomach for it. I have always been a terrible liar. No more lying.

There was chaos among the members of the small group who had held the secret since January. This group turned out to be Matthew and his wife, Emily and her husband, Irena, Anna, Tomas and his former girlfriend, who had all come to the house on the morning of January 9 to help with Henry's funeral arrangements. They had decided to remain quiet for a time, to let me recover from the shock of Henry's death. Matthew had planned a funeral for his best friend while coping with his grief, shock, and profound disappointment. Matthew and his wife had been our friends for years. None of the group had counted on Tomas telling me when he did. But as in much of life, things don't always go as planned.

Emily asked if she could now speak to our other friends. She told me that keeping the secret for these months had been emotionally exhausting. She had felt like a liar. I understood.

And of course there was the little matter of revenge.

Emily raged about the last months—remaining silent, forcing politeness when she saw Cathy in town.

Anna, in a fury as bright as her red hair, said it was time for the Scarlet Letter.

Gossip did the job swiftly. Cathy was now fully exposed in our small community. She stood alone at the school playground, she was shunned at the supermarket, but there was intense shame for me as well. The feeling of whiplash caught me unprepared. The pitying looks, the oblique apologies for my latest tragedy. I was humiliated, quite sure that everyone was talking about the scandal my life had become. In fact, my life felt like a complete ruin. Hell is indeed a small town.

Steve phoned me as news spread. "You lied to me. You told me you would keep things private. Do you really want our children to find out about this?"

"I changed my mind," I snapped back. "I get to do that. And this really isn't a private matter. Henry and your wife kept their secret by lying to everyone, to all our friends. I won't lie anymore."

"You're a liar," he repeated.

"Yeah, right. And the liar in your home, who lied to you for years?"

He had already circled the wagons. He was going to stay with Cathy—his marriage vows were sacred. I pointed out that Cathy had not thought much about her sacred vows.

"I'm going to try to forgive her, and I think you should too."

"I don't give a shit what you think I ought to do. I'll forgive her when and if I decide to forgive her."

.   .   .

Cathy sent e-mails. She was a writer after all, and a good one. She offered articulate apologies about the terrible thing she and Henry had done. She told me that she was determined to win back her husband's love and trust, that she was committed to devoting herself again to her husband and child. She also accused me of ruining her reputation in town.

We were in our separate trenches.

I need to leave this place.

———

I called Leslie Burns, Henry's psychiatrist. He had been seeing her during the last year and a half of his life. Anxiety, he had told me. He couldn't work. He was having panic attacks and trouble sleeping. She had prescribed medication, different from mine. Our house was a regular drugstore.

Leslie Burns agreed to meet with me, but only because I was the executor of Henry's estate. She would need to see that in writing.

I arrived midday in Grand Central Station. I had not been depriving myself much since January had brought its glad tidings, so I hailed a cab and made myself comfortable in the backseat.

Then I looked at my driver to give him directions. He was a very attractive man. Dark, glossy hair tossed to one side. Dark, wide-set, sleepy eyes. Olive skin, high cheekbones. His hack license suggested that he was a recent immigrant from Eastern Europe. His elegant hands rested on the steering wheel like two beautiful, bored fashion models. Tomas's hands, but softer, unused to rough work. Our eyes met in the rearview mirror as I gave him the Upper East Side address.

Suddenly the air in the taxi felt superheated. I wanted to speak to him. I wanted him to pull over so we could make out in the backseat. He looked at me in the rearview mirror, an uncomfortably long look. I rummaged in my handbag for my wallet and, on second thought, lipstick. When I looked up, his eyes met mine again.

I had the feeling of elastic time, like the day Henry died and the last five minutes of his life stretched out. The trip was completely silent, just the rumbling of the car's old chassis on the city streets, the traffic outside.

At last and too soon he pulled up in front of a brownstone on an elegant, tree-lined street in the East Seventies. I paid my fare, lingering as long as I could. I stepped out, and he looked at me and I looked at him. I just wanted an hour with this man in a hotel room somewhere. I didn't want to speak to him or know his name. I wondered if Henry had felt like this when he pursued his women.

I stood outside a bit longer than necessary, arranging my bags. The driver lingered on as well, and I saw him looking again in the rearview mirror while the car idled. I turned away toward the door of the doctor's office. When I turned back for a last look, he was driving off slowly.

Inside the office was the hush of the white noise machine, magazines to browse. I patted down my skirt, fiddled with my tank top and my hair as if I'd had that hour in a hotel room after all.

Leslie Burns leaned back in her comfortable black leather chair, resting her feet on an ottoman. She was a plump woman who wore overalls. "He loved you, you know," she reassured me. "He did not want your marriage to end. He loved you and Liza and really valued that part of his life."

I wondered if she might lie to me, just to make me feel better.

"But what about this other part of his life, with Cathy and other women?" I asked. "Was he ever going to tell me, or was this going to go on and on?"

"I believe he wanted to tell you about Cathy. You know, it took him six months to tell *me* about Cathy. At first when he told me, he made no apologies." Leslie shifted her ample body in the chair. I couldn't keep my eyes off her overalls. In all my many years of therapy, I had never seen a shrink in anything but a tasteful, businesslike outfit.

"As time went on it became clear that his relationship with Cathy was destroying his life. He wanted to end it, but he was afraid to tell you. He was afraid you'd leave him and take Liza away."

You better believe I would've left him.

I looked around on the walls and found the reassuring diplomas from Ivy League universities. I would hear this woman out.

"I believe the other women—there were several—were 'transitional,' a way to end his relationship with Cathy and return to you. I was trying to help him do that."

She told me that Henry showed signs of narcissistic personality disorder. For Cathy she suggested a possible diagnosis of borderline personality disorder. Women with borderline personality are emotionally unstable and intensely needy, and often resort to dramatic gestures to win love and attention.

My mouth hung open. *Holy fucking shit.*

Leslie explained that both diagnoses refer to the behavior of people with low self-esteem, usually the result of particular child-hood emotional traumas.

"Henry often spoke about his difficult relationship with his mother," Leslie said. "She idolized him and expected him to take on a lot of responsibility for the happiness of the family. That's a classic situation."

Leslie described how, as adults, people with NPD are charis-matic extroverts, but inside, in private moments, they are aware of the false social persona. In contrast to the confident personali-ties they project, they are filled with self-loathing. People like this can't tolerate solitude because it forces them to see the true self, hidden below the surface. The false persona might, however, win them many friends, sexual partners, and career success.

"And, sadly, our culture often rewards such behavior," Leslie said, sighing. "Deceptive behavior is very common," she contin-ued. "I have another patient in this situation. Patients like this have affairs as a way of testing the people they really love, almost to prove that they are unworthy of love."

I remembered how charming Henry had been when we met, how polite. I had been suspicious of it at first, but he had won me over. This same strategy had obviously worked with Cathy and other women.

Henry's childhood experiences do not justify him being an amoral asshole as an adult. How much compassion am I supposed to have for him? I had an unhappy adolescence, but that doesn't give me license to lie, cheat, and steal.

Leslie continued. "Borderline or NPD adults are both very needy, given to extreme emotional fluctuations and distortions of reality."

"You don't pay enough attention to me." Henry's frequent

complaint. "You should spend more time paying attention to me and less time worrying about Liza."

Two really messed-up people had found each other, fed off each other. In Cathy, Henry had found a ready worshiper, and in him she had found a love object with an endless need for attention.

Leslie leaned toward me. "Julie, do you mind if I ask you— what would you have done if Henry had told you about Cathy?"

"I would've divorced him so fast his head would've been spinning," I snapped back. But those were just words. Really, I didn't know what I would have done.

"I'm sorry to hear that," Leslie said. She lowered her gaze for a moment. I saw that she really was sorry. She had been rooting for him, hoping that he could repair his life.

I wondered if his death had been not a random medical event but rather the direct consequence of his choices. I left the office with a new feeling about Henry and Cathy. I was not ready to forgive them—my rage was not burned out yet. But to my surprise, I felt sorrow for Henry. He had died before he had a chance to undo the damage.

Matthew had called me every day since Henry's death, always comforting, "just checking in." After confronting Cathy, I'd called him to see what had survived from Henry's computer hard drive. I had actually given him Henry's computer, never imagining I'd need it again. Matthew had backed up everything and now gave me three CDs with Henry's personal journal, *umami* book notes, and correspondence. A few times during the prior months, I'd asked Matthew if I could have copies of material on the hard drive, but he had always been vague, promising to get them to me, hoping I'd forget. Anticipating a good deal of material, I'd dropped the CDs off at the copy shop the day before rather than print it out at home. Further, my idea was to take the package and mail it to Helen, my therapist, without even opening it, so that she and I could look at the contents together in a safe space. I had the addressed envelope all ready in the car.

The copy shop in town is a very local sort of place, where people know you well. It is wedged between a small gourmet shop (where the coffee is good and the tuna fish salad is supreme) and a service station where I took my car to be repaired. One February morning, when my car wouldn't start, I'd played Damsel in Distress, and Tony had come right over with his jumper cables. In this same town center are the grocery store, post office, drugstore, and a knitting shop where I spent a good deal of money on yarn.

As I entered the copy shop, there was the momentary relief of air-conditioning and then the familiar chirps, tweets, and silverware drawer clatter—claws on metal—of two colorful caged parakeets, who greeted all the customers. I dislike the insistent chirruping of caged birds, but in this store, mingled with the hum of the copying machines and air conditioners, it became soothing white noise.

The walls of the shop were covered with snapshots of customers, hundreds of them, pasted one right next to the other in a free-form collage. The overflow of photos was strung across the space like a laundry line of clothes. Some couples had played a game of Exquisite Corpse with their snapshots, cutting and exchanging heads and bodies with humorous results.

I knew many of the faces. My gaze roamed a familiar trail, and I found Henry's face on the right-hand wall. He was in his favorite winter parka and cap, staring out at me with his winning grin.

I had an urge to walk up and rip the picture off the wall. As the woman wrote up my bill, I wondered if anyone had glanced over the pages while they were printed and bound.

What a horrible task Henry left for his friend. Matthew lost his best friend, and the next morning he had to clean up Henry's trash so that I wouldn't stumble on it. The trash is in this envelope in my hands now.

I took my package and headed for the door, feeling quietly relieved that my picture had never made it to the store wall. What remained of my privacy suddenly felt intensely valuable.

The heat ambushed me as I stepped out of the cool bliss of the store. I opened the car door and sat in the driver's seat. The car's interior had warmed up in the few minutes I had spent in the copy shop, and the steaminess softened my brain. I felt safe and relaxed in my car, full of the clutter of empty juice boxes, snack wrappers, and cookie crumbs. Henry had frequently chided me for messing up the car.

Well, fuck you, asshole. This is my fucking car now, and if I want to trash it, what are you—fucking dead guy—gonna do about it?

I looked at the package containing Henry's personal diary, and in a state of terrified vertigo I opened the envelope. I could see the first page of text through the clear plastic cover. My fingers were sweaty and sticky, my tongue raspy and dry. I opened the cover and began to read. The excerpt was from early August 1999. At that time we had been living in our town just over a year.

Journal Entry 8/4/99

We were really going at it. No, no. First I came in and asked for a glass of water, which she got for me. I thought about kissing her in the kitchen, but I'd already done the kitchen, I was bored with the kitchen. While I was looking at her, she asked me what I was thinking. I said I was thinking how great it would be if we were away some- where alone. On vacation in a cottage. Fucking and read- ing books to ourselves and each other. That seemed to make her happy. We sat in the dining room. I was just sit- ting across the table from her and then I asked if I could kiss her. She said yes. We started kissing. During a pit stop I ask her what she's thinking. She scrunches up her face and says something like, I'm not thinking anything, I'm just paranoid. The fucking house is about as open as you get. I feel like I'm dry-humping on Main Street. Any min- ute a FedEx guy could arrive. Then she suggested moving to a more comfortable place. So we move into the TV room. I've got her on her back on the couch and I'm lean- ing down and rubbing it on her crotch. She looks up in surprise for a moment then gets into it. Then she flips me over and now I'm on my back. She's rubbing herself on me. It feels great except the friction of the clothing is giv- ing me a mat burn on the underside of you know what. I ask her whether we can go upstairs. She sort of looks un- comfortable. I decide I have to push it a little. She finally says yes. We go up the stairs. She looks to the left at her bedroom where she sleeps with [her husband]. She looks at the kid's bedroom. I have to say that I admire her sense of the sacred. It's clear that she won't go into either one. Finally I steer her toward the mostly empty room they've been using as an office. We start kissing. She kneels down around my ankles, opens my fly, and takes me in her mouth. Wow. It's like getting head when you were a teenager. It's electric. I feel like I have an electrode attached to my glans.

I take my pants off. I get her pants off. We proceed to fumble around for a few minutes on the hard floor. There's nothing between my forty-year-old ass and that hardwood but an old rag rug. Not only that but this room is close to the eaves, meaning that the windows are about level with my butt. I look down into the next house over. An old lady is in her kitchen baking cookies. Who the fuck is that? I say. Oh that's Mrs. Kettle, she says with her mouth full. Well, Mrs. Kettle is checking us out. Don't worry, she's almost blind. She's worried about every fucking possible thing in the world, except this old lady who's looking up my rectum? I can see her. She's smiling at me with hazy, clouded eyes. I don't come, but we fool around for a while. Finally we just end up cuddling on the hard floor. I've got her in a Clark Gable. We smooch. Then we go get our daughters.

I closed the book—my mouth was open—sucking in air. Once I had some air in my lungs, I cried till my head ached. My chest hurt like it had been cleaved in two with one of Henry's beloved cooking knives.

I called Tomas from my cell phone. I could barely speak.

"Julie, just remember that none of this was real when it happened, it wasn't real when he wrote it, and it isn't real now."

I thought I understood what he meant—that Henry's writing and thinking and behavior during his affair with Cathy was a kind of fantasy. That what had happened between them was part of a game. But something had happened, they had done these things.

The Henry in the journal was wholly unknown to me, a fictional character. This was not the man who had proposed to me over champagne in a romantic restaurant, not the man who had promised to cherish me when we married, nor the man who had written me tender love notes, waited out my long childbirth labor, carried our wailing and sleeping child. Even the man I fought with was never so callous. Which man was real? Had my marriage been real?

"Do you still love me?" he'd asked. "I don't think you still love me. Do you still think I'm handsome?" I had always answered yes.

I sat in the car, mesmerized by the dashboard panel lights, soothed by the hum of the engine and the air-conditioning until I was calm enough to open the book again. I read like I was eating a package of Pepperidge Farm Milano cookies, right down to the bottom of the bag—feeling a slight nauseated bloat when I was finished.

It's like reading Henry Miller. Even though I was reeling after reading Henry's journal entry, I couldn't help but recall similar passages from Miller's novels. Certainly some of Miller's tales of sexual conquest are male-fantasy bullshit, but they are thrillingly written bullshit. I had to admit that page 484 of the unexpurgated Grove paperback edition of *Sexus* was some of my favorite masturbation reading.

But just as Henry Miller used his own life as a point of departure, my Henry's journal entry had the ring of truth about it in all its details. I could picture the scene in the spare room in Cathy's house. I had stood there myself on other occasions and seen the view into the old lady's house.

Breathe deeply.

I was ready to move on to my Henry's e-mails.

six

July 14–18, 2003

The heat continued unabated. People were dying from this heat. While a fan blew heated gusts on my sweaty skin, a part of me was dying as I sat reading the stack of e-mails Henry had left behind.

> January 25, 2002 9:32 A.M.
> Okay, I'll talk to you in about half an hour or so. Do you want me to come over or do you want to e-mail me?

I could not remember what I had been doing that January morning when he e-mailed Cathy. Maybe I had made a run to the store to get milk and eggs or a stop at the post office followed by a few minutes at the bank to take out cash for the week. No, by 9:32, I'd have finished all that, I'd have been in my office, staring at the computer screen, just as I had been doing the day he died. I tried to conjure up images of the alternate reality he had created with Cathy, the signs of which I hadn't wanted to see.

I was like the Bubble Boy, the kid who was allergic to the outside world and had to live his life within a plastic enclosure. I had become allergic to my marriage. Over time I had thickened the walls of the bubble till I could see nothing except the most contained domestic world of mothering, work, laundry, backyard garden, school, and playground.

Their adultery had its own small-town, workaday rhythms. Henry e-mailed Cathy in the mornings, took a shower, read the paper, shut himself in his office, and then went out around lunchtime, often telling me that he was food shopping. Sometimes he did tell me he was going to Cathy's for a coffee, and that he would pick up Liza from school. Not perceiving Cathy as a threat, I had welcomed the extra work time. Steve left most weekdays for his city job on a lunchtime train. This left Henry and Cathy with three hours till school dismissal, at 3:00 P.M., longer if I did the school pickup.

I got up to pace my small office. I stood in front of the fan, taking some comfort in the white noise and the airflow. I closed my eyes, trying to imagine all those days of the last years of my marriage. The details were mostly as hazy as this hot day. The heat drove me out to the back garden, where I hoped that staring at the last of the fragrant, sun-bleached roses in full explosion would calm my rage, the rage that made me want to tear up everything tender that remained from the years I had spent with Henry.

What is real? What do I get to keep? The love notes and poems Henry wrote to me? The contents of our photo albums? Did any of it really happen? Does any of it mean anything?

Liza meant something. Everything. Maybe she was the only thing that was real. I could start from there. How and when would I ever be able to explain this to her, that her father loved her but not enough to do right by her? He had been careless, even reckless with us. I walked back into the house, retreating

from the glare. Inside was a dark cave, and that suited me perfectly.

Back at my desk, I continued reading e-mails. Henry and Cathy
discussed Steve's train schedule, the timing of my yoga classes,
child care. They arranged the purchase of sexual lubricant. Cathy
offered opinions about our couple's therapy and worried that her
neighbor Jenny was onto them. Henry complained about my angry outbursts. Cathy was jealous of our modest vacations and
dinners at restaurants. She asked Henry for advice in preparing
her taxes. She complained when her husband hovered near her
computer. Henry wrote back: "Give him a blow job; that'll get
him off your back."

In evening e-mails, Henry and Cathy compared notes on Am-
bien, Xanax, and Klonopin—medications they took for insomnia
and anxiety. I do not think I was mistaken in detecting a competi-
tive edge to their playful bedtime chatter.

They gushed about how great sex had been the day before.
And how mediocre married sex was by comparison.

On February 11, 2002, Henry wrote,

> We have pleasurable sex that achieves the right ends (I have
> standards), but it is not "exciting" to me anymore. I think that
> compared to most marriages, it would be considered great sex;
> but compared to you and me, it is just sex between married
> partners who know each other well, maybe too well. The sex
> you and I have together is spine-tingling and bone-jarring, on
> and over the edge. And if I have anything to do with it, it will
> only get better.

Reading that hurt me in ways I could never have imagined, every word a spike in my chest. I had lost him long before he died. I had lost a love that had once been central to my life. I felt like the soldier in the opening D-Day battle scene of *Saving Private Ryan*, who searches around for the arm that has been blown off, before another shell takes him right down.

This is part of my inherited property. What to do with this? What to make of it? The bubble is bursting, the bubble I created to shelter myself and Liza.

Still, no one else here in my town had seen it either, the big, whopping It that was Henry and Cathy's affair. No one in our circle of friendly couples had had the slightest clue. Cathy's neighbor Jenny and I had idly speculated that summer day in her backyard, but we had both jokingly dismissed the idea. Henry flirted with every woman he ever met. All my friends in town had reacted with genuine shock.

"But he loved you so much. He always said so. I don't understand," said one bewildered friend after another. Their confusion was a comfort. I felt less like a complete idiot, but only slightly less. Mostly, I felt like I'd been hit by a truck.

I was desperately trying to keep my rage contained to the hours between 9:00 A.M. and 3:00 P.M., while Liza spent her days at a nearby day camp with Anna's son, Leo. I was not always successful. Many evenings Liza saw me crying in my office. You know you have reached a low point when your first grader is trying to comfort you.

I kept reading. I couldn't stop. I was disgusted, outraged, but also ravenous. I had to understand, to have some idea of what his life had been like during those last years. I wanted to understand my own attraction to a man who had done such great damage. I experienced the irresistible, vicarious thrills of reading a trashy tabloid magazine. The same part of me that sneaks furtive peeks at the covers of *People* and *Us Weekly* in the grocery store checkout line and looks forward to the occasional satiating read at a hair salon couldn't get enough of this, my very own small-town celebrity horror show. How bad would it get? How deep would my humiliation be? How would it all end?

And how did he juggle it all? If he hadn't died, I might never have known. Though truly, the more I thought about it, the clues had been everywhere and I had chosen to ignore them. Perhaps he was begging me to find out, by leaving everything so carelessly on his computer desktop in neat, labeled folders. Most husbands are more careful. And they don't drop dead on the kitchen floor before finding the time to hide their correspondence.

It might have gone on until his psychiatrist persuaded him to tell me. We might have continued in couples therapy until he convinced me to give him another chance, all while he continued to have affairs. I would have withdrawn further into the bubble, until, perhaps, one day I would have turned on him, fully enraged, ready with an exit plan.

The bubble was a bad idea.

It was an odd comfort to discover that Henry and Cathy argued with each other at least as often as Henry and I did. The fights must have occurred in her home or in a car. The e-mails referring to their fights were short, testy exchanges.

Later on February 11, 2002, Henry wrote:

> One of the things that bothers me is that you haven't gotten very good at being able to express natural affection for me in public, or in front of others. Sometimes you make me feel as if you just shut me out or changed your mood.

How, exactly, did he expect Cathy to show "natural affection" for him in public? Was he honestly expecting her to snuggle up during a party, surrounded by friends?

> The other things that really get to me are your propensity to blame me for not respecting your feelings, your not allowing me to call a time out in the middle of an argument by accusing me of trying to skirt issues, and your reliance on seeing yourself as a victim of my whatever, when it suits you.

This attack was every fight Henry and I ever had in the sixteen years we lived together. It was truly some bizarre parallel universe. The anger, her anxiety, the intellectual one-upmanship, all masking his own insecurity.

> The sex thing is the hardest. I don't understand why you and Steve are having so much more sex these days, and why you enjoy it so much. Are you having more sex with Steve? Is it anything like what we have?

Of course not, she replied. But he needed to hear from her, over and over again, that he was the most thrilling and perfect lover and that no other two persons could possibly have what they had together.

While I was home, working, being a mom, paying bills, doing his fucking laundry. Sometimes taking care of her kid.

I had to get up and walk again, just to leave the e-mail pile. Pacing around and around the pool, I tried to distract myself with gardening. I crouched low to yank out a dandelion that had invaded my rosebushes. I was too impatient to pry under the deep taproot with a trowel. When I tugged, I held a mere half a root in my clenched fist and pricked my finger on a rose thorn to boot, scattering the shrub's remaining petals.

Cathy's astonishing hypocrisy made more sense to me now. It was perfect that a woman so awkward and needy, so desperate for approval would be able to rationalize a long affair that involved daily deception while singing in the church choir. I tossed the dandelion into the lawn in disgust.

Then I laughed my first dark laugh. At some point, I had to start laughing, because I was all wrung out from crying.

Emily seemed traumatized by the fallout from Tomas's disclosure. By now, I deeply regretted having called her on the afternoon of Henry's death. I also regretted that I had caught her unprepared when I'd called her from Tomas's house. Keeping my secret had been unsettling enough for her. Releasing the secret was like removing the last essential log from an already fragile dam. Suddenly a surging torrent of confused emotion rushed out over sharp, broken rocks.

I had needed and wanted to see Emily as a strong woman the

day Henry died and during the months after his death. But now I was seeing something else. She seemed vulnerable, and shaky. I regretted all the favors I had asked and would likely still ask. I wished I could do something for her—be her happier, supportive friend from before everything bad happened. I was no life preserver. In fact, my own ship was taking on water fast. I couldn't do much more than I was doing for Liza and myself. I was alone, whereas Emily had Justin, a superbly caring husband.

"When do I get my friend back?" Emily still asked me, though less often. I didn't have the heart to tell her that the friend she had spent time with before Henry's death, the woman in the bubble, was gone for good. Standing on my own without the bubble was terrifying. When she told me that she had woken in the middle of the night, anxious about an upcoming art show, and had talked to her husband for a calming hour, I quietly reminded her that when I woke up in the middle of the night (which happened almost every night), I was alone, looking at my sleeping child.

Emily said she wanted to burn sage in my house, to purify it. She brought over a beautifully tied bunch, a gift from a recent trip to New Mexico. Secretly, I thought exorcism would be more appropriate than sage burning.

I wondered what I might say to prospective buyers of my house. *Um, guy dropped dead on the kitchen floor, right here, sort of where you're standing now, but no need to worry, he's a mostly harmless spirit now, just gives cooking advice once in a while and messes with the plumbing, rattles the windows, that sort of thing.*

I was fine with sage burning, or whatever else would make Emily feel better about being in my house. She moved through the rooms holding the smoldering sage in an abalone shell, making shooing gestures, as if she were blowing Henry out the window along with the smoke. I didn't think even the most potent sage from the most sacred pueblo in New Mexico would chase him out just yet. He was in some weird purgatory, trapped in our house, forced to watch everything unravel, including the public image he had cherished. One day I would have to leave this house, seal my boxes tight, and run away as fast as I could, to be sure that Henry remained behind.

I wanted Emily to feel comfortable. I still wanted to spend time with her. She was my friend and I loved her and relied on her, even though there were days when her moodiness and fragility frightened me, because they reminded me of my own tenuous grasp on life.

———————

I felt Henry brush by me in the kitchen while I prepared dinner, such as it was.

"Oh, go fuck yourself, asshole," I muttered under my breath, while stirring elbow noodles in boiling water. "Leave me alone, I have work to do." Liza and I were back to this sort of meal. I could barely muster the energy to rip open the cardboard boxes day after day. At least it was organic. I was maintaining some standards. At least we were eating. I wondered about my earlier sensations of Henry's presence during the winter—had he been trying to warn me? *Well, too fucking late. I'm left with your big pile of shit. Happy now?* I recoiled from the sharp sting of droplets of boiling water that I had whipped into a churning whirlpool in the pot. *I wish you'd just left me and gone off with that twisted bitch. That's what she wanted.*

No, wait. You're better off dead.

Cathy must have hoped for a real relationship with Henry. Her e-mails described her intense love, her wish for a deep commitment that she hadn't copped to when I confronted her in the parking lot near her house. Then she had only been willing to say that she realized Henry hadn't cared sincerely about her. She had hidden the affair from her husband and closest friends and risked everything while waiting for Henry to make up his indecisive mind. I chuckled again, darkly.

Liza stepped into the kitchen, eager for dinner. "Why are you laughing at the noodles, Mama?"

Though it seemed that Cathy had something long term in mind, Henry's correspondence suggested that he had no plans to change his living arrangements. In fact, the secrets in his life served to excite him. He liked the feeling of having it all, even if having it all had created the internal chaos that had driven him to seek a two-hundred-dollar-an-hour psychiatrist.

When Cathy pressed him to offer a clear demonstration of his love for her, he responded with this message.

Dec 29 2001

I just want you to understand that my feelings for you have not diminished since I've been back. . . . I feel great about you; I feel great about what we have and our lives, and our life together. I can't imagine you not in my life . . . we were meant to be together. I have also spent a great deal of time thinking about you and doing things that give me great pleasure, like choosing those earrings, and hunting down your Xmas gift (that hasn't arrived yet).

As I read e-mails, I discovered that after our New Year's Eve party that began 2002 (when Cathy told me she was planning to "get shitfaced"), another secret drama had played itself out.

Jan 02 2002

I'd like you to curb your incredible jealousy. My personal world is very important to me and while you are the most important person in it, your attempts to control or comment on friendships that I have that you feel are threatening are really becoming a burden to me.

You were giving me such a hard time that I was having trouble enjoying myself. I thought we would be able to enjoy our intimate relationship throughout the party as we discussed. You were so aggressive and out of control that I thought you were going to give everything away, i.e. the fact that we are involved.

I love the fact that you love me so much, and I love the fact that I love you so much. I love it when the both of us are able to express this love. What I don't like is when you are irrationally and uncontrollably jealous and use anger to try to control me. It doesn't work and it only sets us back. It is the single reason that our relationship doesn't progress the way you would like it to.

Cathy followed Henry's postmortem with a torrent of self-criticism. She worried that she had ruined everything in their relationship. She apologized for her drunkenness. She felt humiliated, and wondered anxiously what other party guests thought of her behavior. Later that day Henry consoled her:

You haven't ruined things for us; as for everyone else there, you shouldn't worry about it. You don't have anything to be embarrassed about. People knew you were drunk but also thought you were happy. I think they enjoyed the fact that someone was losing their inhibitions.

Just take a few days off and be good to yourself. I love you.

Cathy, drunk on the living room couch and, later, vomiting in my downstairs bathroom on that New Year's Eve had not looked happy or uninhibited. At the time I had not understood why she had willfully made herself ill.

But now I knew why she had drunk herself into oblivion. She must have been miserable, lonely, confused, conflicted, and perhaps even guilty, though not guilty enough to stop trying to get Henry for herself. Perhaps she hoped to force him to pay attention to her, to rearrange his life for her. Perhaps if she was wounded enough, he would leave me, and take care of her.

Henry, burdened with two very unhappy women—this was rich.

Within the next months, their relationship cycled back to mutual obsession and jealousy. Cathy described their energy as so complementary that it was as if they could feed off each other. This imagery of a kind of cannibalistic feast made me shiver. These kinds of relationships never turn out well, in novels or in real life.

Having criticized her for being jealous, Henry expressed his own irrational jealousy, and a few weeks later they were in the midst of another battle over the nature and future of their relationship. Ignoring the obvious conflicts of his life, Henry was consumed with resentment.

March 15 2002

I have to tell you that I am feeling intense anger toward you right now. I keep thinking about how my feelings never get considered. You never ask me what I want, never try and reassure me about wanting to continue our relationship. I feel incredibly cheated.

I couldn't help but notice that Henry's complaint about Cathy was Cathy's very complaint about him. And of course my very complaint about him, the source of many of our arguments.

Mostly, we did things his way, according to his schedule. "All my ideas are good ideas," he liked to joke, though it never felt like a joke to me.

Their battles built up over the next weeks of correspondence, and with conflict came gloom and depression. During this same time, I too had been anxious and depressed. Henry and I had fought continuously. Henry said I was overreactive, overemotional. He said I needed more medication. After several pitched battles of our own, I had finally succumbed. It was my fault, I agreed. I would ask my doctor for different medication. Henry described this private issue in one of his e-mails to Cathy.

It was true that in April 2002 I was a mess—anxious, agitated, and suffering from insomnia. I remembered going to the city with him to see my psychiatrist. I remembered how earnestly he had spoken to my doctor. How caring and thoughtful he had seemed. He had even charmed and deceived my psychiatrist.

I had been off medication for almost six months now. I had dragged myself through the terrible time after Henry's death without the antidepressants that he had insisted were so necessary. And horrible as things were now, my head had never felt clearer.

My college friend Sara called me from her home in England. She would be back in the States in a few weeks, meeting me on the Maine island where I traveled each summer. Anna and Leo would share my rental house with Liza and me. Sara and I talked about the longed for summer holiday; then I gave her a brief synopsis of the latest catastrophe.

"He gaslighted you," she announced tartly.

I struggled to recall the plot of the film *Gaslight,* which I vaguely remembered watching years earlier with my dad. Ingrid Bergman is cruelly manipulated to the point of madness by her husband, the handsome and charming Charles Boyer, who is after some jewels hidden in the attic. Things disappear; the gas lamps flicker on and off for no reason, as if possessed.

I thought again bitterly about the trips to the psychiatrist and the medications I had taken. Then I remembered the desperation I'd felt arguing with Henry over the barking dog next door.

The small barking terrier was named Rebel, of all things.

On the day we looked at the house, Rebel was barking.

"Henry, it's a nice house," I said, as the dog ran manically around the yard. "It's a nice house, but I'm telling you right now, that barking will drive me crazy."

"Oh, don't worry, he'll stop once he gets to know us."

From the day we moved into the house, it was eight hours straight of barking terrier while the owners were away from home at their respective jobs. For days and weeks, until a kind of insanity took over. It was like Chinese water torture.

You can tell a lot about people by the ways in which they inflict their poorly trained animals on others. I did not have high hopes for my neighbors, a Mr. and Mrs. Caine. I suspected that they would prove to be thoughtless, inconsiderate people, who felt, under some homespun Second Amendment, entitled to subject the neighborhood to Rebel, the public good be damned. Henry had grown up in a small, conservative town, so I figured he'd know the best approach to take. I asked him to speak to them.

Henry refused. "Why can't we have a pleasant time in our new town? We just moved here. You don't understand. The dog will stop barking after he gets to know us. You're completely overreacting."

"Henry, I told you I wouldn't be able to stand this. I'm telling you now, again, it's driving me crazy."

Henry said I had to wait. I waited. But even with my office door closed, I could still hear the incessant barking.

I called the prior owner of our house. She sighed with exasperation. "Oh, that stupid neighbor, Mr. Caine!" she blurted loudly. "That dog of his never stopped barking!" She told me that the neighbors had been rude and unresponsive to her repeated requests to keep the dog indoors. I didn't ask her if this was her motive for selling the house, but when I hung up the phone, my first instinct was to pack our belongings and put the place up for sale.

After a few months, with Rebel still barking, I nursed murderous rage, and in passing moments wondered if I could get away with poisoning the animal. A chocolate brownie wrapped in a meatball might go undetected. These thoughts pained me. I'd always liked animals. In rational moments, I realized it was the owners who were responsible, rather than the lonely dog.

When I called the neighbors, they were, predictably, short-tempered and rude. Another neighbor offered to intervene. He'd known the Caines for years, he said. But his efforts didn't help much either.

Fall came, then winter. Rebel was mostly inside during the cold months. Anticipating spring, Henry and I continued to argue about approaching the neighbors more forcefully. Rebel began barking again as soon as the weather warmed.

One early summer weekend in 2000, Irena came to visit from the city for the weekend. I knew that she had never been convinced of the wisdom of our move. I wanted to present our new life in the best possible light. We did have a modestly sized swimming pool and an enviable view across the river. My work in the garden was beginning to pay off. Despite the risk of the barking, it seemed best to stay outside, where these assets were on full display. We arranged towels on the stone terrace and settled in for what I hoped would be a comfortable afternoon together while Liza played with Amy at Cathy's house.

Rebel burst out of the Caines' house into the yard, barking, barking, barking. After some minutes, Irena looked at me quizzically. A deep embarrassment sparked and grew. For this we had left the city? We'd left the relatively tolerable hum of city traffic, occasionally punctuated by sirens and car stereos, to be tormented by this incessant noise? I tried to ignore the barking and carry on our conversation. An hour went by, the barking continued.

"Is it like this all the time?" Irena asked at last, her brow furrowed with concern.

I couldn't answer her. The truth—that moving to this house

had been, possibly, the most wretched mistake of my adult life, with this infernal dog the most potent metaphor of that error—was too painful to bear. I had left behind my comfort and my closest friend, a woman who had been my steady cheerleader for nearly ten years. I had no friend like her here, with such long and meaningful history. Despair flooded over me, and I felt tears coming. The barking became the main event in my head, blotting out everything else around me—the river view, the sparkling pool, the roses in their full glory. The effort of maintaining calm became so much of a distraction that I couldn't focus on anything Irena was saying or my responses. A surge of humiliation and rage exploded, sparkling upward, right up to my eyeballs, where I felt a sudden pinging and throbbing, the precursor to one of the migraine headaches that plagued me in periods of intense stress.

"That fucking dog!" I screamed. "I can't stand it anymore. It's ruining my life! I'm going crazy!" Irena stood stunned as I stormed down my driveway. She ran after me onto the main road as I charged around the corner to the Caines' driveway and up to their door. I rang the bell again and again, but there was no answer. I was sobbing now, my chest heaving. Irena was comforting me. I kept ringing the doorbell, then, accepting defeat, we came back, the barking continuing as we walked into my house.

Henry, who had been out shopping for the barbecue planned for later that afternoon, returned.

"That fucking dog!" I screamed at him. "It was barking for two straight hours while Irena and I were trying to sit outside! I can't stand it anymore. You have to go speak to them, because I can't stand one more day of this shit!"

Henry looked at me with rage and disgust. As Irena stood amazed, he grabbed me by the arm and dragged me into the hallway, where he pressed me against the wall. "You're out of control, you're crazy and out of control. You're not rational, this isn't rational, your way of looking at this. It's just a dog."

"I told you I wouldn't be able to stand it, I knew I wouldn't be able to tolerate it. Why are you defending those people instead of helping me? They won't deal with me. Why can't you do the husband thing and deal with them? Why won't you do it?" I was sobbing again. "Why?" I was terribly alone. I was married, but I was alone and isolated, feeling crazy and unbalanced. I learned that day that there is no more lonely state than being lonely in a marriage.

Later that afternoon, Cathy, Steve, Amy (bringing Liza), and other friends from town came over for the barbecue. I performed my hostess duties. Irena still seemed troubled by the afternoon incident. At one point I observed her in close conversation with Henry. She was talking, with a serious expression and urgent hand gestures. Henry was listening, but he was not his usually sunny host self.

After that weekend, I didn't see Irena again for some time.

"I don't understand why we're drifting apart," I lamented to Henry one night as we lay in bed. We had by this time contacted a lawyer to deal with the Caines (the attorney told us that a good deal of his practice concerned barking dogs and fences). We were also seeing a therapist, one that Cathy had recommended. The issue of the dog came up immediately and repeatedly. To me it showed one of many ways Henry ignored my feelings and my clearly stated needs. To him it showed that I was unreasonable and overreactive, and probably needed more medication. Outside the therapist's office, Henry was less diplomatic. He told me I was crazy. As I thought about Irena, I began crying again, something I did a lot. "She's been my closest friend for years, and now it's like she doesn't want to see me. I have no friends like Irena up here, Henry. I don't know if I belong here. I feel lonely."

"Cathy is a friend, isn't she?" he said.

"I don't get Cathy," I replied, sitting up in bed and turning toward Henry. "I don't feel comfortable around her. She's very hot and cold. And she and I never do anything together on our own anyway. It's not like we're real friends. We'd never spend so much time together if Liza and Amy weren't so close."

"Well, I think you should give Cathy a chance," Henry said gently. "I think you should make some new friends. You don't need Irena."

———————

I called Irena now, on one of these sweltering July days. She told me that she had seen It—Henry and Cathy. She had the advantage of being from outside our small town. During that weekend three years earlier, she had seen Henry and Cathy interact, put the puzzle together. Unknown to me, or anyone else at the gathering, Irena had confronted him directly.

"I said to Henry, 'What's going on with you and that woman?' And he said, 'Is it that obvious?' I told him, 'I don't want to know anything about this, I don't want to be your confidante. Julie's one of my closest friends. I just want you to deal with this now and tell me when it's over.' So he said, 'Irena, you understand that if this gets out my marriage is over.' It felt like a threat. If I told you, then he would blame me for the consequences.

"I couldn't spend time with you while he was doing this," Irena continued, recalling her confusion and the anger she had felt toward Henry. "I didn't know what to do—I was caught in such a bad place. I felt like I was lying every time I saw you."

Listening to her, I recalled one strangely strained lunch during this time. Irena had asked me pointed questions: whether I was happy in my marriage, how I really felt about supporting Henry's writing career, did I feel fully appreciated, weren't there dreams of my own that I should be pursuing? These queries had prompted a performance of loyalty on my part that felt less than authentic, as I tried my best to create the vision of Henry and myself on a path together with common goals for the future.

"I didn't want you to go through what I had just been through. I had just been through my divorce," Irena said, recalling the painful drama I had witnessed as her friend. I shivered, wondering how difficult it would have been to tangle legally with Henry, a man who never liked to lose an argument.

"I hoped he would just end the thing with Cathy, quickly, and this would be a small blip in a long marriage. And mostly, I was afraid that if I told you what I knew, you would just defend him and reject me, and then our friendship would be broken forever."

Here I had to admit, sadly, that she was probably right. I would have continued to defend Henry, because making allowances and excuses for his behavior was part of living in the bubble.

"But, Julie, I know he loved you," Irena said. "I know he did. That's why he kept it secret. I worried that he would never let you go if you found out and wanted to end your marriage. He wouldn't have made leaving easy for you. He didn't want to lose you or Liza."

My life in those last years of marriage was like a blister that forms on your heel from a too-tight shoe—the body's imperfect attempt to create a protective layer over a wound. *Now I will have to lance the blister, endure the pain, and then try a different life, one that fits me better.*

seven

Late July 2003

The days crawled by, the heat relentless. At least Liza was out of the steamy house and safely away from most of my unpredictable bursts of rage. Anna and I took turns ferrying the kids back and forth from day camp, morning and afternoon. One morning Anna returned unexpectedly after camp drop-off, carrying a large manila envelope.

"What's in the package?" I asked grimly. The two of us seemed dogged by bad luck. No packages were innocent now. We both looked like hell, exhausted and miserable. I'd stopped eating again, and she looked haggard as well. In moments of dark humor, we called it the Death and Divorce Diet.

Anna held out the package. "It's all the e-mails John exchanged with his little chippie," she said, confirming my fears. "I was going to ask you if you could keep this here for me. It's too painful to keep in my house. But I might need it."

I took the package from her, and we chose a place on a high shelf in my office, so that I would not be tempted to open it. I had enough of my own toxic waste to read through.

We wandered back into the kitchen, where I poured us each a glass of iced tea. We sat at the table quietly, clutching our sweating glasses.

Anna, twirling the end of her red braid, broke the silence. "Julie, do you ever think about moving back to the city?"

"I think I'll go crazy if I stay here too much longer," I mumbled, doodling a city skyline in the condensation on my glass. I pressed the cool, wet glass to my cheek.

Oh, for Star Trek *technology, whereby Liza and I and the cats and our stuff could be beamed into a decent and not too expensive two-bedroom Brooklyn apartment. Maybe with a little garden, like that place Henry and I had when Liza was born.*

"My brother says I shouldn't run away," I said, feeling tears well up. "He says I have to be patient, and wait out the first year. But I don't know how much more of this shit I can stand."

"Yeah, I hear ya," Anna said, laughing bitterly. She came over and gave me a hug. "I hate being here, kicking around such a big house."

The knowledge that we shared the same vast loneliness helped me stop crying.

"Anyway," she said, "I'll never be able to afford it after the divorce."

"I am a bit scared to uproot Liza right now," I said, my mind momentarily tangling with the thousand small details a move would involve.

"It would be tough," Anna said. "But I bet we could do it," she added with sudden brightness.

We had already made elaborate shopping and packing lists for our August trip to Maine. We were the List Queens. I wondered if we could plan a move back to the city together the same way. We could make lists; accomplish tasks. This woman was not flaky, even though her life was splitting at the seams, just like mine. If we decided to do this, we'd do it. But I wasn't ready, not yet.

"Let's think about it," Anna said, looking at me intently, sensing my uncertainty. "Promise me you'll think about it."

....

Late at night, Liza asleep in my bed, I was still wide awake and reading again in my office. Here was a jaw-dropper. This, from a man who prided himself on his self-awareness and sophisticated understanding of human nature.

> I don't feel conflicted about you. I may feel a little conflicted about what our relationship does in terms of me coming to terms with my marriage.

A little conflicted? Ya think? How could he be so detached? How did he not understand that his actions, even secret ones, were causing damage to our marriage, and his daughter?

I had never enjoyed smoking pot or taking drugs, though I had certainly made futile efforts to be cool in high school. In the end, I hated the sense of dislocation that drugs produced. I was not comfortable taking on roles. It was enough of a daily struggle to identify my true self. But clearly Henry loved playing games.

My brother, David, sent me an e-mail he had found while going through Henry's financial records months earlier. He hadn't understood everything at the time; he didn't even know to whom Henry was writing. But he had guessed enough to know that he couldn't send the e-mail to me then; its content was too combustible.

When I read the exchange, dated September 20, 2002, I could imagine something of the situation. Henry wrote:

I thought we left each other today with some sort of understanding that we would try to take some baby steps forward
with our relationship. I don't expect us to get back together in
the old way. I do expect that we will eventually be able to have
physical intimacy with each other because that is what we want.
If things are exactly in the same place, I am going to be very
upset with you.

He was trying many roles, alternately bewildered, seductive,
pleading, condescending, and belligerent. There was something
cold in his way of shutting Cathy down at the end. "I am going to
be very upset with you."

Cathy followed with a note to Henry about her joy seeing him
again after not speaking for several months but insisted that they
must not resume their sexual relationship. Her note read like the
"no, no, no, we mustn't" that is, in fact, an invitation.

I wondered if Henry was looking forward to the game of winning her over again, just so he could despise her more. It was clear
that he liked fucking her, he liked that a lot.

No later correspondence survived. I could only imagine how
this drama would have turned out. In her phone conversations with
me, Cathy had taken credit for ending their sexual affair the summer before he died. Henry's therapist had suggested to me that he
wanted to end the affair. There was no way to know the truth now.

When I recalled the scene as Cathy wept over Henry's body at
the wake, it seemed most likely that on the day of his death this
relationship wasn't over at all, not by a long shot. The game hadn't
lost its appeal for him, and perhaps she hadn't yet given up hope
that he might still leave me for her.

Although most of Cathy and Henry's e-mails had been lost or
destroyed at some point following their discovery, there was

plenty of other e-mail from the months before his death. I turned
to that next. In one long letter, Henry unburdened himself to Christine, the woman in California—the woman Henry, and then Tomas,
had told me about—the knitting divorcée, with ex-husband, two
kids, and a messy house. For Christine's benefit, Henry glamor-
ized Cathy in his tale. It's good to believe one's own stories, and
he could be sure that Christine would never meet Cathy. Henry
was what my high school English teacher would have termed an
"unreliable narrator."

There were certainly prettier women than Cathy in our town.
Her availability and willingness to play a dangerous game by his
rules must have been sufficient compensation. But the danger was
key, the big bad-boy thrill.

October 22, 2002
Christine,

Okay, on to the subject of my girlfriends or the History of
My Infidelities. I'm still a little bit wary about telling you all of
this. I kind of feel like I'm handing you the gun you're going to
shoot me with in the third act . . . but here goes.

I've had five sexual affairs in the past three years as well as a
few romantic dalliances, ranging from a few dates to an ongoing
thing. Early on in my relationship with Julie, even before we got
married, I had an affair and a couple of near misses.

Then really nothing until about three years ago when I met
this woman Cathy. I happened to be playing with my daughter
on the school playground (doing a headstand for her) when this
beautiful black-haired, blue-eyed woman shows up with her
own daughter and proceeds to chat with me.

She started to woo me via email for about six months. I then
sort of confronted her about it over lunch one day, and about a
month later we were sleeping together. We saw each other for
nearly three years. It was like a second marriage. We saw each

other every day. Our kids were best friends. I would say that in some ways we saw more of each other than our own spouses. It was also a tumultuous relationship because she has some emotional volatility.

The thing that kept us together was the sex. It was amazing. So anyway, we had sex a lot.

Then we had a huge falling out last May. I broke it off with her. She got really pissed at me. Then I wanted to go back to it. Then she didn't want to. And on and on. Finally I decided not to talk to her or interact with her at all. It has been difficult, but I think I've broken the addiction.

Let's see. I had a short affair with an advertising executive in New York that I had once had strong feelings about. We slept together several times, and then she turned really cold on me. Unfortunately she had the twin qualities of being really sensitive, but also unable to express her emotions. I suspect she thought I would have a more intense reaction to our relationship after sleeping together, perhaps to the point where I would leave my wife.

I had a brief fling last summer with a tall blond woman in Sonoma. We picked each other up at a party. She was sort of between boyfriends and we had fun for a few days, and she had a beautiful hilltop house with an amazing view, as well as a hot tub and a swimming pool. But she was remarkably unaware of her own body for someone so beautiful and athletic, so sex with her was a little unsatisfying for me. (I like it best when my partner is really having a great time, and that takes self-knowledge as well as technique. There is only so much a boy can do on his own.) But she was a genuinely warm and loving person so the time together was great.

Oh yes, and there is a woman back home who I met at the gym. She has a wonderful body. She works out five days a week and can do ten one-handed pull-ups, and yet is as slender as a reed. She is however not as smart as I would like for a romantic companion.

Otherwise, there was the woman who picked me up in her Mercedes. We had a great time flirting around, but it didn't really click for me. I met a 25-year-old Argentinean girl over the summer whom I had a great flirtation with. Even though she is young she is an old soul as you said, and a "fellow traveler." She didn't want to have sex with me at that point, but wants me to meet her on some future vacation somewhere to have an affair.

When I was in Willapa [Washington] recently a woman picked me up over breakfast. I literally chatted with her for a few minutes in the morning, only to find a note at the front desk in the inn inviting me to dinner later that evening.

I was walking down the street today in the rain on Haight-Ashbury and I was missing my wife very badly.

What's your schedule tomorrow? I think if I do this, I'll just go over to Oakland airport in the morning and take an afternoon flight. Can you pick me up? Or should I take a cab? How much time can you spend with me on Thursday?

In a fury, I slammed the e-mail down on my desk, crying as much in rage as from my own shame, that I hadn't seen all this before. More pacing in the garden, more yanking of weeds. *I may not have wanted to see this before, but I will look at it now, every fucking square inch of it. I am sick of feeling like the town idiot. It can't be that I am the only woman in this situation. This must happen every day, just like it happened to Anna. Just that most of the assholes don't drop dead and leave all this debris behind.*

I stomped back to the office. The practical planner in me—who made lists, paid bills, completed work on deadline, boiled water for endless spaghetti dinners, made sure that Liza's homework was done and that she had clean underwear—began a research project. I took out a fresh ruled pad from my supply cupboard, made a list, and started calling up the women.

I found Christine's phone number, and I left a message for her. I returned to Henry's long letter and hunted for the other women in his address book.

Another muggy afternoon. Liza had returned from day camp, but I felt unable to be her mother. Instead I sat alone in my office thinking about the last years Henry and I spent together, comforted by the drone of the TV in the living room. SpongeBob had been steadily babysitting Liza for months now. Television had been an acceptable distraction from the sadness of Henry's death, and now the horrors unfolding in my office.

I had been distracted long before Henry's death, in my marriage, even when we had sex. Nestled in a familiar tangle under our sheets, I'd run through to-do lists in my head. When I opened my eyes, I'd muse on the sparkly dust on our windowpanes and the moonlight outside, while he was inside me, making me come. I was tired a lot, and tired of fighting with him. The truth now settled hard upon me. Of course there had been signs of his bad behavior, but I had willfully ignored all of them.

"I want you to be more like my girlfriend, less like a wife," he told me several times during that last fall.

"You should pay more attention to me, less to Liza." This had been a continual refrain since her birth.

It was clear that Henry's well-known flirtatiousness was not innocent fun but in fact a well-used modus operandi that had been wildly successful, not only in charming our immediate social world (*hundreds of people at his funeral!*), but also in winning female ad-mirers in many corners of the land. I smacked my fist down hard onto my desk so it would hurt, a better choice than smashing it into a wall.

I had been afraid to look at the truth, because there was so much at stake. I had been afraid of being alone. Now I was alone. I had accepted intolerable behavior because of the fear that I couldn't live without him. But here I was, living without him.

February 14, 2002

I've been kissing you all over your body today, especially the pink tender bits. And I have a valentine waiting for you on the end of my penis. I am dying to deliver it.

Henry had sent the same Valentine message to Cathy and Mandy (the hot-and-cold advertising executive he'd identified in his letter to Christine) within several minutes of e-mail time. I had to smile at the efficiency of it all, a savage little cut-and-paste job.

I had not received that naughty Valentine. That year Henry gave me a handmade card, penned with a freshly composed poem, as well as a gorgeous arrangement of roses, iris, wild thistles, euphorbia, and hydrangea, flowers he knew I loved. Which Valentine offering, I wondered, represented the more authentic sentiment?

Years earlier, when Liza was a new baby, Henry and I went to a party at Mandy's uptown Manhattan apartment, where she lived with her longtime girlfriend, Dinah. At the time, Mandy and Di-nah were in that category of "friends of friends." I sat on their couch, bouncing Liza on my lap, attempting to take sips from a glass without spilling wine everywhere. The loose gray dress I had chosen did not make me feel sleek or urban, but it did hide my soft postpregnancy belly as well as the constant baby mess of spit-ups that were my new life.

Amid the crowd of twenty-odd people, Mandy, Dinah, and Henry clustered intimately across the room at the kitchen counter, laughing and talking. In any other context, where the women identified themselves as heterosexual, I might have wondered if both women were pursuing Henry. Mandy was a tall brunette, thin lipped and mannish looking. Not Henry's type, I would have guessed. I sat with my baby, feeling bored and boring, a piece of inconvenient baggage in the corner of the room. I desperately wanted to go home.

"Mandy looks great in an Armani suit," Henry commented when he returned home with trousers and shirts from one of his occasional trips to Neiman Marcus in New Jersey. I thought of Mandy as his gay shopping friend, just as Anna talked about clothes shopping with her "gay husbands." Shopping trips had seemed harmless enough. I didn't have to like all his friends, I reasoned, just as Henry didn't like all mine. He could spend time shopping with his friend and I wouldn't ever have to deal with her.

I hoped that he was planning to be more aggressive about finding new work so that he might have opportunities to wear the crisply tailored trousers and shirts he happily tried on for me to admire.

When Henry told me that Mandy and Dinah had broken up, I only briefly registered concern. By then, I had a toddler, and not too much penetrated from the world outside motherhood and work.

A few months later Henry mentioned that Mandy had taken a new job in Australia. The other side of the world was far away enough.

Two years later, in 2001, she returned to the United States following another romantic breakup, this time with a man she had planned to marry.

"Hey," Henry asked, "can I invite Mandy up here for dinner?"

"She's always completely ignored me. I really don't like her, and I don't want her here."

"Can I tell her that?" He laughed.

"Go right ahead," I replied stonily.

"Did you have an affair with Henry?"

A moment of silence on the phone line.

The advertising executive searching for workable spin?

"No, I didn't have an affair with him. We were very close," she continued. "We were good friends."

"I remember that you went shopping together. So that's all it was, then? Just good friends?"

"I was really upset after 9/11. I saw everything right from my kitchen window. It was horrible, and Henry helped me a lot right after they let me move back into my apartment."

Henry had told me about her apartment in Battery Park with views of the twin towers. As she sat reading the morning *New York Times* and drinking coffee, the planes came in, one after the other.

"It's terrible that you had to go through that. But now I need to know what happened between you and Henry."

"I think we shared a bed one night, but we didn't have sex."

When does that ever happen?

I didn't inhale. I did not have sexual relations with that woman.

I couldn't respond to such a tale. Henry didn't tell me anything about sharing a bed, just about helping her get back into her apartment and the eerie scene at Ground Zero. He said a friend was staying with her. He called me from the city to say that he was staying in a room at his college club in midtown. I wanted to believe him, so I did. *I was busy, worrying about the important stuff, like earning a living, taking care of our child. Okay, I was an idiot.*

During the frantic days and weeks after 9/11, I stayed home, close to my child. I wasn't able to think about anything except that I needed to be near Liza. When Henry told me about Mandy losing access to her apartment, I did not suggest offering her a room. I felt sorry for her, perhaps a bit guilty that I couldn't feel welcoming, but I still did not want to have her in my house. I wanted to trust Henry to help her move back into her own apartment, so that Liza and I could be home and safe.

I had overlooked Henry's ability to make all situations, even a traumatic national tragedy, work to his own advantage.

Several days passed before Christine, the knitting divorcée in California, returned my call. At last she left a message on my phone. She had been away on a camping trip with her sons, but she wanted to talk to me.

"What the fuck did you think you were doing, getting involved with a married man with a kid?" I demanded. I gripped the edge of my desk with sweaty fingers, relieved that this woman was many miles away, so that I wasn't tempted to smack her.

"You weren't really thinking about me, were you? How would you feel if some woman did this to you?" She did not hang up, which impressed me. She apologized, quietly.

She told me how she met Henry at a food event while he was on the West Coast researching his book. At the time, she was recently divorced from the father of her two young boys. Her boyfriend had callously broken up with her as her mother began her final decline from cancer. Henry arrived in her life during that time, offering something that must have felt like real comfort. His wonderful home-cooked meals, which had once wooed me, went a long way with her.

"At first Henry didn't tell me that he was married. And he wasn't wearing a ring. When I pressed him, he admitted to being married but claimed that you and he had 'an arrangement.'"

"I assure you," I snapped, "there was no such 'arrangement.'"

"My boyfriend and I had an open relationship at that time, so I accepted Henry's story at first. But he was so secretive about his home life. I figured out pretty quickly that he hadn't talked to you about anything. I really only knew Henry for a few months. We met in October, and it was pretty much over as a sexual thing by Christmas."

Christmas, when Liza and I had flown out to meet Henry in Seattle. Two weeks later, he collapsed on the kitchen floor. His last December seemed a long time ago. As did that entire fall season, when he was seeing Christine.

One morning during that autumn came back to me now, with startling clarity, the morning of November 8, 2002. Henry and I were in the car, traveling up Route 9 to the private school where we hoped to transfer Liza.

Our local public school wasn't working out. Liza was being

bullied by some girls in her class, and the administration did not handle the issue aggressively or gracefully. I had spoken to the mother of one of the other girls, a conversation that had produced some modest positive effect, but the damage had been done. Liza hated going to school. She was only in first grade. We had eleven years of her education ahead of us.

Now we were driving up the road to look at the only alternative in a one-school town, a private school about forty minutes from our home. Emily's two daughters went there, as did the children of a few other friends in town. The public-private school issue was controversial in a town already sharply divided between the longtime local families and the recent urban refugees. We felt our share of guilt about our impending defection. When I quietly mentioned our plan to Cathy one afternoon at school pickup, her face crumpled in dismay at the thought that our girls would end up in different schools. Cathy herself had spent years at an elite private day school, followed by an even more elite boarding school. I resented her attitude toward our choice.

I didn't like thinking about how Henry and I would afford a private school. Paying for babysitters and day care had been hard enough, but I hoped I could scrape money together, with some family help and some scrimping. Henry was certainly no saver, which was a constant source of anxiety. The whole project worried me as I kept my eyes on the crazy Route 9 traffic and Henry's cell phone rang.

He took the call. I hated when he talked on his cell phone without a headset while speeding up this congested highway, but I was most immediately startled by the intimacy of the call. I could tell that he was talking to a woman. With hand gestures, I tried to get him to end the conversation. He ignored me.

"Get off the phone, Henry," I hissed. "This just isn't the time. It's dangerous and it's illegal."

Enraged, he ended the conversation and swerved the car over to the shoulder of the busy highway with a hasty and violent lurch of the steering wheel.

He shoved my shoulder. "Why are you such a fucking selfish bitch? Why can't you understand that my friend is upset? She's calling from California! Her mother is dying! Why can't you understand that? I hate you when you're like this!"

His anger terrified me. I thought he was going to hit me. The wind generated by the speeding cars shook our car. My body started shaking, though it was warm inside and I was wearing my newly purchased sheepskin coat.

We were married. We knew, without speaking, that we needed to maintain some pretense of calm for the upcoming school tour. After a minute, during which I felt ashamed but still furious, Henry pulled back onto the highway, and we drove on to the school in stony silence.

Once in the lobby, escorted by the director of admissions, Henry pulled off a theatrical performance that stunned me as much as his earlier anger had. Suddenly he was all warmth and charm, eager and enthusiastic, full of thoughtful questions. We were the perfect dedicated parents looking at a wonderful school for our beloved child.

Now I understood that Christine had been the caller that day.

Oct 23 2002

You are not the first woman I've done this with. But I'm on some kind of search, and whatever I'm looking for I haven't found it yet. There is something about you, about the combination of your intelligence, your openness to life, and your physical beauty that calls to me at the moment. I have not met someone like you until now. It's kind of like call and response. I'll play a tone, and the tone you play sounds right and true.

You may not think what I'm doing is romantic. I'm making great effort and making a great investment in our emotional relationship. I know that at the least I'll have a new friend, and I make friends for life. I think you know that I want more. I want us to have a very intimate friendship whose dialog also includes physical love.

I want to pal around with you. I want you to feel comfortable, and be able to be affectionate with me when we're away from your children. I just want to enjoy each other for who we really are. Whether I've slept with other women . . . I think these things should be put aside for a few hours. Let's just see what's drawing us together.

Love you

Henry

Christine's responses to the flattery, his gifts of expensive jewelry, the home-cooked meals, the fact that he cleaned up her kitchen and loaded the dishwasher? As any harassed single mother would confirm, she was near delirium. I would have been thrilled myself, if Henry had returned home from his trips and lavished such attention on me, instead of pleading exhaustion. His returns home were actually the worst parts of that year.

In her e-mails to Henry, Christine mostly sounded tired and drained. Her mother was dying, she had two young boys, her boyfriend was about to dump her, perhaps because he didn't want to deal with the two young boys, her house was in disarray, and it looked like she couldn't afford to keep the house anyway. After returning from a three-hour class for divorced parents, she remarked in an e-mail to Henry that her advice to all was to stay married. Probably not exactly what he had hoped to hear.

When Matthew called Christine the morning after Henry died, she was just another unknown name in an extensive address book.

"I told Matthew about the affairs," Christine recalled. "I was sure Henry had been careless and had left everything in plain view. I told him that he had to hide everything from you. I knew there was a lot to hide."

By the end of our first talk, I had the odd feeling that if we had met in some other way, I might have chosen Christine as a friend.

"This was Henry's nightmare," she said, "that you and I would meet and get along famously, go off into a corner to talk and knit and forget all about him."

We both laughed, and I could feel the truth of it. Our laughter softened the space between us.

I asked Christine to send me a photo of herself. She sent a JPEG file via e-mail. Before I opened it up, I thought to myself, *I'm going to find a cute little brunette.*

She was, in fact, a petite, sweet-looking woman, about my age, with a toothy smile, short, dark, curly hair, and gentle features. She could have been my cousin—or Cathy's better-looking sister.

I felt a strange sense of loss. I had to admit that I liked Christine. She had a great sense of humor. She was bright and witty, and of course, I wanted to like anyone who could talk with enthusiasm about knitting.

"Hey, there's a photo this month of me holding some mittens in a knitting magazine," she told me with evident delight. I drove to my local yarn shop, bought a copy, and admired again her appealing, open face. Henry was right about us—we got along just fine. And as I reread Henry's long, confidential e-mail to her, I envied her ability to draw him out of his life of many secret boxes.

But what happens to you in the moment when you decide that it is okay to have sex with a man who is married and has a child? Christine was never willing or able to explain her thinking about this line-crossing moment.

I had some idea about this experience. Once, years earlier, before I met Henry, I had crossed the line.

Roberto and I had been quietly attracted to each other for years. We saw each other almost every day as part of a postcollege group of Upper West Side friends. We went to parties in smoke-filled apartments on Riverside Drive. We ate in cheap restaurants. We drank beers at The Gold Rail on 110th Street and Broadway, and on weekends we went dancing.

Roberto was married to Annette. A green card was involved (he was from Italy), but his wife demonstrated an adoring devotion. They had no children. Roberto was dedicated to academia and had been completing his doctorate in linguistics.

In September of that year, 1984, Annette went for three weeks to do research in Chicago. One afternoon after she left, Roberto called me up at my office to see if I would go out with him to the movies that night. There was a Wim Wenders film festival in a small art theater in my neighborhood. The movies were a wonderful reason to leave my terrible apartment.

Small, cheap, hard-won after years of ever-changing sublets and shares, my apartment was a nasty railroad array of four rooms on Broadway and 107th Street, with a view of a dimly lit air shaft.

The lonely male inhabitant of the apartment across the airshaft liked looking into my windows. The shades I put up to gain some privacy blocked out most of the remaining light. The only regular male in my never-sunny apartment was Chester, my imposing tabby cat.

Chester helped me chase down mice and the water bugs whose antennae and shit brown whiskered feet startled me awake at 2:00 A.M. My panting screams were followed by long hunting expeditions. Chester had nothing but time. He could wait stock-still by the radiator for hours until the water bug ventured out again. Chester's twitching tail alerted me that our quarry was on the move, followed by much use of Raid foam and a Manhattan phone book or shoe, whichever was closest at hand.

Roberto and I saw *Alice in the Cities, Kings of the Road, The American Friend*. After the movies we ate rice, beans, and oxtail stew at La Rosita, a narrow restaurant on the north corner of my block. We drank steaming cups of *café con leche* and ate our stew as the last summer flies buzzed lazily near the grease-fogged windows. He walked me home after the movies and often came upstairs for a cup of tea. We talked about the movie we had just seen, his endless thesis in linguistics (something to do with Noam Chomsky, about whom I still understand nothing). When we ran out of movies, we just went to the restaurant.

The night before his wife returned he stood outside my halfclosed doorway at midnight and finally told me what he wanted. He pressed his body on the door and said he did not want to leave. I opened the door and let him stay with me. The initial euphoria of fulfilled sexual attraction was followed by several brain-numbing migraines. I found myself stumbling up Broadway to the corner market with a half-moon of vision loss in each eye. Insomnia kept me awake till 3:00 A.M. I wasn't cut out for an affair with a married man, though I had certainly fallen deeply in love. I ended the affair after a month.

Roberto pleaded with me to give him time. We began seeing each other again. At Christmas he gave me a pair of long black lace gloves. I didn't give him anything for fear that Annette would notice. The migraines returned with greater intensity, snowy vision, pain, and nausea. I begged Roberto to make a decision and to tell Annette about the affair.

He told Annette. He told me he couldn't decide what to do. He wasn't in love with Annette, he said, but his marriage provided him with support and comfort. He didn't know if our relationship would work. I told him I didn't know either, we would have to try first, but I couldn't continue this way. I ended the affair and the friendship. We never spoke to each other or saw each other again. It was like quitting smoking cold turkey.

On Valentine's Day, I opened the white envelope that had arrived in my mailbox eagerly, half-hoping it was from Roberto, whom I still missed with gut-wrenching misery. The card inside was crudely drawn in black ink, a black heart decorated with dead cockroaches, their antennae and legs perfectly preserved, carefully glued onto the white paper.

It was from Annette. She called me a bitch and a cunt and a slut. These words still had the sting of high school days. I felt frightened, knowing that there was a woman a mere twenty city blocks away who hated me to the core of her being and might do me harm if she saw me. But I also thought that I deserved her anger.

I wondered about her careful effort in the creation of the card. Were the roaches from her kitchen? Had she hoarded and then emptied a Roach Motel for this purpose?

I quietly suffered over my lost love, still hoping that he might change his mind and return to me. With a lesson well learned, the pain of this loss gradually softened until I met Henry, a year and a half later. That brief affair was the most chastening experience of my early adulthood, and I kept that card for many years as a reminder of a path never to be taken again.

Christine in California was in her late thirties or early forties, not an inexperienced twenty-five-year-old. And though she expressed genuine regret about what she had done, she was vague and evasive when I pressed for details. She seemed to understand that she owed me an explanation, but at a certain point I hit a wall.

In our conversations she tried to minimize the sexual aspect of the relationship. Perhaps she wanted to spare me some pain. And it's true that sometimes sex is just sex. Some people pay for it. It's not always interesting or meaningful, though Henry's e-mails made it clear that he was eager to continue their sexual connection. Christine suggested that she had really felt more drawn to Henry intellectually, that it was their conversations that had been important and meaningful to her, and that these conversations had even changed the course of her creative life.

She apologized for these conversations. She told me that she understood how wrong it had been to engage so emotionally in conversation with Henry. She understood that this kind of intellectual engagement was as wrong as the sex they had, because it must have provided a huge distraction from his marriage.

But the more I thought about it, the angrier it made me. The emotional intimacy of their relationship over those few months had been significant enough to deeply affect my marriage that morning in the car on Route 9. With Cathy in and out of his life, Christine had temporarily satisfied Henry's need to be the center of the world.

. . .

My conversations with Christine never felt "done." I felt like there was something more she had to tell me, but lacking Henry's charms, I couldn't pry it out of her. Nevertheless, I called Christine again one morning from my kitchen while taking a break from packing boxes of foodstuffs to take to our island rental house in Maine. I couldn't wait to leave town again. Piles of sheets and towels were stacked on the table. There were more piles of clothing upstairs. Even in August, Maine can be unpredictable. I had taken out everything from fleece jackets to bathing suits. It was good to be busy.

"I am so sorry that you are dealing with the results of Henry's poor life choices and I am so sorry for my role in such a yucky mess," Christine said.

Yucky. A word children use to describe a bowl of pudding overturned on the kitchen floor or the foul-smelling contents of their diapers. I sensed her wish to be done with me, and this whole sordid tale, to move on to a happier life chapter.

But I did not have such a luxury. For reasons I was just coming to understand, I needed to dig much deeper. It was not cathartic, the digging, it was horrible in every imaginable way. Yet I did have the sense, clearer with each passing day, that in order ever to have a new life, I would have to strip away the veneers of the one that was over. I knew that Christine had finished confiding and wanted to return to her life, and that whatever else I discovered would be elsewhere.

I wondered how many other people, maybe even close friends, were not telling me what they knew, to spare my feelings.

Who could I trust but myself? Though it felt like I was jabbing myself in the chest with a scalpel, by the following morning,

Liza safely at day camp, I was ready to head back to my office to continue down the list of women.

A pleasant woman's voice answered the phone.

"This is Julie. Henry's wife."

Ellen—the wiry muscle girl who could do ten one-handed pull-ups—began crying.

"I've thought about you so often," she sobbed. "I heard that Henry died. But I didn't go to the wake or the funeral." I heard her sigh, and she paused for a moment. "I knew I didn't belong there."

Weeping continuously, Ellen told me that, after they met at the gym, Henry had flirted with her and pursued her. Her mother had been very ill, living in her home, requiring constant care. Her daily trips to the gym were a welcome escape from the burdens of her home life. She and her husband had been going through a difficult time.

Ellen said that she and Henry had sex twice. Consumed with guilt, she had then told her husband, started marriage therapy, and rearranged her gym schedule so that she and Henry would no longer meet.

"Out of curiosity," I asked, "what do you look like? No, don't tell me. I bet you're a little brunette." She was.

The day after that phone call, Ellen called me back. She cried some more and asked for forgiveness. I'd read through all her e-mail exchanges with Henry. Her letters suggested that she was gullible, but perhaps no more than I might have been in her situation.

Henry had complained to Christine in California that Ellen wasn't
that intelligent, but she was no dimmer than I had been while
married, and while he may not have seen her as his intellectual
equal, in all other ways she was his superior. She had a working
conscience, and she was capable of authentic emotion. She had
come quickly to a clear understanding of right and wrong, a clear
sense of her own culpability. She had made a mistake but had cor-
rected herself. She did not run away from her responsibilities to
her marriage or to me.

I wished Ellen a good life. I told her that I hoped her marriage
would improve. She said she was grateful. Now life could move
on, for both of us.

I was surprised at how quickly my anger passed after our conversations. Perhaps I was just worn down, desensitized. But I felt
mostly pity for this woman who had stumbled briefly into the
mud pit of my marriage and fallen for Henry's charms. She never
knew about Cathy, and even if she had lingered longer in his life,
he probably would not have told her about Cathy or Christine or
anyone else. She was a plaything for him. Ellen was, in my mind,
a kind of innocent bystander, briefly tantalized by something
Henry seemed to be offering at a time when she herself was exhausted with obligation. I noted that Henry had been good at
finding vulnerable women. In matters of romance, illicit or otherwise, timing is everything.

———

I sent an e-mail to Alicia, the Argentinean woman Henry
had mentioned in his letter to Christine.

I had only one e-mail, from December 3, 2002, from Alicia to

Henry. My friend Sara had found a printout of it during her searches in Henry's office when she had visited in the spring, folded at the bottom of one of his travel bags. Without understanding its full significance, she had saved it for me and mailed it back after I told her about Henry's affairs. The subject header was telling enough: "Re: My North American Boyfriend."

In the e-mail, written in stilted English, Alicia told Henry that she would be happy to talk to him about "my sex matters." She suggested a time to talk on the phone and included her phone numbers.

I had met her twice, at parties, one at our own house during the prior summer. She was a friend of Tomas's former girlfriend, Lindsay, who in this case had unwittingly acted as matchmaker.

I sent Alicia an e-mail, and to my surprise, she responded promptly. Our correspondence was hampered by her poor English, but we muddled along for a few rounds. Her life seemed confused and sad. She was a university student. She lived with a man, a relationship that was by her account troubled and unhappy.

"Nothing really happened," she said. Was this the truth? Were Henry's fantasies of a future affair overblown? Clearly they'd talked about something and had made plans to continue talking. I understood from her description of her own relationships and culture that infidelity was more flexibly tolerated in Argentina. I guessed that Henry had counted on that. His ideal woman would come from somewhere outside the United States—we are known worldwide for being prudes, the sins of Bill Clinton et al. notwithstanding.

In a peculiar twist that seemed to suggest the extent to which he had compartmentalized his life, I recalled with bitter amusement that Henry had come down quite hard on our former president, both for his adultery and for lying about his adultery.

During this first terrible week after I found out about Henry's affairs, Tomas and I corresponded daily, a welcome relief. I knew he was having his own hard time after having told me what he knew. Some of the same people who had viewed his involvement with me suspiciously judged him even more harshly now. But I felt liberated and grateful.

Tomas invited Liza and me to a dance event in a large barnlike building on the grounds of a local summer camp. A band played, and we danced exuberantly, sort of a mock boxing match, which perfectly released the anger I'd felt all week. Tomas tossed and twirled Liza in the air. I knew many in the crowd and had the uneasy feeling that they were beginning to view Tomas and me as a couple. After a time, Liza tired and Tomas and I were sweaty. We walked outside to rest and get some air on the beautiful grounds. Liza enjoyed the last daylight and began playing with some other kids. The ten-year-old daughter of a friend recognized me. She looked at me and then at Tomas, then back at me.

"Are you *dating?*" she asked, still looking back and forth between Tomas and me.

I wasn't sure how to respond to her question, the bold and direct type that kids are famous for, the type I usually encouraged. I didn't really know what Tomas and I were doing. We were trying to be in a relationship that couldn't be classified in such traditional terms as "dating." As the time of my trip to Maine drew closer, I sensed these might be some of our last times together in this way. The fall was bound to bring changes.

But to my surprise and relief, Tomas salvaged the awkward moment. He stepped toward me, put his arm around me affectionately, and said, "Yes! She is!"

There was one woman left. Her name was Eliana. She was not mentioned in Christine's letter. Once the news was out in the open, Matthew had come over to talk with me about what he knew about Henry's women. He remembered that it was Eliana who had called early on the morning after Henry's death, and that it was this woman's screaming voice I'd heard from my bedroom.

After I found Eliana's name in Henry's address book, I waited a few days before trying to reach her. I had saved her for last. I needed time to work up courage.

eight

....

Late July 2003

I had met Eliana once, just a few months before Henry's death.

The same November 2002 that found Henry and me driving up Route 9 to tour the private school for Liza provided a welcome night out. Lindsay, Tomas's former girlfriend, invited us to her birthday celebration. I thought she had broken up with him rather shabbily the summer before, while he was living in our attic, and in the inevitable way that people choose one or the other party of a fractured couple, we had remained closer to Tomas.

Our town provided little drama. Lindsay had a talent for making her own, however, and I was happy enough to be included. The event was to be a costume party. Our children were invited, and Liza happened to have a blue pinafore-style dress, so I volunteered the idea that we might go as characters from *Alice's Adventures in Wonderland*.

"I hate costume parties," Henry responded dismissively. "What a pain in the neck."

"Yeah, okay, but it's Lindsay's birthday and *she* wants a costume party. Tomas is even going. Can't we just humor her?"

"Everyone always humors that girl."

"You might have a point there."

. . .

I fastened the row of buttons on the back of Liza's blue ruffled dress. I put on a wine-colored velvet dress, one of my vintage favorites, and the crown I had sewn from pieces of scrap brocade and ribbon. I was quite proud of my eleventh-hour effort. Henry reluctantly agreed to say, if asked, that he was the Cheshire Cat after I suggested that his smile was enough of a costume. He grumbled on the drive over, but I had to admit that, in spite of my mixed feelings about the hostess, I looked forward to the evening. Gray autumnal melancholy was seeping into the house, a bit more each day, with its signs of quickly encroaching winter isolation. And every night out in company was a night when Henry and I didn't fight or head off to our separate offices. A party might provide the stage for some family togetherness.

As we entered the noisy, crowded space, I spotted an ebony-haired woman, slender, dressed in black, supervising the food and drink table. In New York City this attire would have been unremarkable, but in our town it was a noticeable dark mark. Her wrists were encircled with black leather studded bracelets. Her long hair shimmered blue-black under the overhead light. Her eyes were framed with dark liner and mascara. If this was a costume for one of Lord Voldemort's followers, it was convincing, but she moved with such ease in it that I wondered if she dressed like that all the time. She smiled at me, but I felt chilled.

Other distractions filled the room. One woman, reincarnated as a young Elvis, with hip swagger and blue suede shoes, sang a stirring version of "Heartbreak Hotel." Jesus wandered through the crowd, dressed in white robes and leather strapped sandals. Tomas was frighteningly convincing as a Mafia goombah, a pillow stuffed under a stained wife beater, his hair greased back. As I forced a smile, he joked about exorcising his inner demons and angled his beer can in the direction of the hostess.

Lindsay, the birthday girl, turning twenty-five, was as pretty as ever. Everyone had been at least a bit in love with this golden girl when she and Tomas had first moved to town. Tonight she did not disappoint. She wore a mandarin-collared dress that elegantly displayed her long-limbed body. She brandished a vintage cigarette holder in one hand, and with the other she smoothed her blond hair, twisted in an updo, with nervous excitement. She waited expectantly for Henry and me to respond to her costume. Anaïs Nin, the famously petite and dark-haired early-twentieth-century writer of erotica, she told us, her scarlet-glossed lips briefly pouting after neither of us guessed. Aha, we smiled.

I sighed, suddenly wishing I had a long cigarette holder, with a cigarette burning in it. But, alas, I had finally quit years ago, in the interest of becoming a good mother. I was already experiencing an all too familiar urge to glue myself to the wall. I took Liza's hand and directed us toward the corner where I had spotted Emily and her children.

Emily's costume also featured a long cigarette holder. She would have looked more convincing as Anaïs Nin, I thought, with her dark bobbed hair and red lipstick. Like the Parisian bohemians she admired, Emily flowered in the chatter, her cheeks flushed with the warmth of the animated room, the otherwise peaceful studio where Lindsay led our yoga classes. I wondered for a moment if Emily ever got bored living in our small town. Life for a nonworking mom must have been much more fun in Berkeley. Food co-ops, women's circles, progressive schools, and genuine political activity. No one really did much about that around here, though everyone talked a lot about what we could do to save the world for our children. Here we were too busy redecorating our houses.

It was a good party: Lindsay was a welcoming hostess, there

was plenty of food and drink, there was music, and the guests were feeling free enough to dance. I was the problem child in the room.

I left Liza with her friends, walked over to the drink table, and accepted a glass of red wine from the woman in black. She smiled again. I returned her gesture weakly and retreated quickly to my corner. The wine soon softened the edges of the day and my irritation with the world. Henry, who had been cheerfully circulating (his grumpiness faded quickly with wine and company), appeared, then disappeared to mingle some more. I was happy to stand around the edge of the room with Emily and a few other friends, while our kids entertained themselves on top of a pile of coats.

During a pause in conversation, I glanced over to check out the dark-haired woman again. She and Henry were talking and laughing. When our eyes met, his were shuttered into narrow slits against the overhead colored party lights, and he was grinning madly. *The Cheshire Cat, to perfection.*

Liza's voice distracted my gaze.

"What did you say, sweetie?" I asked, turning away from Henry and the noise in the room.

"Can we go home now, Mama?" *My thoughts exactly.*

"What did you think of Eliana?" Henry asked me a few days later. He looked up from the clutter of papers on his desk as I handed him his mail. I couldn't bear to set the stack of new envelopes on top of the already chaotic pile of unopened bills. It was one of the many times when I was relieved that we had separate checking accounts.

"Who's Eliana?"

"The woman I was talking to at Lindsay's party."

"The woman in black? I thought she was scary looking. Who is she anyway?"

"Lindsay hired her to help at the party. And Tomas knows her too. I'm planning to have lunch with her next week. I was thinking of asking her to help me with my book, you know, as an assistant. What d'ya think of that idea?"

"Whatever happened to the idea of a smart English major from one of the local colleges?" I shot back, amazed that I needed to point out the obvious. "Does this woman have any research background? Does she know anything at all about food? Is she a professional writer?" I edged away from his desk, desperate to retreat downstairs to my office before a battle broke out.

"She isn't really a writer," Henry said. "She'd be more of a"—he paused for a beat, searching for the right word—"spiritual guide." Henry looked at me, almost plaintively, but still provocatively, melding the two facial expressions into a kind of dare.

"A 'spiritual guide'? Since when do you, Mr. Rational Man, son of Voltaire, go for 'spiritual guides'? I can't even get you to take another yoga class."

This was becoming stupid. The dark-haired woman with the black leather wristbands—an assistant? With regard to his book project, this was the most laughable idea I had ever heard him propose. I wanted to get out of his office, immediately, before I exploded, but I was paralyzed at the doorway with frustration and a sudden paradoxical compassion for Henry, who looked so mournful and lost.

"I feel blocked," he continued. "I can't seem to get started writing my book. I need some help getting organized and focused." A silent beat passed as we both acknowledged the untamed piles of paper. "And why do you always have to be so negative about everything?"

"I had lunch with Eliana today," Henry announced one evening after dinner the following week as he rose from his seat at the kitchen table. Liza was finishing a dish of ice cream. "I really think she'd be great at getting my research together."

I turned off the faucet and set down the scrubby sponge and the pan I was laboring over. He was heading into the hallway toward the stairs. I followed him up to his office, already conflicted about leaving Liza to finish her dessert alone.

"Look, Henry, you asked me before, and I told you what I thought. Why did you ask me for my opinion when you have no interest in really listening to what I have to say?"

He sat down at his desk gloomily.

"Henry, it's crazy in here." I surveyed the clutter of papers on his desk. His was a long desk, a seven-footer. There were no visible empty spaces. If Nature abhors a vacuum, his office had become a kind of rain-forest jungle without a patch of bare earth. Since our talk the prior week, more stacks of unopened mail and magazines had sprung up on the floor, this in a room lined with custom-built bookshelves.

"I honestly don't understand what you do all day. I mean, I get up, I go into my office, I work. I don't visit Cathy for coffee. I don't take naps, I don't go to the gym three times a week. I work and take care of Liza, and I take a yoga class once a week." I paused, hoping my voice sounded measured, not hysterical and angry.

"I can't fix this mess for you," I continued, wrapping my arms around my waist self-protectively and perhaps bitchily, "we'll just get in a fight about it. But I really think you need someone bright and capable, not some weird girl in black leather wristbands."

"You never like any of my ideas." His lower lip curled down in a pout, like that of an indulged child who still, after all, wanted my approval before he misbehaved.

"Yeah, well, then just keep doing what you're doing since it's working out so well," I said. "But I don't want that woman in my house. And don't complain to me when you miss your book deadline. I'm going back downstairs. I want to keep Liza company and I have work to finish before her bedtime."

Before we could have yet another argument about Eliana, she was gone. Henry, visibly disappointed, told me that Eliana had decided to leave the area and move home. I didn't care where home was, just that she was far away.

"A piece of work, isn't she?" Matthew said, forcing a dark laugh. He'd come over to show me Henry's computer photo files, previously hidden from view. I looked at the picture of Eliana, in full Queen of the Night regalia, her eyes peering out provocatively between two curtains of dark hair, and I sighed. Now I understood Matthew's stoic mood during Henry's funeral. He had known all this already. He had protected me, and I loved him for that. We were happy to close the computer window after a moment. Eliana's image was already seared in my brain. *This is going to be very bad.*

"Something sexual happened between Henry and this woman," Matthew pronounced quietly. "I read through some of the e-mails. It looks like Henry saw her while he was in California on his last two research trips in the fall." As if echoing my thoughts, he added, trying for some of his trademark dark levity, "I imagine, you know, sordid hotel room scenes." I tried to conjure up the very worst, to avoid later surprise.

Afterward, Matthew and I sat on the porch. I felt unsteady, almost dizzy, with the heat and my anxiety about getting in touch with Eliana.

"Henry really had no spiritual life," Matthew said, shaking his head and looking down at the stone floor. "He rejected all that as nonrational thinking. I was always trying to get him to read some books on spirituality. I thought it would help him. I wanted him to be happy." He looked at me very directly. "I wanted both of you to be happy. I loved you both. A couple of times I think he might have been trying to talk to me about what was going on with him and Cathy, but I cut him off, I just didn't want to hear this at all. You were my friend too. I told him so."

I thanked Matthew for his loyalty to me and to our marriage. Intense fury rose in me again, though I tried to stay calm. Just as he'd done with Irena, Henry had tried to place another person very close to me in a situation where he would be forced to lie.

"He and I didn't spend that much time together the last year or so," Matthew continued. "He hardly ever called me. I could see that there was something really missing in his life. He could be very self-destructive, ever since college, when we all drank too much and did drugs."

"Yeah, he loved telling those stories, didn't he?" I closed my eyes for a moment, remembering the adventures he'd told about his college days (the most colorful tale involved buying LSD preserved from the sixties from a nameless dealer at the Syracuse airport), and our own times together before Liza was born, when we'd all gone to parties and bars together.

Entering our thirties, we'd cleaned up our acts. I was never much of a drinker anyway. Henry had stopped drinking for a year, and when he resumed, he drank only modestly. Therapy seemed to have been instructive—he spoke to me about how he had used alcohol to "self-medicate." He understood finally, he said, how to drink in moderation. But I wondered now about the weekly dinner parties Henry insisted on throwing. Perhaps at some level they were about trying to recapture some of that time, to create an atmosphere of lawless abundance.

"Maybe"—Matthew sighed ruefully—"considering how everything turned out, maybe he was better off just drinking."

I wondered about the transference of his addictions—drugging, drinking, adultery, it was all a kind of risk-taking for its own sake.

By this point, I hoped that nothing could really shock me, that I had reached the end of the line. I had been reduced to the level of silently praying (I, the skeptic) that Henry had cared enough about me to use a condom. Eliana looked like she got around, more than I had anyway in the last sixteen years. I had been a faithful wife.

I called our local doctor to arrange for an HIV test.

"I am so relieved to hear from you," the doctor said, with an audible sigh.

It turned out that Henry had requested an HIV test in early December 2002, a month before his death. Confidentiality agreements had prevented the doctor from calling me to have me take a test as well. I did recall that Henry had avoided sex with me right after his return from that West Coast trip. He was exhausted, he'd said apologetically. And he certainly had looked tired then.

So, perhaps he had cared enough about me to wait to have sex till he got his negative HIV test results. Though I seethed, wondering what he would have done if the results had been positive for something less immediately devastating, such as a more garden-variety venereal disease. Would he have let that go, hoping that he hadn't infected me, waiting till unavoidable symptoms presented, rather than tell me about his infidelities? How ill would he have allowed me to become before he confessed? Perhaps it had been fear, not just exhaustion, I had seen in Henry that early December. He must have understood that his situation was dangerously unraveling.

The doctor suggested I get tested just to be sure and rushed the tests, which, to my intense relief, all came back negative. Somehow, miraculously, I had dodged at least ten bullets.

The number in Henry's address book turned out to be the home of Eliana's sister in Canada. Her sister gave me another number, in a nearby town. Eliana answered this time.

"I have been expecting you to call. In these last days I have felt your presence strongly." Her voice had an airy, singsong quality, her sentences floating upward. My imagination conjured a palm reader or a crystal ball gazer.

"You were expecting me!" I was shouting at her already, though I'd wanted to remain calm. "What does that mean? Did you think about me when you were fucking Henry in a goddamned hotel room?"

She did not hang up. Like Christine, she listened to me. She apologized quietly.

Now we could get somewhere. I got my yelling out of me, and we started talking. After that first conversation, I wasn't ready to talk to her again for several months, but we began an e-mail correspondence that very first day.

Since the moment he passed, I have visualized your essence and what you must be living through. I have known since that day, you would find the thread and come asking. I did not expect you so soon. Thank you for having the courage.

There are spiritual dimensions and doings of this relationship between him, you and me that are beyond logical comprehension. I can only unveil to you what I sensed and experienced in my friendship with him. I ask you to listen to what is relevant for you to understand in all this and release the rest.

Eliana used language I couldn't work with easily—a "New Age" lyrical vocabulary very uncomfortable for me. I was familiar with its forms from the college health-food co-op I had joined, and many yoga classes I had attended. I understood it, but I didn't like it, not one little bit. I had been educated to write clear sentences with identifiable subjects and predicates. I had learned to diagram sentences. I practiced again, on some of Eliana's sentences, but it was like taking a walk in an overgrown forest, through thoughts intertwined like vines.

I was bewildered. Henry himself had always been brutally dismissive of New Age culture. My decision to buy organic milk, eggs, meat, and vegetables peeved him, as did Emily's occasional Berkeleyesque meanderings about astrology and goddesses, and the spiritual aspects of my yoga practice. Had he truly gone off the deep end having a relationship with a woman so nonlinear in her thinking?

To her, the word "sphere" did not represent a round ball, a social group, or an arena of geopolitical influence. It was a kind of spiritual energy force. "Congestion" was not nasal, pulmonary, or coronary but a kind of emotional and spiritual phlegm. She spoke about visions, energy waves, and the paranormal with the certainty of a scientist cataloging research data. I didn't know what to make of this woman, but I knew I wanted to smack Henry upside the head, with a swift kick in the ass for good measure.

Whatever else she might have been, Eliana was possibly the true witness to Henry's last, very troubled months, during which time he was, at the least, in a crisis of confidence about his book and desperate to entangle himself with and untangle himself from Cathy, before I found out about their affair.

I speculated about the lost correspondence between Cathy and Henry. What exactly had happened between them during the last six months of his life? Had Cathy threatened to tell me? Anything was possible, but without evidence, Cathy could hide—and I was left to wonder without any hope of really understanding the truth. The best I could hope for was a glimmer into his world through this woman.

I had to admit that Eliana's voice was soothing and kind. But for all her airy-sounding language, she was clearly wary about revealing everything right away. I would have to prove to her that I could handle it. I needed her to tell me what she knew. I wanted to see everything now. Something had changed in Henry's thinking, and whether from anxiety about the book that wasn't writing itself or out of a sense of being more profoundly lost, he had reached out to this woman for guidance and she had answered.

Eliana had presented herself to him as nonjudgmental, liberated, and unchained from convention. She told me that she had lived for years this way, seeing herself as a free spirit who could make her choices without consequences, moving in and out of relationships with men and women. She said she was reassessing this path in the aftermath of Henry's death.

Eliana had spoken to Henry on the phone, she told me, the

evening before his death. I must have seen them talking as I passed in and out of his office while Henry organized his papers.

And when she sent me their e-mail correspondence, I saw that they had exchanged important ideas about the future in his last days, after our New Year's Eve party.

On January 3, five days before his death, Eliana wrote:

> Well, this can be a long journey of discovery . . . in the path of spirituality, emotions are a part of our beings that we need to learn to observe and have distance with . . . feelings reflect our inner ways of knowing truths, value, honor, so they differ from the games we as humans use in the emotional spheres . . . if we are truly conscious of our actions, when an emotion arises, like anger, if we are in truth of ourselves and wanting to nourish our inners in the strongest way, it is by feeling what this emotion brings to us, allowing ourselves the place creatively to let it go through us and find peace, calm, balance within ourselves with it. . . . I am working at looking at the emotions which get triggered when I am with you and let myself breathe with them, yet always keeping the love flowing.

My first response was that this was all a turd wave of bullshit, that she was the expert surfer girl riding the big turd wave and Henry was the newbie, thrilled to discover the newest surf shop, filled with all-new gadgets he'd never tried before.

When I made an effort to be more generous, though, I thought her e-mail also could have been a preclass talk a yoga teacher might have offered on the topics of nonattachment and compassion, ideas I certainly struggled with but whose wisdom I appreciated. In her way (very different from my way, I had to acknowledge), Eliana was explaining to him how much damage we create for ourselves, and others, when we have no understanding or mastery of our emotions, when we are too attached to the outcome of a situation.

I thought about what Matthew had said, that Henry had no spiritual life. Perhaps, just at the end of his life, something had changed in Henry; perhaps, having dug himself into such a deep mess, he was trying to understand himself in a different way. Having exhausted the patience of other women in his life, he had at last found a most welcoming listener. His long e-mail response devolved into a self-involved rant about his anger at Christine for ending their sexual relationship.

> I am "congested" at the moment as you say. It really isn't in my temperament (or anyone else's that I've ever met) to be able to transcend emotions. I'm just honest about it. I don't want to transcend things; I want to meet them head on and work through them.
>
> But I am trying to learn to let things go (at your urging). At the moment I am having difficulty emotionally with both Cathy and Christine, I admit it. It's nothing that I can control; I am just trying not to be compelled to act on these emotions, which is an entirely new thing for me.
>
> [Christine] was most probably pissed at me for a variety of things: (1) seeing other women, (2) seeing other women who are younger, (3) hearing from her friend that I thought she was in love with me (which is not exactly what I said).

This was followed by a longer rant about Cathy, which confirmed my suspicion that their relationship was very much in play throughout the fall until his unexpected death. He recounted the scene at his final New Year's Eve party.

As for Cathy, let me describe some ugliness.

I suppose it was my own stupidity that caused me not to delete those emails (yes, stupid). But for her to generate all that hate after seven months is just too much.

At first I thought it was going to be okay. I gave her a lot of space at my party. At one point she grabbed me by the arm to ask me to get some more champagne for one of her friends. But basically she spent the whole time clinging to her husband, or talking to two of her friends who go to the same church as her. Other than that, she spoke to no one.

She drank heavily and toward the end she spilled wine on these two above-mentioned friends. I handed her a stack of napkins and mildly joked by asking her if she needed a permanent supply, to which she hissed, "No." At that point, I knew that things weren't going to go well. Then, as she was getting ready to go, she looked really tired and drained. I asked her very gently if something was wrong, and she said, "With whom?" Then she said I should "check my paperwork" to understand what was wrong. I think that was a reference to the emails she had discovered. I then asked her if she would like to get together and talk about it, to which she sneered and said, "Nah." She comes over to say goodbye, again in a really hostile way, and when I get up to see her and her family to the door she shoves it closed in my face.

Part of me so desperately wants to call her up and set things right . . . but I know it is hopeless and I'm just going to have to live with the situation. What I have to learn, and what I did learn by listening to you is that there is no way I can apply "reason" to this situation. The fallacy, the projection that I had been operating under for the time I was seeing her (all the way until a lightbulb went off in my head five mornings ago) was that she was like me . . . that she has a psychology that resembles mine. But this is not true. The reality is that she is emotionally unstable. The reality is she is certainly too small emotionally. She is one of the most rigid, fearful, and narrow-minded people I have ever met.

And the larger reality? Any energy I am directing at these two women is really some sort of pathology on my part. I need to keep that energy inside of me and conserve it for my wife and for my new husband/boyfriend—you. So, instead of obsessing about these things today, I was able to convert this negative energy to thoughts about a positive path for myself. That indeed is a change in my behavior, and I have you to thank for it.

I noted, with more confusion, that Henry seemed to think of her as his male partner, which revealed something about the nature of their sexual-emotional relationship. Eliana had taken control of the relationship in a way that was new for him, and because of that, he was listening to her in a way he did not listen to his other lovers or me, his wife. A minute later he sent her this note:

Sweet Eliana:

Really, you don't have to read that email. It really was just a way for me to clear. I can't tell you how much lighter I feel.

Light and clear like water . . . like a flowing crystal. If you want to read, just read the last few lines—that's the important part.

Snow is falling outside. I'm getting ready for bed. The world is hush, and I feel, by some miracle, some peace. We are good for each other.

Love, Henry

A flowing crystal? These were new words for Henry. He had been in treatment with his psychiatrist for over a year. Though

Leslie Burns had told me much in our meeting, this mystery woman with the leather studded bracelets had managed comparable insight into Henry's personality. Eliana had also allowed him to really hope that he could repair his life. She was telling him that this would be hard work, and that he would have to make real effort. He was still rationalizing his affairs, and still making excuses, but he was starting to understand that he alone had to make changes. Perhaps, for a few days, he had that hope. Then, he died.

There had been hints of Henry's brief time with Eliana. During our last Christmas vacation together, in Seattle, Henry and I went out for a drive without Liza. After an obligatory trip to REI, he insisted on taking a detour to a sex toy shop he had heard about. He was sure that this would be fun for us and was disappointed at my lack of enthusiasm. "Jesus, you have no sense of adventure, Julie."

His insistence, which to me felt harassing, was, of course, incredibly unsexy.

He must have ventured to the store at another time during our trip. During the last week of his life, I walked into his office while he sat at his desk. I noticed a small, unmarked corrugated box on a chair, flaps open. A peek inside revealed its colorful contents: red leather wrist restraints and other sex toys. He had often suggested using toys in our sexual relationship, but since I wasn't that interested in sex, or at least sex with him, during our last years together, the idea had not been appealing. Restraint was not appealing at all—some part of me didn't trust him. But I hated being thought of as a poor sport, and I was hoping very much that the new year would bring some joy and spontaneity back into our marriage.

"What's this?" I asked, looking up from the box.

Henry laughed. "Go on, take a look inside." I lifted out a black metal-studded leather belt. Examination revealed a central metal ring, a holster for a dildo.

Suddenly, I felt silly and playful in a way I had not experienced for years. I tried on the dildo belt over my jeans. In an instant, I was transformed into a tough S & M chick or perhaps a pocket-size version of fearless Samantha from *Sex and the City*— she'd try anything at least once. He laughed again, looking up from his papers.

"I wonder what people would say if I wore *this* down Main Street?"

Henry laughed again, this time a broad actor's stage laugh, which abruptly broke the spell with its forced timbre. Now I just felt stupid and uncomfortable in the belt. I took it off, happy to place it back in the box. Dress-up game over, I returned to my work.

After an intense week and a half of e-mail correspondence, Eliana was ready to tell me the story of her relationship with Henry. She said that Henry had described me as needy and vulnerable, which explained her initial caution with me. But as our correspondence continued, we both saw each other more fully.

Intrigued by her metal-studded leather bracelets, Henry had approached Eliana at Lindsay's party. He was particularly interested in her itinerant lifestyle. Eliana had no fixed home at that time but wandered, visiting friends, moving where her relationships took her, a life focused on sexual adventuring. She was happy to live this way, and was open with her partners about her lifestyle choices, though she said that several of her partners were less content.

After their lunch, Eliana and Henry talked several times while she remained on the East Coast. She said that he expressed immediate interest in a sexual relationship. Henry also spoke to Eliana about Cathy, about her neediness and possessiveness. The level of anxiety in his relationship with Cathy had escalated, and he was looking for some way out, to a different, more liberated life. Eliana suggested that his trips out West might also have opened up ideas in his mind about living very differently, in a different kind of marriage. A marriage I never signed on for.

Eliana told me that the day before Henry died she had experienced pain in her own body and sensed strongly that he was ill as well. At another time I would have quickly dismissed this account, but after my own unaccountable "visitations," I was more open to the idea that some experiences could not be explained in purely rational terms. In fact, it was a relief to write to her about Henry's visits. She received my accounts with the same calm as had Maya, the massage therapist.

I tried to imagine Henry and Eliana together. During his penultimate trip out West, in late November 2002, Henry had called me every day.

"I miss you and Liza so much," he'd say before signing off. "I can't wait to come home."

He had often called me while driving. I could hear the whooshing of passing cars on some western coastal highway. He told me about the meals he had eaten that day, the food people he had met. Eliana told me that she had been in the car with him during several of these conversations, witness to what I had thought were private exchanges. She was, literally, the fellow traveler he had been searching for.

In L.A., he brought out all his toys and I was thrilled. It had been awhile since I had a fun playmate, particularly one who was new to the world. At the beginning, I was the one in the wrist constraints. It was interesting, as it had been awhile and I too had to adjust again to letting go and feeling trust and no control. However, when he put them on, this is when I saw his inner reality. As I have seen with many other men. Particularly those with control issues.

He said it was the most intense experience he had had and I do believe for the first time in his life, he felt the inner force of another, equal to his own.

A wave of nausea consumed me after reading this. The gap between the reality of our marriage and what he had wanted was like the Grand Canyon. My eyes drifted out of focus. I put my head down on the desk. I needed air.

Rebel the dog ran out of his house, barking. I picked up a small rock and threw it at the dividing fence, and Rebel ran off. I tried pulling up weeds, usually a cathartic pleasure. The dog circled back and began his plaintive barking again. At last Mr. Caine appeared and shooed Rebel back inside.

Maybe I am better off without him. I remembered an afternoon nine months earlier, standing in my autumnal backyard, when this entirely radical thought had come to me, moments after one of our last screaming phone fights. While Henry's mind had been opening to new ideas out West, mine had been slowly opening as well during that final year, when he was frequently absent, permitting brief moments of clarity.

We had spent sixteen tumultuous years together. I had loved Henry and remained attached, even when I had felt repelled physically and emotionally, because this was the commitment I had made in front of my family and friends and a benevolent rabbi. *No, things will get better; they are just really bad right now.* On that afternoon, I had chased away the jangling thought: *Maybe I am better off without him.* But perhaps at some later point, after a few more fights, I might have begun listening to myself, concluding that Liza and I would be better off on our own. Though Irena, the experienced veteran, was surely correct—it would have been a terrible divorce.

An amusing idea flitted past, that Henry had been struck down by the Big Guy himself, flattened onto the kitchen floor by the strong hand and mighty arm I remembered from all those Passover dinners, the guy who thought nothing of setting rivers of blood and swarms of locusts against his enemies. I was laughing again, a good sign, considering the situation.

Eliana told me that Henry often spoke to her about our marriage and our life here in a small, conventional town. Though he had wanted to have a family, support from a partner, and success in the "real world," he also had urges to live freely.

She described an evening in Los Angeles. They went out to a restaurant, and while they sat at the bar, Henry flirted with an attractive woman while Eliana charmed the same woman's husband. Henry told Eliana that he had ideas about opening up his marriage, but of course he never spoke about that to me. He knew I did not want that kind of marriage. The one we had was hard enough.

Eliana said that Henry talked to her about feeling like a useless member of the family, that he was "not good enough." This idea felt outrageous to me. Were not these the specious excuses of a coward and a liar, the rationalizing of bad behavior he was too lazy to correct?

I could never have listened to his confession, even if he had spoken in the most sincere way. There was no more trust, and not enough faith in our future. A happy marriage is about having faith in a future together, a shared worldview.

Eliana admitted that she had "boundary problems." But she had never been involved before with a married man who had a child, or with a man who lived in such a conventional world as ours. She wrote to me that her relationship with Henry had showed her the consequences of ignoring boundaries. She would not repeat this pattern, she told me. She was in the process of radically changing her life.

I felt my initial repulsion for this woman softening. She was not like me at all, and yet, as the days passed I felt that we were drawing closer, that we shared a real bond, one I valued. I was starting to enjoy the idea that there could be a woman like me and a woman like Eliana in the same world and that somehow we were finding a way to connect.

We began to write to each other about our families. She wrote about a niece she loved and asked about Liza in a way that showed me she understood and appreciated children. She knew plenty about me, from her conversations with Henry. She said that he had admired my mothering, my sense of honor, and the discipline of my work life, regretting his own lack of focus. When Henry first approached her about helping him organize his book, she told him that she didn't understand why he hadn't asked for my help. I replied that by that time Henry and I were barely able to have a peaceful conversation, let alone a collaborative working relationship. I was pleased, however, to hear the ways in which Henry had appreciated me.

She also offered the first hopeful words about a future life I could not imagine yet. And the idea that what had happened was a kind of gift to me, a chance to start over, a chance to be free.

Now that you have asked for guides, trust they will come. It may take some time. You may also not know the signs until they appear. But when they do, your instincts will tell you. They will create the bridges for you. In your healing, you will find what you need intimately for you, in your style. And you will attract it to you again. You have this gift. Be clear on what you want.

I told Eliana that I was leaving for Maine but that I hoped we could continue our correspondence when I returned. I decided that even if she was editing her version of events, what I had now gave me a clearer picture of Henry's last months.

I had learned a lot from my correspondence with Eliana. I saw more clearly the ways I had sheltered myself in my married life. I had learned that opening my mind to someone so different from myself could have great rewards. I had an urge to make something new for myself, to heal myself.

Healing would require full forgiveness. I wasn't ready for that yet. Cathy's long involvement with Henry, her disregard for my family and the idea of friendship disgusted me. I was still too furious to forgive Henry. But it was already refreshing to look at Henry's dark side with eyelids peeled open, to make myself see how lost we had been as a couple. This was the man who had so frequently told me that my version of reality was damaged. Now I could see that my version of reality was quite fine. My mistake had been allowing him to make me doubt what I was seeing. There had been deception and self-deception.

————————

My therapist, Helen, shared a strange story with me during our last session before I left for the August holiday. She recalled a private session she'd had with Henry before he left on his final trip out West.

"Henry said this to me, at the end of the session, 'I am coming to feel that the purpose of my life is risk.' That's quite a thing to say about oneself. I wasn't sure where he was going with that comment. He was leaving my office after that last appointment, his hand was on the doorknob—we therapists call this kind of moment 'doorknob therapy.' Then Henry asked me if I thought it was possible to have more than one intimate relationship. I had some idea then where things were headed, so I told him that we could take up that topic at your next couples session. But of course, there were no more couples sessions after that. Henry died a month later."

It occurred to me now that Eliana might have made headway persuading Henry to come clean, and that during that last session with Helen he was testing this idea out in the safest shared space we had, our therapist's office, the place where you pay to share your secrets.

———

While I had wanted to see everything in terms of absolutes, right and wrong, good and evil, it was clear that I would have to settle for something gray and muddled. I could talk to Christine or Ellen or Eliana every day for a year, and still I would never really be able to understand what had happened to Henry, to the marriage I had clung to, to me in that marriage. I would have to go forward into the gray, muddled place and bushwhack some clear path of my own. And while I had scattered moments of gratitude for my "second chance," I was mostly furious, raging, and brokenhearted.

On a superheated early morning toward the tail end of July, Anna found me pacing in my office, still in a nightgown, my hair disheveled and damp with sweat, crying while talking on the phone with my brother.

It was my turn that morning to drive the kids to day camp, but it was clear that I wasn't ready to go anywhere. Anna sighed, and her expression betrayed exasperation. She stood for a minute watching me on the phone, then left abruptly and strode off to the kitchen. I ended the call to David and sat in my office, praying silently that Anna would bail me out one more time. It wasn't fair of me, I knew that. Her life was a mess too. Her divorce was in progress, and she and her soon to be ex-husband, John, were fighting over property and child support. But just in that moment, mine felt messier, a disaster, more than I could dig out from in the next ten minutes.

I listened with relief as she got the children organized with their daypacks. She soothed Liza, who was confused by my condition. The refrigerator door opened and closed several times, and I heard the reassuring bustle of Liza's lunch being prepared and some welcome childish laughter. Skittering footsteps headed for the back porch. The screen door opened, buoyed for a second or two by the antique drop weight tied to a string, then smacked shut. The house was silent. A moment later I heard Anna's tires crunching the gravel in my driveway.

I was staring out the window, still in my nightgown, sweating and crying, when Anna reappeared in my office doorway. I had not noticed the half hour pass by. She gave me a moment to take her in, then spoke.

"Julie. I had to make lunch for your child because you couldn't do it. I had to drive your child to camp because you couldn't do it. I had to give her a hug good-bye because you couldn't do it."

She paused, but she needn't have worried. She had my full attention.

"Julie, I love you and I want to help you, but there is a limit to what I can do for you. You need to get it together. Because if you let all this take over your life, then *he* wins, and *he can't win.*"

I looked up at her. My mouth opened to take in air. I was exhausted, my head hurt, throbbing hotly at my temples, the top of my skull ready to blast open. I started crying again.

"You're right. I'm a mess," I said. "Everything is a mess. But how could he do this to me? It's so fucked up, Anna, and it just goes on and on and on. When is it going to stop?"

"I don't know, honey, I ask myself the same question every day."

She gave me a hug, one that I really needed, and smoothed my damp hair.

"But I'll do better," I said, my tears, snot, and sweat dampening Anna's clean tank top, "starting right now, this minute. I promise."

"I know you will," Anna said, with a confidence I welcomed. "You're tougher than this. I know you are. You need to have a nice cool shower, take care of yourself, and eat some food. Here, have a tissue." I tried to wipe my eyes and dripping nose with a sense of purpose.

"Things will get better, right?" I asked her, like a pleading younger sister. "Just tell me it can't get any worse."

She smiled and began to laugh, and then I laughed, just because it felt good to laugh.

Anna and I completed preparations for our three weeks in Maine. We had gone up together the year before, while Henry was away on a West Coast trip and John had chosen to stay home. At the time we never imagined the vacation in Maine would be a sort of dry run for our future lives. Foodstuffs and a few essential kitchen tools were now carefully stacked in corrugated boxes I'd snagged from the grocery store. Our clothing and linens were folded into duffel bags. I was almost ready to leave.

I drove the familiar route to Tomas's home. I was pretty sure I would return home from Maine to find another woman in his life, perhaps even someone he had kept from me to spare my feelings. But I wanted us to end as friends.

We stood in the grassy meadow, behind his studio, where there was a bit of shade.

He said he had taken a lot of criticism about being with me. People had said he was taking advantage of me, the lonely, distraught widow.

I knew that. I'd heard the same rumors. "You didn't take advantage of me. I didn't do anything I didn't want to do. You and I know that, even if those people don't."

Sometimes my emotional turmoil had frightened him, he said. I knew that too. I thanked him for the companionship that had kept me going longer than we'd both planned.

I told him I loved him. He said he loved me. So, we loved each other, in some way that was meaningful.

"I think," I said, "that one day, we'll both understand this better, what happened these last months."

He nodded.

I felt intense sorrow and loss but also some freedom. Now I could start to walk away from his twenty-eight-year-old world, and he could walk away in the other direction and find whatever it was he wanted next.

He gave me an old stone roof slate from a pile in his backyard, leftovers from his house renovation. "You know, a clean slate," he said with a smile. I took the gift with pleasure.

When I got home I wrote on it with some of Liza's colored chalk: "Things will get better, things will get easier." I propped the slate up on the counter in my kitchen as a reminder for future dark days.

part three

ON THE COVE
From Henry for Julie's Birthday, 1996

A fog-shrouded inlet, a cove
Cupped in granite, the God-Mind's
Vaporous pinkie paused in the geode
Of the child-planet's teacup. On the island,

We are delivered into ourselves. Doubled over
Your pregnancy, you peer through the viewfinder
Into Earl Grey milkiness, your camera-mind blessed
With a momentary panorama of stress-free nothingness.

And mine, coursing the shoreline with Labrador
Randomness, is arrested with doggy wonder
At the eroded, abandoned armatures of dog-whelk.
Urchins, periwinkles, and other minute hulks

Which lived to prove that time passes. I pray
What we have paused to reproduce blesses
Us. That the signs we fail to see in this inlet's
Sublime anagoge are already written into a sandy tablet

Beyond us, of some larger unseen felix mundi,
Growing now around the double-helix
Of our love, our part in the many-chambered future.

nine

August 2003

Blue sky, feathery clouds, a supreme August day. Barefoot in a bit of mown grass, I was hanging up laundry, wearing cotton underwear and an old tank top. My mother had bought this tank top for me, Calvin Klein no less, the summer I packed up to go to college. It had faded from black, through many washings, to a charcoal gray.

The laundry line was strung up between two arthritic, lichen-covered crab apple trees. One by one, I pulled out clothespins from an old half-gallon plastic milk container, the top cut away for easy access. The clothespins were as gray and weathered as the cedar shingles on the farmhouse just down the gentle slope of open meadow, edged with wild rosebushes and thistle.

Anna was a small moving form in the middle distance, recognizable in her cheerful red canvas sun hat, wandering the low-tide mudflat beach. Her son, Leo, and my Liza, in their colorful swimsuits and billed caps, trailed behind her with plastic beach buckets, filled with a collection of small blue crabs, hermit crabs, and periwinkle snails, a mucky, messy adventure. We'd have to hose the kids down later and wash all those clothes. The kids loved rinsing themselves off with the coiled green garden hose, and I looked forward to the ritual of laundry. I would have been happy to spend every noontime on this island hanging up clothes and taking them down.

You never can tell much about weather out here. The sheets and towels, T-shirts, shorts, and sundresses snapping and ruffling in the breeze might be sopping wet with rain or invisible and clammy in a pea soup fog within the hour. It's what I've always liked about this place. You must surrender control and just enjoy whatever happens.

Sometimes it takes several days to get clothes dry. I hang them up, rushing back half an hour later to take them down as rain clouds approach, and hang them back up again when the storm passes. During longer damp spells, I reluctantly drive to the coin-operated Laundromat on the other side of the island to use the dryer. But I always feel cheated. Hanging the laundry is both a meditative ritual and a game, never a chore, not here.

Henry and I started coming to this house the year after Liza was born. I enjoyed hanging up the laundry in those early parenting years, with my baby crawling about at my feet. Liza liked to pull the wet clothes out of the wicker basket, or follow grasshoppers through the grass, trying to catch them in her still clumsy hands.

Henry never really learned how to relax here. He had trouble with solitude, and after a few days was desperate for social activity. He organized dinner parties for our small collection of island friends. He needed off-island trips to shop for these events, to reconnect with "the real world" and buy a same-day copy of *The New York Times*. Two Augusts earlier, he had insisted on paying for dial-up Internet service and spent many days indoors, in front of his laptop. He'd said he was researching and writing, but now I thought it more likely that he'd been corresponding with Cathy.

Fortunately, my new understanding did nothing to ruin the island for me. I was happy to hang up laundry, go on walks in the woods or on the pink rock ledges, make paintings of the rocks and sea, think about how I missed kissing Tomas, take down laundry, take my turn making macaroni and cheese for the kids, play evening games of Monopoly, make pancakes, hang up more laundry.

Anna and I had caravanned in our separate cars, each packed with gear and groceries, wending our way up the coast, stopping off to visit friends in Portland. The final push led us to the dock where we waited our turn to drive onto the car ferry. Life slows down as soon as you arrive at the ferry terminal—there is no rushing this situation. Anna and I spent the one-hour wait happily eating a crab roll from a nearby restaurant while the kids played at water's edge until one of them spotted the ferry coming into view. Driving onto the ramp was a mental journey, signaling the end of worries about work, and the turmoil I had left behind at home. Once we were parked on the deck, the four of us were giddy with anticipation.

"I can't wait to see the big tide pool again!" Liza shouted above the noise of the ferry engine. She and Leo began planning their first creature-hunting adventure. Anna and I smiled, delighted to see the children so eager. The wind whipped her red ponytail back and forth like a flag on a mast. Despite the long driving days, she looked more relaxed than I'd seen her in months. I hoped that her divorce battle in progress wouldn't press too much on our time here.

After unpacking our groceries and making up the beds, we slipped quickly into an easy routine. Anna and I rose early to make coffee and breakfast, while the kids lazed around the house. Sometimes Anna and I tried to do yoga on the lumpy lawn in front of the house. Liza and Leo watched on amused, occasionally inverting into a Downward Dog with us before we all headed down the path to our tidal pool to do some crab catching. By lunch I'd hung out the wash for the day, and we had planned an afternoon activity.

The first days were filled with simple discoveries and amusements—caterpillars and butterflies to inspect, a colony of funnel-shaped spiderwebs in the tall grass, a brightly painted lobster buoy washed up on the shore. There were apples and raspberries to pick along the road. Herons and cormorants came to feed in our inlet, and an occasional eagle perched in the tall firs. One afternoon the kids staged a hermit crab race on our deck, unbeknownst to the hermit crabs, who skittered as they pleased. Other days Leo and Liza played with toys in the grass or we read them books while lounging in the hammock.

Nighttime was less lonely as the four of us climbed the staircase of the house, with steep treads so narrow that it resembled a ladder. There were three bedrooms on the second floor, all in a line. The kids shared the end room, and Anna took the middle bedroom. I slept in the room Henry and I had always shared. A twisted maple tree with small, ashy silver leaves gently tapped its branches against the glass panes. The owners of the house had planted another maple nearby, anticipating the death of this crooked old lady, but I was praying she had a few more years in her yet. Every year, as we packed up to leave the house, I wished her a healthy winter and a fond farewell, just in case. In the middle of winter, back in New York, when I felt a yearning for the sea and that house and that cove, it was the sound of the brown leaves rustling on the oak tree in my own yard that brought the island back to me.

One morning I drove with Liza to visit a longtime friend named Jim. Now in his late sixties, Jim had originally come to the island as a summer visitor like me but had been living there full-time for many years, making the most of his quiet life by developing his gifts as a glass artisan. Jim had one of those New England faces that you might encounter in a novel by Nathaniel Hawthorne: long, vertically lined, with an exuberant head of white hair—a retired sea captain came to mind. I always saw him in the same clothes—a pair of well-worn trousers once white, now a mottled putty; an equally worn pale blue, short-sleeved button-down shirt flecked with stains; leather boat shoes or old white sneakers—all of which looked as dignified on him as a tuxedo would on any other man. As we approached the house with its lush vegetable garden, his two elderly Jack Russell terriers trotted out to greet us.

In addition to his skills as an artist and gardener, Jim was an excellent and adventurous chef. He and Henry had met through other island friends and bonded over the stove. He led us into his home, which felt like being aboard ship, full of marine hardware, shells, dried seaweed, interesting rocks, books, and artwork. Liza was particularly fascinated with a thermometer he displayed on his kitchen counter—a tall glass cylinder in which glass balls filled with colored liquids rose or fell according to the temperature. Jim took Liza's hand and led her to his back deck so that she could feed the koi fish in his rectangular lily pool. I accompanied

Jim back to the kitchen, where he offered me a glass of wine and I filled him in on the events of July. Though Jim came from another, more discreet generation, he was, in private, one of the most irreverent people I knew, unshockable, with a sly sense of humor.

"Ah, so I see Henry was a bad boy," he said in his raspy baritone.

"Yes, indeed," I said with a sigh.

"You know, I saw him," Jim remarked, matter-of-factly.

"Oh?" I asked. "Tell me. I've had plenty of visits myself, but I didn't realize he was making the rounds."

"Well, now, let me remember," he said as he began lunch preparations. "Yes, I was in my truck one morning, coming back from the post office, and I looked to my right and there he was in the passenger seat, smiling at me. Just that one time. I was happy to see him. I miss him."

"Henry was a good friend, though maybe not the best husband. There sure were a lot of people at that memorial service who loved him. I loved him."

"I wish he'd been better to you, my dear," he said, giving my hand an affectionate squeeze. We stood quietly for a time, then we carried lunch out to the elegant table he'd set on the porch. Liza looked up hopefully at the sight of the smoked salmon and homegrown tomato salad.

Over the years I'd become part of a circle of friends on the island, other families with more or less same-age children. We were artists, writers, musicians, and teachers on summer vacation. Some days we all met at the island's sandy beach, where we could hunt for sand dollars at low tide and I could channel my inner architect and help build elaborate castles and water canal systems to temporarily house the hermit crabs that scurried in the shallow waves. Liza was game for a swim in the frigid water and once a season managed to persuade me to take a quick dip. By late afternoon, we were home again, preparing a meal, setting up a board game. Anna and I had some peaceful hours together preparing food and cleaning up afterward, before the evening call from her soon to be ex-husband, John, who called nightly to speak to Leo. If I answered, I greeted him in the most business-like way before passing on the phone. I couldn't help notice that even this brief intrusion from outside caused Anna distress.

I was trying as hard as I could to keep my home life far away. In addition to being separated from work, I was separated from e-mail. Cell phone service from our house required walking to a certain spot on the lawn, which discouraged long conversations on blustery or rainy days. I called Tomas every few days, but our conversations were brief.

"I hope you're getting out to paint a lot," he said, with a sincere interest I appreciated. He told me about his preparations for a fall exhibition. We didn't talk much about our parting at the end of July, nor did we dwell on the events of the recent weeks. I hoped we would still be friends when I got back home.

My college friend Sara arrived from England with her family. For several years, two weeks every August had been our yearly time together. They were staying in a rented house nearby.

On our first group outing, we walked to the other side of the island, the wilder side, which faces the open sea to a place the islanders call Hero Beach. The landscape is heroic, though it's not exactly a beach, if sand and swimmable surf are what you expect.

A professor who summers here once explained to me how the island was formed. A wayward piece of Scotland smashed into a small chunk of the North American continent. At Hero Beach the primordial smashup is visible, like a still frame from a Discovery Channel TV reenactment. The pink granite resembles a lava explosion of strawberry soufflé, folding over the crags of charcoal black basalt. When I stood still with the sea and sky around me, I felt a witness to something elemental. I tried to imagine the sound of the original event, which must have been even louder than the ominous roar and smack of the seawater rushing up to meet the basalt crags. After each crash, the sea sucked the wave back, producing a shimmering clatter through millions of rounded pebbles.

We lunched on peanut butter, cheese, and tuna sandwiches. Food on the island was another adventure. There was no real store that year. We'd brought everything on, ordered up a resupply after two weeks from a mainland grocery, and bought milk, eggs, and other staples from the island family gracious enough to set up shop for the summer months in a tumbledown trailer propped on cement blocks. No easy conveniences out here, but the proprietress would bake you a fresh raspberry pie.

The kids—Sara's two daughters and young son, Liza, and Leo—climbed up and down the ledges; the one we'd named The Brain was our favorite. A huge rising mound, as tall as a two-story cottage, pink, and creviced, its summit offered a view of the heaving sea, the jagged far reaches of the island, other small islands, and rocks covered with bits of windswept seagrass, where seals sunbathed at low tide.

Sara and I sat close to each other on another pink ledge watching Anna and the kids.

"He loved you, you know," Sara said, as if sensing the essential question that had tormented me these last weeks. "No matter what he did. He loved you. He did like to flirt." She paused, gazing out to sea before continuing, "He even flirted with me."

"You're kidding."

"I think he flirted with every woman he found attractive. If I were a different kind of woman, if I'd expressed interest, he would have pursued."

"Yeah, leave no stone unturned, I guess that was his policy."

"But I know he really loved *you*." Sara, not the most effusive woman, took my hand and gave it an earnest squeeze. "He wrote you those poems. Whenever I talked to him, he always spoke about you so adoringly. Don't let this ruin everything you had in sixteen years. That wouldn't be fair to either of you."

"I'm not sure what's left to cherish, really. I'm still trying to understand what kind of love that was, what he supposedly had for me." I looked off, because tears were coming and I still felt so ashamed and lonely and afraid. "Sara, you are so lucky to have found someone loyal and decent." Sara put her arm around me, and I relaxed for a moment into her shoulder.

"I'm so lucky to have my child," I said, as Liza reached the top of The Brain with the help of Sara's older girls. "I don't know how I would've gotten out of bed these last months without her. I'd go through all this mess again to have her."

The kids climbed down The Brain and seemed ready to head home. Sara asked me if I would like to have some quiet time to paint. Happy and relieved to accept her generosity, I watched the party pack up and move off toward the trail. As they disappeared into the woods, I was suddenly and wonderfully alone, a different, more exhilarating alone than when I was home working in my office.

At first my mind exploded with frantic activity. I darted around, moving close to the surf's edge, working on different paintings, backing up as the tide rose. The sun burned away some remaining cloud and haze. Heat and postlunch stupor caught up with me. I stopped working and just sat, staring out to sea. Then my eyes fluttered closed.

I had to lie down. The rocks were warm. My eyes closed again. The engine of a passing lobster boat whined and hummed over the noise of the surf. The warm rock heated my pelvis. I was thinking about Tomas kissing me all over my chest as I lay in his bed. The sadness of losing him was physically both painful and arousing. My hand slid into my underwear. The lobsterman continued hauling up traps, rebaiting, dropping them down, the engine noise quickly swallowed by the crash of the surf.

After a short doze, I began packing up my painting supplies. I wondered about something Eliana had written in one of her letters. That I had been blessed by Henry's death, set free.

Mary Oliver asks at the end of her poem, "The Summer Day," "Tell me, what is it you plan to do with your one wild and precious life?" What *would* I do with my one wild and precious freedom?

THE SUMMER DAY
Mary Oliver

Who made the world?
Who made the swan, and the black bear?
Who made the grasshopper?
This grasshopper, I mean—
the one who has flung herself out of the grass,

the one who is eating sugar out of my hand,
who is moving her jaws back and forth instead of up and down—
who is gazing around with her enormous and complicated eyes.
Now she lifts her pale forearms and thoroughly washes her face.
Now she snaps her wings open, and floats away.
I don't know exactly what a prayer is.
I do know how to pay attention, how to fall down
into the grass, how to kneel down in the grass,
how to be idle and blessed, how to stroll through the fields,
which is what I have been doing all day.
Tell me, what else should I have done?
Doesn't everything die at last, and too soon?
Tell me, what is it you plan to do
with your one wild and precious life?

ten

On the last Saturday night of November 1986, a friend invited me to an early holiday party. I was happy to go to a party
and dressed carefully. A lonely but instructive year had passed
since my affair with Roberto, the married friend. Apart from one
demoralizing one-night stand, I had been celibate and was eager
to meet someone new.

As we headed out of the subway toward the host's apartment
in a tenement building on Rivington Street, my friend Carrie told
me that she couldn't wait to see her friend Sally, whom she was
sure I'd love. She said that Sally had a great new boyfriend.

We went to the makeshift bar, set up on the kitchen counter, to
get glasses of wine. Carrie introduced me to Sally, who was slender and stylish, with dark hair cropped into a fashionably asymmetrical cut draped across one eye. She wore a startling shade of
scarlet red lipstick.

The new boyfriend was medium height, with dark, wavy hair,
a rich olive complexion, high cheekbones, and dark, almond-
shaped eyes. When he laughed, his face opened into a wide grin.
When he spoke, he focused completely on one person, his concentration both flattering and unnerving, as he tipped his head forward to create an intimate space in the crowded, smoke-swirled

room. There was a delicacy and elegance about his slim hands. He dragged off the cigarette in his left hand and with the right held a wineglass exuberantly poised between his thumb and pointer and middle fingers. Dressed in khakis and a white polo shirt, he didn't seem like the sort of man who would take even a conversational interest in me. I was neither skinny nor glamorous, but rather grungy and curvy, with a lot of dark, frizzy hair, dark clothes, and black eyeliner. I smoked, contemplating his cheerful preppiness with gloomy severity.

To my surprise, he strolled toward me and struck up a conversation.

"So, do you live around here?" he asked.

"No, I live uptown," I answered, staring off. Not having expected to speak to this man, I felt unprepared. For something to do, I flicked my cigarette ash into my now empty wineglass, enjoying the hiss of extinguished embers. I loved smoking, a godsend for socially awkward girls like me, who could never keep their hands calm otherwise.

"What street are you on?" he pressed further.

When I told him the location of my nasty railroad apartment, his smile electrified like the strings of holiday lights draped crazily across the apartment windows.

"Hey, we live in the same neighborhood. We should have dinner sometime." I looked over at Sally, engaged in happy banter with my friend Carrie. I was sure that she would be unthrilled if I had dinner with her charming, handsome, and possibly slippery boyfriend. I made a move to step away, with the mumbled pretense of settling my ash-filled glass on the kitchen counter.

Undeterred, he put down his own wineglass on the windowsill, reached into his pocket, withdrew a conveniently placed pen, wrote his name and phone number on his paper cocktail napkin in an elegant, looped script, and handed it to me with a smile as wide as the universe.

"Call me sometime, and we'll have dinner."

I was all done with boys like that. Back home I called up my high school friend Chandra and told her about the incredibly good-looking but sleazy guy who had tried to pick me up at a party with his girlfriend standing, like, ten feet away. We agreed we were all done with that sort of boy. But I did not throw away the paper cocktail napkin, which remained on my table for another week amid a stack of unpaid bills until I realized that I couldn't read the handwriting anyway and I had forgotten the guy's name.

Several Saturdays later, Chandra herself asked me to accompany her to another Christmas party. Once in the apartment, a penthouse one-bedroom, impossibly luxurious compared with my railroad apartment, I was immediately plunged into the old feeling of nausea and unease from my outsider adolescence. I turned away, rummaging for a cigarette, wondering how long Chandra would want to stay. She was talking to friends on the outdoor terrace, her expressive cigarette hand tracing a twirling path of burning orange.

I saw that I was not alone in the hallway. Across from me was a good-looking man, with dark hair and olive complexion. He was wearing khaki pants, a white T-shirt, and a gray cardigan from an earlier era. A handsome, preppy guy, like the Amherst boys I had avoided during my Smith College years, but his dark skin and the vintage sweater added something. I was trying to figure out what that something might be, when he looked at me, smiled gorgeously, and spoke my name in a questioning musical phrase.

"I'm Henry, remember me?" He offered his elegant hand with well-practiced but still appealing formality.

The napkin guy. I hadn't recognized him without the girlfriend with the asymmetrical haircut and scarlet red lipstick.

"Oh, now I remember you," I replied. The coincidence of meeting this man again suddenly seemed to have significance. "Are you here with—I'm sorry, I forget her name. Your girlfriend."

"Can I get you a glass of wine?" he asked, by way of reply. "Don't go away, I'll be right back," he said, smiling. He strode off to the bar while I waited. I ventured out of the dark hallway into the living room and looked through the crowd. Sally was nowhere in sight. A quiet and secret thrill bloomed in the space between my ribs. *Maybe they broke up. Maybe he isn't sleazy after all. Maybe.* I felt giddy and special.

Henry returned with two red-wine-filled glasses. "We've been having a difficult time," he began soberly, giving a brief history of his three months with Sally and concluding, with a look of exasperation, "and she takes forever to get ready to go out, putting on her makeup and picking out her clothes—it drives me crazy."

I nodded, not knowing what to say, relieved that I wasn't much of a style maven myself, though in fact being one was something I aspired to, just couldn't afford.

"We had a fight tonight because she was taking so long," Henry continued, "so I came alone." He smiled at me. "I'm glad I did."

We unraveled the connection to this party—he had gone to college with the hostess, who was a high school classmate of mine.

Now I felt like the luckiest girl in the world. Sally was not here; we were here, the meeting point of two tangent circles of acquaintances. We were being given another chance to know each other.

He spoke about his college years with humor and some bitterness, dwelling on the story of a lost love. He described a woman, brilliant and intellectual, whom he had adored and pursued, despite her wealthy parents' disapproval. They didn't want a writer for a son-in-law, and that was his great ambition.

"What snobs those people must have been!" I sympathized, as he described the girlfriend's Greenwich, Connecticut, parents. I thought my own parents might like a smart writer for a son-in-law, if I ever got married, which of course I wasn't going to, because marriage was a failed institution, bad for women.

We spoke with reverence about books we loved. It was the time of Gabriel García Márquez. I had just finished reading *Love in the Time of Cholera*. I was now plowing through *The Brothers Karamazov*.

He spoke with enthusiasm about the poet Joseph Brodsky. I felt embarrassed, being underread in modern poetry. I could barely summon up a line or two memorized during a college Yeats course: "I bring you with reverent hands/The books of my numberless dreams . . ."

He told me about a book he had given his college love, a first-edition copy of Shakespeare's *Macbeth* with illustrations by Salvador Dalí. "I should never have given her that book. I'm sure she didn't really appreciate it."

"Wow. Salvador Dalí?" I had grown up in an apartment where art books especially and all books generally were valued like fine jewels. "I would've loved to see that book. Too bad you gave it away."

"Maybe I should write to her and ask her for it back, but that would be so tacky." He sighed, then added, as if encouraged by my interest, "I gave her something else even more valuable."

"What was that?" I asked.

"My beloved old aunt gave me a family heirloom ring that was meant to be an engagement ring, to give to the woman I married. It's gold with a pearl in the center. There's a great story about the ring. Do you want to hear it?"

I did.

"Well." Henry stepped closer to me and bent his head forward in a way that shut out all the noise of the other people now crushed around us—the hallway had become quite rollicking in the half hour since we had found each other. "The story is that my grandfather found the pearl in an oyster he was shucking—he worked as a chef in a restaurant. He wasn't a very rich man, and he wanted to give his wife a present, so he had a jeweler set the pearl in a ring to give to his wife. It's a very unusual ring. It's like a gold claw holding this large pearl." He formed the fingers of his left hand energetically into an open fist. "Maybe I should ask her for that ring back. I wonder if she still has it. My aunt really meant for that ring to be given to my wife. In the end she and I broke up, and she went off with this other guy at the end of senior year. I was completely devastated. Now she's married to some other guy and lives in Cincinnati and has a couple of kids already."

"Really?" I responded, frowning. "She must have started so young." We were twenty-something New Yorkers. None of us at the party were married, let alone parents. "Anyway. I don't believe in marriage. I think it's a failed institution that's bad for women."

He laughed. "Yeah, all that expensive education and now she's changing diapers."

We both dragged on our cigarettes.

"I should really ask her for that ring back," he repeated, looking at me intensely, and then, as if my opinion mattered most in that moment, he asked, "What do you think?"

I didn't know what to say. He seemed still heartbroken about losing the woman, the book, and the ring. I thought how I would love to receive such meaningful gifts from a man who could love someone as he had loved this woman.

"Maybe you could write to her and ask her how she feels about that," I said, hoping to sound helpful and diplomatic. "I bet after all this time she'd return the ring to you, especially if it's a family heirloom." I was now thoroughly intrigued by the man, the book, the ring, the college girlfriend, even the beloved old aunt.

Henry and I left the party together and walked uptown. At a small local bar on Amsterdam Avenue, I spontaneously ordered a Scotch, liquor I normally avoid, which I hoped would give me an aura of toughness and adventure. I drank it down and another, while talking and talking about more books I loved, my job, my family, anything to fill up the silent spaces, not that there really were any in a noisy bar at holiday time.

Henry leaned over and kissed me.

"Just to get you to stop talking," he often joked later.

Henry told me a bit about his unusual childhood, what he ruefully called his "riches to rags" story. He had spent his early childhood in a luxurious expatriate community in Seoul, Korea, complete with cooks, servants, a driver, and Kunja, his *amah* (nanny)—by his own account, a pampered life. His father worked at that time for Texaco California as an executive, and his mother was the considerably younger, beautiful Korean woman he had married. His father had taken an early retirement and resettled his wife, along with Henry, two older half brothers, and younger brother and sister, in the small town where he had grown up. He had become quite a hermit since retirement.

"And of course," Henry remarked with regret, "that was the end of the cooks, servants, and driver, not to mention my beloved *amah*." Then, with alcohol-induced honesty, "I don't think my mother ever recovered from the shock of that move."

Two more Scotches later, as the sky turned from wintry black to first light, we stumbled the remaining blocks to my apartment. Though I normally slept nude, I made a point of putting on pajamas, so that nothing would happen. All that whiskey allowed just enough energy for some more kissing before we fell asleep. When we woke at midday, I was bewildered but thrilled to see his eyes open in front of mine. Despite a leaden hangover, I made us breakfast and sent him home.

After he left, I sat down at my rickety round table and cried. I was very attracted to this man, but I was still recovering from the affair with married Roberto. I had determined never again to settle for being the "other woman." After a Sunday meal at my parents' apartment, I cried some more over their kitchen sink as I rinsed dinner dishes. I told my mother about the man I had met, how it felt like an act of fate to have met him a second time, how much more I liked him the second time, but how I couldn't go through a mess again.

My mother remembered the married man fiasco. I had camped out for four miserable days with my parents after I ended the affair with Roberto, days I had spent mostly crying, curled up in the fetal position on my childhood bed, wrapped in the threadbare remains of my satin-trimmed, crocheted baby blanket.

My mother agreed. The only solution was not to see Henry again, unless he broke up with the girlfriend.

Henry called me at my office on Monday morning.

"I'd like to see you again, very soon," he said confidently.

"I really like you," I answered, "and I had a lot of fun Saturday, but I don't think I can see you again." I told him firmly that he would have to end things with Sally if he wanted to see me again.

"Please give me time," he urged. "I'll take care of things. Can I at least take you to dinner?"

There might be women who could refuse such an entreaty, but fine restaurant meals were too few and far between on my salary, so I accepted the invitation. Henry took me to Raoul's, a bistro in SoHo. He ordered frogs' legs, which seemed a bit show-offy, but he ate every bite with great relish. In later years, when he knew I'd laugh, he was famous for eating things like frogs' legs or squid, allowing a wee leggie or tentacle to dart in and out of his mouth like a viper's tongue. After our first meal together, he held my coat while I struggled to get my arms in the sleeves, desperately trying to look graceful. He held the door open as we walked out into the street. I took a cab home, hoping that he would take care of things with Sally very soon.

We spoke on the phone almost every day after that. One evening I was bold enough to ask him if he wanted to have dinner with me. He said he couldn't make it; he had "something important" to do. The next day he told me that he had ended things with Sally. I was so startled and thrilled that I didn't ask for the details; it was enough that he had chosen me, though when I gave some thought to Sally, I imagined it had been a wretched evening for her. I weighed my own delight against her misery and selfishly relished what seemed like long overdue good luck.

And then, of course, we had sex and I was a goner.

At the end of our first month as a new couple, he had knee surgery for an old injury. In those days before arthroscopic surgery, ligament repair was a big open-knee operation. I visited him daily during his five-day hospital stay, bringing him food treats from the outside world. After his discharge, he navigated the city on crutches while I carried his computer, the original Macintosh 128 (Henry always was an "early adopter"), back and forth from my apartment on the Upper West Side to his new apartment on East Second Street and Avenue B. I was delighted to take care of him, delighted to be with a man who wanted to be with me, who was so attentive, who made me laugh a lot, and who told me often how much he loved me. We even found ways to have sex in a single bed with his leg brace on.

As our relationship progressed, I overlooked the occasional red flags. There was the night he went to a poetry reading promising to be at my apartment by nine.

"Wait for me," he said, "we'll have dinner together." He showed up cheerfully drunk at 1:00 A.M., after I had waited frantically by the phone all evening.

There were the heated debates about politics, where I discovered the ways in which our thinking had been influenced by our very different family environments. But the arguments were also exhilarating, a reminder that we were young, alive, thinking and therefore opinionated.

I especially tried to ignore the outsider feeling I had the first and every time we traveled to his small upstate hometown to visit his family. There I was confronted with the emotional distance between Henry's withdrawn, elderly New Englander father and his younger Korean wife, though I immediately adored crinkled Aunt Rose, who lived next door.

At seventy-two, Aunt Rose was still vital. Till her death at eighty-six, she read *The New York Times* daily and could debate any current topic. She was more "motherly" than Henry's own mother, whose poor English after thirty years in the States seemed an almost willful defiance of an American life she had refused to embrace. Aunt Rose baked apple pies and banana muffins in her perfectly preserved 1940s kitchen, which featured an old, still operational, green Westinghouse refrigerator. She was thrifty in the manner of Depression-era survivors, yet with us, her "children" (she'd been unable to have any of her own), she was warm and generous.

I sensed that Henry's mother had profound, even bitter regrets about the comfortable life of servants and cooks, driver and *amah* she had left behind in Seoul for the small town where Henry, her half-Korean son, was called Chink in the public school. As a city girl myself, I couldn't blame her for that—the town seemed forlorn, with its abandoned rail line and tattered Main Street, though the surrounding countryside presented a gorgeous array of rolling hills and farms, where I often walked alone with the family dog as escort.

I was disturbed by Henry's adoration of his father, an almost childlike, worshipful love. No parent is so perfect, especially not one who forced a move that satisfied only his own needs, though of course this was common for his generation. I concluded it was perhaps my family that was the anomaly, where my working mother wielded equal decision-making power with my father.

The dinner table seemed to represent the field of battle. When evening came, Henry's mother set out two spreads—American meat and potatoes as well as a selection of Korean dishes, which created a pressure of superabundance, the two complete meals in uneasy competition for table space like neighboring but not altogether friendly nations.

An unhappy smell—mildew, cooking grease, sour milk, overflowery room fresheners, and something else at first unnamable—permeated the house. Liza noted and tried to identify the smell as she grew older; for me it was the odor of disappointment.

At the point in our marriage when we began thinking about moving away from the city, Henry, perhaps caught up in a momentary fit of nostalgia, laid out a plan to move back to his hometown, where he fantasized that we might build a house on a portion of the hundred acres owned by his family.

"Henry," I said, "let me just be very clear before you do any more planning. I won't ever want to move to that town or live so close to your mother. No way. That's just not happening."

The town we ultimately chose had seemed an acceptable compromise, positioned at roughly the halfway point between the city and his family. I maintained what I hoped was a courteous but detached relationship with his parents and spent my time there with Aunt Rose. When Rose died, in 2000, I was heartbroken to have lost her, my only meaningful connection to Henry's family. With her death, I also felt that Henry had lost a powerful emotional anchor in his life, a moral rudder, someone who understood him, loved him, and for whom he willingly made sacrifices.

One evening about six months into our relationship, I met Henry and Eric, one of his close college friends, at a restaurant near their shared East Village apartment. Henry had his back to me when I entered the restaurant. Eric smiled as I approached the table. Feeling giddy, I put my hands over Henry's eyes. It wouldn't be much of a surprise. My gesture was meant as a sort of rhetorical joke.

Eric looked at me with a steady, affectionate gaze and said to Henry in a quiet voice: "It's not Michelle, so don't make a fool of yourself." The huge unanswered question cast a shadow over the rest of the evening.

Michelle turned out to be his physical therapist, a woman Henry had described in some detail, without naming her, who put weighted sandbags on his postoperative knee in weekly sessions that he had described as excruciatingly painful. Yes, they were having an affair, but it wasn't a serious thing, he assured me.

"I promise you that this will never happen again," Henry said.

And soon after, we seemed on a happier path. I gave him keys to my apartment, where we had lots of joyful sex. I was in love. He told me he loved me. I became part of his circle of friends. Matthew, one of his closest college friends, lived nearby with his wife, and we were a frequent foursome.

Henry and I made plans. We traveled to France and Italy together and struggled at our low-paying jobs, dreaming of a creative future. Henry would write a great novel. I had many unfocused urges and envied his single-minded ambition. I had never been in a long relationship, but now this seemed to be the right person— smart, challenging, worth adoring.

"You are so lucky," my friends said. "Henry is so handsome, and he loves you so much." Sometime, I thought, I might even rethink my early edict on the topic of marriage. After all, I imagined, I didn't have to love everything about him, and I didn't have to love all his family.

Always, from the beginning, he cooked for me; frequently elaborate events with many courses. But for me the humble meals were even more memorable.

Two A.M. on a Saturday in early 1987 found us returning to Henry's apartment after a long night in the emergency room at Beth Israel hospital. We had been mugged on Lafayette Street immediately following a showing of David Lynch's *Blue Velvet.* One of the young perps who surrounded us on a quiet street corner hit me on the head with a piece of wood. The one-inch laceration had released a dramatic quantity of blood, which the ER doctor had cleaned up; now the wound was neatly sutured with a metal staple inserted into my scalp.

We were shaken and famished. Henry began rummaging in his tiny kitchen. Half an hour later he offered me a soup: chicken broth from a can, some Korean seasonings, frozen peas and spaghetti noodles, with a swirl of sesame oil. We devoured it all, supercharged with the lingering tension of having survived real danger. That night I began to fully appreciate Henry's joy and creativity in the kitchen. I even wondered if maybe it wasn't a novel he needed to write but a cookbook. We made love ecstatically after that meal. I would always remember that night—we were more connected and intimate after the ordeal we had experienced together.

"*My Supreme Loveliness* (this, I swear, was one of his nicknames for me), I love you as I love life," he pronounced dramatically as he handed me a small antique green jewelry box.

It was late December again, and we were drinking champagne at a table at Café des Artistes, one of New York City's most over-the-top romantic restaurants. We had been a couple for two years. Henry had moved into my nasty railroad apartment (it was way cheaper than his tiny sweatbox-in-summer, icebox-in-winter East Village apartment), and this anniversary warranted a celebration. Several times during the autumn, Henry had asked me how I felt about marriage. I was careful to soften my prior strident position. Marriage could work, I said. We could have a different kind of marriage, where we wouldn't slip into typical patterns. There would be no *Diary of a Mad Housewife* for me.

So when he offered me the green box, I thought I knew what was going to happen next. There would be a tasteful engagement ring, recently purchased, I hoped not too expensive.

But when I flipped open the lid, I found inside the gold claw ring he had described the night of our second meeting, which was the day we thought of as our anniversary. It indeed resembled a golden fist holding a small white stone. The stone itself didn't look like a pearl to me.

"This is the ring, isn't it?" I asked. "When did you get it back?"

"Oh, ages ago, along with the *Macbeth*. I wrote to my old girlfriend right after we met."

When I took the ring to be resized, the jeweler told me that the center stone was actually a piece of coral, not a pearl. But the original story was so wonderful and romantic I decided it should remain intact.

Our April 1989 wedding was a no-frills affair. We borrowed my brother's loft work space, and I arranged for economical catering. Henry wore a vintage midnight blue tuxedo. I wore a simple long white cotton dress, something Jane Austen might have chosen, with red satin shoes, because the white bride thing was starting to get to me. A rabbi sang the traditional Jewish prayers as we stood beneath a chuppah. Henry stomped with enthusiasm on the napkin-wrapped crystal wineglass he'd purchased for the occasion. Irena's unforgettable offering—a homemade wedding cake—was a chocolate extravagance sheathed in edible gold leaf. My parents looked pleased and proud, and happy toasts were made to our future together. We danced to the music on a series of tapes I'd made.

A few days later, we subjected ourselves to shots for yellow

fever and hepatitis. Our young doctor handed us prescriptions for
malaria prophylactic and just-in-case antibiotics. The shots hurt
like hell. I winced when the needle went in my butt.

"Haven't you kids ever heard of the Bahamas?" the doctor
asked with a sigh.

We laughed. The Bahamas—indeed.

We were off on our "honeymoon" (we enjoyed the ironic us-
age of that word to describe this trip) to visit Sara, my college
friend, who was serving in the Peace Corps in Malawi, a sliver of
impoverished nation in southeastern Africa.

After an English lunch of smoked trout on British Airways in
coach class, we stepped out of the air-conditioned plane onto the
metal stairs at Lilongwe Airport. The sun glared on the hot tar-
mac. I rummaged for the sunglasses Sara had insisted I pack. I
glanced around and saw the edge of the airport. The very edge,
where the watered lawn ceased and the wild bush began. There
would be no smoked trout till we got back on a plane in a month
to return to London. We were precisely in the middle of nowhere.

Sara's boyfriend, soon to be husband, was there to greet us.
Just past the airport exit, the road quickly changed to rust red dirt
where we passed adults and children in rags, walking barefoot,
malnourished children with bloated bellies, strange skin conditions, and discolored hair. I had grown up in New York City, I
had seen poverty, but this was something entirely new.

When we reached Sara's village, we found her living in an
ample-size house with concrete floors, cool to the touch of our
bare feet. I unloaded the supplies she had requested: shampoo,
conditioner, soap, and chocolate. "You'll be eating rice and beans
three meals a day from now on," she said. "But at least we can
have a treat now and then. I haven't had visitors for a while."

During our first walk alone together, Sara told me that she was pregnant. At thirty years old, I still had only one close friend, Irena, who had a child, but having been married a week earlier, I was optimistic and thrilled for her. A baby in Africa—what an adventure.

I learned to tuck in the mosquito netting good and tight at bedtime. While I tried to cope with large, hairy spiders, I never did overcome my aversion to snakes. The rule of thumb in Africa seemed to be "better dead than alive." People loved terrifying us with "can you top this" tales featuring puff adders and mambas. The stories always ended with a just-in-time hatchet.

We reassessed the concept of garbage in a place where almost nothing was thrown away. Ingenious toys were made out of bits of scrap metal and wood. Clothing was worn till it literally fell off the body. Any piece of plastic could be put to some good reuse.

In addition to poverty, we glimpsed the political upheaval in that part of Africa. We were drinking beers one night in a bar on Likoma Island with the town's only doctor when the local priest opened the door and announced somberly that there had been "an incident." Henry and I (he was more eager) followed the doctor back to his crude clinic. No painkillers were available for the stoic patient, who had been shot in the back of his right calf by Renamo guerrillas in a village across the border in Mozambique. The doctor was quite drunk.

Two weeks later, having adjusted more or less to a steady diet of rice and beans, spiced with generous dollops of hot piri-piri sauce (marked, helpfully, "Friend, Take Care"), Henry and I found ourselves in the back of a dusty Malawian government Land

Rover. We were ascending the Nyika Plateau, a mountainous area that is part of the Great Rift Valley. Sara had sent us off for this week with careful instructions on hitchhiking etiquette, but since so few cars passed by, a scant handful a day, we just took the first ride that would take us.

Three Malawian men who worked at the national park on the plateau squatted quietly with us, barefoot, wearing rain slickers. Henry and I looked at each other in silent speculation. Unlike most Malawians, we had clothes and shoes aplenty, but no rain slickers, because the rainy season had already passed.

About twelve kilometers from the government-run inn at the top of the Nyika Plateau, the Land Rover stopped in the middle of the road. The khaki-uniformed driver told us that we had to get out, right here, in the middle of nowhere. It was illegal for government vehicles to give lifts in the first place, he had done us this favor, now, please get out.

We climbed out with our backpacks, which were loaded up heavily with food for our stay, as there were no stores of any kind on the plateau. The rain-slickered Malawians eyed us—with, was it generosity or pity?—and came forward to help us with our load. I felt guilty but grateful.

We walked silently on the dirt road for several miles. Zebra and eland darted over the bracken-covered hills, as well as black birds with long, ribbonlike tails whose official name I determined to look up later. These were truly rolling hills, which appeared to be made of green cloth, gathered and draped. The sky was clear, a startling blue dome that seemed to press down upon us, until from somewhere, low-hanging clouds approached at great speed, intermittently blocking the sun, marking dark patches on the green hills. Sun darts blasted through the clouds in long laser beams.

Then came the rain. Henry and I walked on, soaked to the skin in minutes. The Malawians weren't complaining about their bare feet, so complaining about being wet seemed childish. Miles later we arrived at the inn. The proprietors laughed gently at the sight of the drenched and shivering white travelers and offered us tea and bananas.

Once we were installed in our enormous six-dollar-a-night chalet, Edward, the caretaker, made us more tea and homemade biscuits. We huddled in front of the fire Edward made for us, and later we huddled together in the narrow bed. Henry held me close. So far our marriage had been a great adventure. We were alone together in Africa.

It was this image of Henry, generous and loving, embracing the unexpected, that I had kept with me during our years together. We'd had plenty of fun together: we loved our friends, our books, and our own private jokes. He was the best loyal soldier during my long childbirth labor, comforting me during my contractions and catching sleep on an unfolded Saturday edition of *The New York Times* when our labor doula relieved him. In those precious times of presence and real connection, I forgot about the fights that increased in frequency and bitterness, the times when we seemed so miserably incompatible that I wondered how we would be able to raise our child amid such daily discord.

Now, I didn't feel I had many of the good memories left. I had fallen in love with a man who had appeared to be confident and charming. Over time, I had seen some of his weaknesses and had refused to look at others. The overall picture that Henry presented to the world was undoubtedly a mirage, designed to shelter a sadder self, one that he was afraid to reveal to others, even to me.

I recalled how coldly Henry had dismissed Cathy the previous summer with the comment that she was "the most conventional person I know." After that, he had moved on to Christine and then Eliana, who represented in his mind a truly liberated person.

I thought about that idea of perfection. Every woman he fantasized about was a new opportunity to imagine perfection, just as every meal he prepared was another opportunity to reach a kind of nirvana. But just as shallots burn in overheated butter, so these relationships disappointed. He must have known that I no longer saw him as any kind of perfect, though I had once felt we were well suited. Perhaps his comment about wanting me to be more like a girlfriend was a wish to return to the time when we both were more innocent, and ignorant of each other's flaws.

I remembered Henry's comment to Helen—that the purpose of his life was risk. Henry had wanted adventure, all the time, every day, like those days in Africa. Quotidian tasks bored him. He wanted to feel like he was facing down danger, so that he could emerge a hero. It occurred to me now what an epic amount of risk he had required—more and more throughout our years together—to re-create that heroic feeling. I wondered grimly if this was a guy thing, the famously satirized "midlife crisis."

Henry needed to create Big Stories: The scar over his eye. The car accident when he broke his leg. The time he went skydiving two weeks before the end of his final term at college to make up a missing gym credit. His rock climbing—a recent interest. He, Cathy, and Steve had taken classes with a guide in the lower Catskills. After one attempt at a climbing gym in New Paltz, I had backed away—my fear of heights created vertigo at about twenty feet, and I didn't think hanging off the side of a sheer cliff would do much for me. I was never sure if Henry loved the rock climbing itself or the specialized gear he bought—a velvet chalk bag (I had given that to Cathy after he died), the tight-fitting, pointed shoes designed to nestle into cliff cracks, the sweat-wicking outfits, the all-important pulleys, ropes, carabiners, and safety belts. These props were perhaps all part of the real, vivid, and (for him at least) thrilling risk of injury and even death.

The charismatic, charming man I had met when I was a shy and naïve twenty-seven-year-old was, perhaps, a type that I could now recognize and avoid in the future. The man who can take charge of a room with a kind of invincible glamour, win at poker, make a lot of money, be (or at least seem to be) a "success." As Cary Grant (born Archibald Leach) famously said, commenting on his debonair persona in films like *The Philadelphia Story,* "Everyone wants to be Cary Grant; even I want to be Cary Grant."

—————

At the tail end of summer, Anna and I left our Maine house. I felt the same dread about my return home as I'd felt when leaving Italy earlier in the summer. There wasn't much to look forward to: the routine of school, more conclusive evidence of the end of my time with Tomas and, with it, the growing anxiety about my solitude.

Now our bags were unpacked, and Liza began second grade at her new private school. She loved her two teachers. One was a gentle man who made up songs for the kids as part of their study of the Hudson River; the other, a warm and affectionate woman

with a comforting lap who magically erased Liza's math anxiety
from the previous year.

With Liza settled, I found myself in my office again, studying
the objects on the altar that had once been a comfort to me—the
Buddha snow globe, the gold ring, the shells and pebbles. Unwilling to keep Henry's ashes in my office, I had moved the wooden
urn to a high shelf in Liza's bedroom. One morning, as I began
my workday, I picked up the Buddha snow globe, turned it a few
times, enjoying the goofiness of the fake snowflakes serenely
drifting down over the gold plastic seated figure. I would cherish
peace like that. Henry had loved this globe, delighted by the idea
of the Buddhist icon encased in Americana kitsch. What had he
seen when he looked at the globe? What had Henry been searching for?

Justin, Emily's husband, telephoned me. He and Emily were
invited to a black-tie dinner and he needed a tuxedo. Would I
mind lending him Henry's?

Justin came over to the house. I took Henry's vintage midnight blue suit from the closet and lifted up the plastic covering.
We admired the suit's clean lines and narrow lapels. Justin tried it
on, and it fit wonderfully, just as it had Henry at our wedding. I
felt a pang of sorrow remembering the day and its promise.

When Justin patted the chest pocket, something crinkled inside.
He withdrew a small rectangle of lined yellow paper on which
Henry had listed in neat print: pick up flowers, wineglass wrapped
in napkin, and more items in a hopeful list of prewedding tasks.
On that day, as well as the days on the Nyika Plateau in Malawi,

and the day our Liza was born, Henry had been fully committed and present.

We had shared some real moments. With effort and patience, I might find something I could keep at the end of all this, though I had an overwhelming urge to throw out all my life with Henry and start over with just Liza, the two of us heading off down a long road to somewhere in an old jalopy, one suitcase rattling in the backseat.

eleven

October 2003

The last Saturday afternoon in October arrived bright and chilly, with late autumnal sun breaking through fast-moving clouds. At least it wasn't as cold and blustery as it had been some years. Liza and I made our final preparations before the 5:00 P.M. start of the local Halloween Day parade. In other years, this had been an event to look forward to, but now I was dreading this brief hour in public view.

The first two months back from Maine were already a blur. At least I did not have to see Cathy at the school playground every day. In fact, our schedules were now so divergent that if I took Liza to her van at 7:20 and drove straight to the grocery store (nearly empty at this hour), I could do my food shopping and get home without seeing anyone at all, which was just how I wanted it.

I even avoided Tomas. I had visited him once at his house. We sat at the picnic table in the meadow. He complimented me on my tan and summer freckles as well as the landscape paintings I had made on the island. He seemed uncomfortable just talking and eating a sandwich until I pried from him what I already suspected— that there was indeed a new woman in his life, and that this woman was uneasy with the idea of me. I had no interest in getting in the middle of his new relationship, and I left after we agreed to keep in touch but maybe not too much. I determined to make myself as scarce as possible without actually disappearing.

I could not, however, avoid the Halloween parade, which was a town tradition. Townspeople and their eager children gathered at the intersection of Main Street and the northbound state road and strolled in a friendly mass down the quaint street, while those not up for costumes and marching cheered from the sidelines.

I doubted that Cathy and Steve would miss this opportunity to present themselves as a family. True to his word, Steve had stuck by her, and they had been seen walking hand in hand in town.

In other years I had not bothered with a costume, but this year I felt a strong urge for disguise. While browsing in a local antiques store with Liza a few weeks earlier, I'd found a long red satin evening gown, which I seized upon with evil glee. A red devil. I hoped that at least my friends would enjoy the irony. The rest of my costume was easily purchased on my next city trip at a party store in Greenwich Village. I smirked as I boarded the train home with plastic devil horns and pitchfork.

So now, with me in red dress and horns but without the red face paint I planned to put on for the actual trick-or-treating night, Liza and I walked to Main Street to assemble for the parade. Liza, dressed in a white angel costume (which I had strongly encouraged), could not have known the panic I experienced as I reached the corner of Main Street and saw Cathy standing on the opposite corner, looking around anxiously for Steve and Amy. It did not help to know that she was possibly more uncomfortable than I was.

Gripping Liza's hand firmly, and praying that she would not see Amy, I guided her toward a group of other friends, to whom I did not need to explain anything, as the crowd shuffled down the street. Just a bit onward, where the roadway curved over the railroad tracks, I found Anna and Leo. The return home had been hard for Anna as well—she and John were fighting over their house, though I hoped the end was in sight for her divorce. Anna and I plodded on in our sullen way, plastering on smiles for our children when they looked our way. She grimaced when I told her that I had already seen Cathy at the top of the street.

"Bitch," she muttered, out of earshot of our children.

At the bottom of the street, everyone milled around the waterfront, chatting. In previous years this had been a time to hang out with friends or reconnect with infrequently seen neighbors, but now I couldn't bear the ordeal of one more acquaintance tipping her or his head sympathetically while asking, "Julie, how are you doing?"

Anna and I surveyed the crowd and, without exchanging words, reached the same conclusion, that it would be best to avoid conversation with those who were not real intimates. We guided our children toward an empty bench away from the crush. They soon found entertainment attempting to climb a grouping of three ornamental cherry trees, now mostly bare. A light wind loosened a few of the remaining leaves and swirled them across the brick path. Anna and I sat close, feeling relaxed for the first time that afternoon.

Until Cathy slipped out of the crowd, her daughter trailing after her. Cathy caught sight of us on the bench. Anna and I looked at each other curiously, assuming that Cathy would immediately take Amy away, but instead she lingered on the edge of the crowd, as if contemplating her next move.

"Take your kid and fucking leave," I mouthed through gritted teeth. "Anna, what's she doing?"

"Bitch. She better not come over here."

But Cathy did not leave, despite my efforts to look fearsome when our eyes met. I was regretting what now seemed like a ridiculous costume. I would not feel very assertive confronting her dressed in a red satin dress and plastic devil horns. I felt silly and petty, and remembered the ugly thing Steve had said to me during one of our brief conversations in July, "You are a vengeful woman."

Amy looked over at Liza; then Liza looked up and saw Amy. They smiled at each other with sweet delight. Liza looked at me, for permission. Amy began walking toward Liza, then looked at me for permission and saw my glowering expression. She began to back away from Liza, with downturned lips and widened eyes.

I had frightened this child, one who had spent countless afternoons playing at my house, a girl I had fed, lifeguarded, hugged, disciplined, whose pale tush I had wiped with tenderness if not love. I really felt like shit.

But I'd had enough. I leapt off my seat and walked toward Cathy, right up close to her, so that I would not have to shout. "Get your kid away from my kid. Do it right now."

"You need to start behaving more like a mother," she replied calmly, like a kind but firm teacher. I could hear in her response someone else's speechwriting, perhaps that of her husband, perhaps that of a well-meaning friend from her church, who had been offered a sanitized version of the doings of the last few years. I had thought nothing about this woman could still shock me, but I was wrong.

"Don't you ever tell me how to behave," I said with barely controlled fury, "you who have the moral center of a worm." She flinched. I was happy to see that. I was feeling mean and ornery. "Do not speak to me," I continued. "Do not send your daughter over to speak to my child. I will not allow you to manipulate this situation using our children. I have separated them with great difficulty, and I want it to stay that way." My right hand twitched as it had during that first confrontation in the parking lot near her house, longing independently to smack her, restrained only by a more desperate urge not to make a scene. "If I ever see you again in any public place, I will not acknowledge you. As far as I am concerned you do not exist."

I returned, shaking, to my seat on the bench. I called over to a now distraught Liza. Anna hugged me. "Like I said, it's time to bring back the Scarlet Letter." I was grateful for her solidarity but overwhelmed, tears blurring my vision.

Liza was in tears as well. I comforted her on my lap for the next half hour, while she sobbed on. Why couldn't she just say hello to Amy? She just wanted to say hello. Why wouldn't I let her say hello?

There was no doubt now. This town was too small for the both of us—Henry's wife and mistress. One of us was going to have to move. I had a feeling that Cathy and Steve were digging their heels in, and that this episode was just the beginning of a full-scale attempt at social rehabilitation. Too bad this wasn't Jane Austen's day, when adulteresses like Maria Bertram in *Mansfield*

Park were sent away to live in forced isolation with crotchety old-maid aunts for the rest of their days.

Liza cried for days after the Halloween parade. I was relieved that we did not see Cathy or Amy on the actual trick-or-treating night. Recalling Amy's early bedtime, we began late, kept to our friends' houses, and headed home as soon as Liza had achieved a reasonable quota of candy.

"Oh, Julie, how are you? And how does Liza like her new school?" one of Cathy's churchgoing friends inquired kindly as we passed her family on our way home.

"We're fine, thanks." I squeezed Liza's hand and kept walking at the same pace, to discourage even a minute more of polite social chatter.

I continued to time my movements in town to avoid Cathy and people in general. Some weekends I escaped with Liza to my brother's house in Brooklyn, where I felt gloriously anonymous. I walked around my old neighborhood curiously, wondering with fragile but growing enthusiasm if it might be possible to resettle here.

"The first year is almost up," David said while monitoring barbecued chicken on his backyard grill. "You shouldn't be the one who has to run away. Just try to hang in there till January and we'll see what we'll see."

I had wondered if I could stay in the house if I made some big changes. While away in Maine, I had conceived a scheme to renovate the third floor, a large, unfinished attic space, to create a painting studio. My brother liked the idea. Even if I sold the house later, he said, it would be a profitable investment.

By late September, I had joined many of my neighbors in welcoming a contractor into my attic. By late November, renovation
was completed. On the last workday I walked through the new
studio, inspecting the insulated, pine-paneled walls, plentiful
electrical outlets, new windows and skylights, and the wide, old
floorboards, now patched and painted an olive green not unlike
the color of Anna's kitchen, where I had enjoyed the glass of wine
and the glowing sunset.

From my basement, the contractor's assistant moved a large
drafting table upstairs. Sitting on the high stool in front of the
table, I admired the late afternoon light in the studio and the view
of the mountains across the river. I paced the room and tried out
the new dimmer switches and the variable-speed ceiling fans. Then,
abruptly, I flipped off the lights and the fan, and walked downstairs. I was done with this project and maybe with this house.

Emily came over one morning to see the results. But even as
she walked through, admiring the now open, loftlike space, I had
a piercingly strong and sad sense that no paintings of mine would
ever get made here.

"You could buy yourself some canvas in those long rolls and
just tack it up on the walls. You could get some big brushes and
go really wild!" Emily urged with an enthusiasm I had so often
envied.

"Yes, I'll do that." I knew as I was speaking that even this big
effort would never be enough. I couldn't continue living here. But
I still wanted to please Emily, to acknowledge her suggestion and
pretend for a moment that everything might return to the time
before Henry died. We'd make paintings here together and do
yoga and maybe set up an informal artists' salon.

"That's a great idea, Emily. I'll order canvas right away,"
I said.

After she left, I walked straight into my office, where I ordered canvas, brushes, bottles of gesso, and tubes of paint online. It felt strange to go through these motions with the certain knowledge that I would carry the roll of canvas and the rest of the supplies, still sealed in their original corrugated boxes, right to the moving van, whenever moving day came. I could visualize the scene in my mind like a vividly recalled dream.

I had heard that another marriage had collapsed in this house, two owners ago. During an argument, one party had apparently taken a sledgehammer to the toilet in the half bath off the kitchen, the one I had lovingly painted in the earth tones of houses in Tuscany. With some amusement, I wondered if the house was doomed. The sooner I got out of it the better.

Henry himself was still very much in the house, both as an occasional visitation and in physical form in the ashes in the wooden urn. Liza, when asked, said she wanted to keep her father's ashes in our house. Emily thought I should scatter them. A part of me liked the idea of having them out of the house, but Liza's wishes were paramount.

I suggested the compromise of a partial scattering. Emily seemed to wish very much for this ceremony, so I arranged an afternoon while Liza was at school. Emily came over, I scooped some ashes into a plastic bag, and we drove to a rocky ledge overlooking the river, where a stiff autumn breeze blew our hair to and fro. It didn't feel like much of a good-bye, just a ritual I was performing to try to please my friend.

Still, Emily did not seem happy around me. I tried desperately to summon up loyal-friend interest in her concerns, but I felt too overwhelmed with the mess of my life to deal with the logistics of hers. With regret, I acknowledged that none of it meant much to me. Getting through the next day intact meant everything. As she spoke, my mind felt utterly blank and spaced out.

"Is it always going to be about this?" Emily lamented as we walked back to the car, perhaps sensing my lack of real presence. "Is it always going to be about Henry?"

I would have loved to talk about something else, like my desperate need to get laid, but I didn't think she wanted to hear about that either. These days, I thought sullenly, it was faraway Eliana who was the most receptive audience. How twisted my life had become: I was now finding comfort from one of my dead husband's mistresses. I'd sent her several e-mails a week since returning from Maine, and she always took time to answer me with warmth and encouragement. I continued to be surprised at the ways our unlikely friendship was evolving. Mostly I felt paralyzed and exhausted, knowing I needed to step forward but unsure what to do next.

Now I understood why the single mothers I'd been hanging around with couldn't get through school, find satisfying jobs, or carve out time for their private pursuits. We were all just trying to get through the day.

twelve

October 2003

After the terrible dancing I am ready for fighting.

—OVERHEARD AT A PARTY IN THE EAST VILLAGE, 1987
(SPEAKER, A SHAGGY-HAIRED,
CRAGGY-TOOTHED POLISH POET)

While I contemplated what to do with my house, I had also begun to think about ways to escape the loneliness that had overtaken me since my return from Maine. Now that Tomas was no longer part of my daily life, a kind of panic set in. I'd begun pacing rooms again. I missed his companionship and cursed myself for relying on its comforts. I wondered if it was time to start looking around for someone new, if there was a man, anywhere, someone my age, available, who would be interested in being part of my life with Liza.

With respect to the mysterious world of men, there was the enormous question of baggage. I saw myself as almost nothing but baggage. Large cruise ship trunks and valises, filled to the brim with old, cracked shoes, moldering clothes, and damp, tearstained letters tied up with ragged rose-colored ribbon. I hoped this was resilient, tough survivor kind of baggage and not Dickensian Miss Havisham baggage. I did not want to wake up in thirty years and find myself in a sunless room, fingering the crumbling remains of my wedding album.

Actually, I was worried that I might, in a rash moment, take my wedding album and toss it, along with all evidence of my married life, into the fireplace. Liza deserved some mementos of her parents' marriage, however sadly things had turned out. Just to be sure, I took all the albums and tucked them away in a large dovetail-jointed wooden trunk—one of Henry's family heirlooms. Henry's father had hired carpenters in Korea to make several of these trunks to transport belongings for the move back to the United States. I placed the albums inside and sealed the lid with the heavy brass latch, hoping to forget about them and the day they recorded for a time, until I was tough enough to look through them again with either compassion or humor.

There was the question of trust. I had married the only man I thought I could trust, and this had proved to be a spectacular error in judgment. I didn't trust myself to choose anymore. The old methodology—he's cute in a way I like, he's smart, we have compatible tastes in home decor, he's well mannered enough to bring home to my family—none of this seemed to apply anymore. I would have to start all over again at zero.

I'd go about this in a practical way this time. I would not be swayed by superficial qualifications, like immediate physical attraction. This had clearly been my greatest mistake, I reasoned as I recalled the party where I'd met Henry—the dark hallway, how cute he'd looked in the gray sweater and white T-shirt, how charming he was. The charming thing would be the first thing to go. After all, it is charming Mr. Wickham in *Pride and Prejudice* who turns out to be the low-down scoundrel. And Darcy, Mr. Grumpfest, emerges as the honorable fellow who also, fortunately for our heroine, is the fellow with the big bucks. At least, my whatever-it-had-been with Tomas had shown me that there was nothing wrong with me as a sexual being. Although damaged in some ways, in this way I was intact, ready to flower, perhaps, with someone else.

There was also the question of age—middle age, that is. Like many women in our culture, which enshrines youth and beauty, I had spent most of my life plagued with varying degrees of self-loathing. I'd come of age during the seventies, when the female aesthetic that continues to dominate fashion strode fully and unapologetically out of the closet. The skinny, boy-hipped, leggy girls with straight blond hair and blue eyes were appreciated, the perfect display objects for low-slung, ragged-bottomed hip-huggers and skimpy tops. Girls like me—petite and curvy, with dark, curly hair that frizzed on a bad day—we were something else. At my best, dressed up in a 1940s vintage dress with my Mary Quant lipstick, yellow stockings, and platform huaraches, I evoked other time periods. I was not *now*.

Since Henry's death, and the undeniably flattering, albeit temporary, attentions of a handsome twenty-eight-year-old man, I suddenly and surprisingly found myself in a belated love affair with my body. The new body I lived in was light and airy. For the first time in my adult life, I often found myself admiring my body in the mirror. I bought some belly-skimming T-shirts and hip-slung jeans, once again in fashion. The clothes fit, right off the goddamned hanger.

My body was definitely not "perfect." My legs hadn't sprouted another four inches. Cellulite still burbled up and outward where it wasn't wanted. I tried to avoid certain lighting situations that were guaranteed to produce a feeling of gloom. Bathing suits were to be purchased by mail and tried on in the safe haven of one's own home. And there was that crinkled belly skin, the souvenir of my pregnancy. But this true friend and loyal companion had carried me through a terrible year. When I looked in the mirror, I saw a fine-looking woman, someone I wouldn't mind holding and touching. I wanted somebody kind to love and appreciate my body.

Close inspection in my bathroom mirror revealed that there really weren't that many wrinkles, yet. One of my brows pulled up in a quizzical way; a wrinkle had formed as a result, adding to the asymmetry of my face. Two "laugh lines" had creased the skin on either side of my mouth. I had to laugh at the irony of that. *Laugh lines, indeed.* There were new creases around my eyes. I wondered if crying so much had created wrinkles.

I noticed that Anna's face was looking—suddenly—much more rested and peaceful.

"Oh, it's Botox, my friend," she told me with a chuckle. "I had this permanent worry line across my forehead. My son thought I was upset all the time." She gave me the phone number of her dermatologist.

I longed to erase, if just for the few months' duration of a magical injection, the effects of this anguished year and the last sad years with Henry. I made an appointment with Anna's dermatologist, unsure of what she would propose or even what I wanted her to do to me.

On the train to the city, I ran into an acquaintance. Usually I saw this beautiful woman at the supermarket with her young sons in tow. An occasional fashion model, today she looked the part—her makeup perfect, every shiny brown hair in place, no boys.

"Wow, you look incredible!" I burst out upon seeing her in a nearby seat. "Are you working today?"

"I'm going to an audition—nothing wonderful, just catalog work," she said as I settled myself next to her. She spoke about her modeling career, mostly sidelined after the birth of her sons, emphasizing the workmanlike aspects of the job rather than the glamour. She knew just where she stood and seemed clearheaded and pragmatic.

"Are you going in for a client appointment?" she asked, while I continued to look at her face, as an object now, wondering how she would do at her audition, wondering how many other women of her age—early thirties perhaps—would audition for the job. My gaze wandered down her length, taking in her long legs in slim jeans, the stylish, well-shined black boots.

Noticing for the first time a tiny scar on her forehead, just faintly visible under makeup, I wanted to ask her about this blemish, an urge I quickly suppressed, guessing that this was not the best time for her to dwell on any of her flaws. I realized with deep, flinching shame, that I was too sheepish to admit the real purpose of my own city visit.

"Yes, just work." *Oh, I have a lot of learning to do if I can't even tell this woman, who earns a living with her face and body, that I am going to have a few wrinkles filled in.*

"How are you and your daughter doing?" she asked me, as many acquaintances had. Breathing deeply, I prepared to launch my short response designed to deflect the subject when, through her mask of makeup, I saw that her brown eyes were warm with genuine concern, though we were not intimate friends. She wanted me to tell her the truth.

And so, to my surprise, I found myself telling her how we really were doing, how hard the last months had been. She hadn't heard much about Henry's affairs, but I told her. We shared a few stories of marriage and its difficulties, the work of balancing career and motherhood, a challenge she seemed to manage graciously.

When we arrived at Grand Central, we shared a taxi downtown. At her stop, we said good-bye. I wished her luck and watched for a moment as she strode off in her high-heeled boots; then the taxi continued on to the doctor's office.

An hour later, I slid out of the dermatologist's procedure chair, gently touching my face where the laugh lines had been, still tender from the half dozen needle pricks. The dermatologist, a woman whose placid face suggested she practiced what she preached, said the collagen injections would last four months or so. In the reception area, I glanced briefly at the bill—an astounding eight hundred bucks—and slapped down a credit card. I wouldn't be able to make a habit of this. On the way to the door, I stopped for a long look in the oval mirror. My younger face looked back at me, the face in a photo Henry had taken when I was newly in love, on a hot city afternoon, gazing at him from across a café table. *Wow. Great to see you again.* That younger version of me had been optimistic, idealistic even, and on the brink of big change, just as I was now.

Back home, people said, "Hey, Julie, you're looking so refreshed and rested." It was just like a commercial.

Of course not all body parts can be changed so easily, and mostly we have to live with the package we get born into even as we encounter examples of near-perfect aesthetic design—people who seem to have stepped off a pedestal in a museum.

In the small Italian seacoast town where I briefly lived when I was twenty, I often found myself waiting at a certain café along the curving main street that surrounded the harbor. In those pre-cell-phone days, with unreliable landline service, everyone did a lot of waiting. The phone booths on a few street corners accepted only the mysterious *gettone*—a slotted coin, worth so many minutes, if you could correctly estimate the initial charge your call required. If you guessed wrong, the machine digested your coin, requiring another trip to the corner *tabacchi* to change another thousand *lire*. No one in Italy ever seemed to be in a hurry. With only the one main street, friends and even my unreliable lover eventually turned up at the café. Rather than fumbling with the *gettoni*, which risked bringing on fits of homesickness for the comparative efficiency of New York City phone booths, I would take a seat at a small outdoor table and order a coffee while enjoying the inspiring view of the bay and mountains.

A tourist shop offering flashy swimsuits, sunglasses, candy, and a brand of chewing gum called Brooklyn (the packaging featured a drawing of the famous bridge) adjoined the café. When the shops closed for three hours in the middle of the day, the young salesgirl stepped out into the bright sun to lock up the store.

This woman had unimaginable legs, long, tan, and tapered. I watched her totter across the cobbled street on turquoise high-heeled sandals, the breeze flipping her teeny tiny miniskirt this way and that, revealing a flash of white bikini bottom. She clearly spent her lunch hours working on that tan. She navigated through the slow-moving traffic of Milanese weekenders and foreign summer sun-worshipers, frequently stopping it altogether as she crossed to the beach side of the curved boulevard.

Even here, in this beautiful land of beautiful women with beautiful legs, these two specimens were utterly breathtaking, like an authentic Botticelli painting startling the eye in a gallery filled with more than acceptable copies.

"Una scema, ma due belle gambe," Giancarlo commented as he

arrived at the café and followed my gaze. A stupid girl, but two beautiful legs. His indirect compliment to my other good qualities was reassuring. Maybe in my next life I would get legs like hers.

Chloe, my good friend, city shopping companion, and adviser on all matters related to young widowhood, said it would be good for me to start dating, in a focused way. She had much experience in this area. Chloe had muddled through four years as a young widow, slowly rebuilding her life. Now she had a good job, one of the last rent-stabilized apartments in Greenwich Village, and, most amazingly, a boyfriend, a really nice boyfriend. She'd met him online. In spite of Chloe's success, the whole online dating thing sounded awful to me, so unromantic. I still wanted to believe in Fate, despite the fact that She hadn't done so well by me in the past.

My alternatives, though, were unpromising. I lived in a small town where the unattached men were the ex-husbands of women I knew. I also knew why the women had divorced their husbands. The discarded men were drinkers, philanderers, pains in the neck, or otherwise shiftless nonproviders. In a few cases, couples had just grown apart and no one was to blame, but I didn't want to connect myself to any of them.

And then, worst of all, there was The Crush: a man I'd clapped eyes on one Saturday afternoon in the summer, while loitering with Liza in front of his antiques store during a weekend in Brooklyn. Liza was rummaging in a bin of old kitchen tools he'd set out and held up a few prospects for approval. When I looked up, he was standing in the doorway.

"Is this your store, then?" I asked, checking him out. Slim, short-cropped hair, a smile that formed pleasing triangles of creases near his eyes—clear blue. *Why is it that on men, crow's-feet are attractive and mature, and on women they're just reminders that you're heading into middle age, to be quickly followed by decrepitude?*

"Yup, this is my place." His soft, lighthearted voice rose slightly at the end of the sentence, with the practiced optimism of a salesman.

It was one of those crazy things where you look at the guy, and that's it, you're done for, and you can't quite figure out why.

The Crush violated all the plans I'd made. I wanted to be clearheaded. This was no time for teenage crushes. I adamantly did not want to fall head over heels for anyone. But I bought a bowl and an eggbeater for Liza, my junior chef, mostly to give him a chance to register my existence, to give me a reason to say hello the next time I could create an excuse to pass through the neighborhood.

Chloe gave me advice as I set up my online "profile." I listened to her several horror stories about creepy men and weird bungled dates. I chose a photo of myself standing next to Tomas—taken on a day I'd been cheerful. I spent a bemused fifteen minutes Photoshopping him out of the photo—too bad it isn't this easy to detach people in real life—but resisted doctoring the image in any other way before uploading it to the site.

I should say that I was completely ignorant about dating. Dating wasn't what we, or at any rate I, did in the New York City of the seventies. I went to an all-girls prep school, so any boys I met were on weekends at my then best friend Lucy's house. She went to a different school, rollicking and progressive compared with mine. She lived in a dark and cavernous apartment on East Ninety-sixth Street near Central Park. She had lots of friends and gave parties, or we went to other kids' parties in exciting, less savory neighborhoods. We drank in bars that didn't exactly observe the letter or spirit of the underage drinking laws. Later, I might find myself French-kissing some guy I'd met, perhaps on the floor alongside Lucy's bed, my bare toenail caught awkwardly on the frayed hem of her Indian-patterned bedspread. Occasionally things progressed from that point, but usually I never saw the guy again.

During my college years, a man had taken me to Windows on the World (I am happy I ate there at least once) followed by the opera. That's when I understood what a date was supposed to be. Except that I went home with him that night, when I should have asked him to send me home in a cab. So I still didn't really understand what a date was supposed to be. Six years of misadventures later, I met Henry, who had taken me out for precisely the one restaurant meal before we slept together.

As I pondered the potential adventures awaiting me, I wished I'd grown up absorbing the dating concept along with my morning Wheaties and milk. Dating. Maybe if I said the word enough times, some understanding would penetrate.

thirteen

October 2003–March 2004

Our heads are round so that thoughts can change direction.

—FRANCIS PICABIA, PAINTER AND POET

"You are so sexy! I'm coming again!"

Is anyone counting here?

I was in bed with a sex machine, and not happy about it. Tragicomically and now much too late, I realized that I would have been happier with a good warm hug. I had failed utterly at my first attempt at dating. This was now a pathetic bungle that would require a laundry load of sheets—perhaps boiled—at the rate this guy was going.

Rich was an intelligent, driven man. These qualities had seemed key a week earlier. I reasoned that, among other flaws, Henry's despair over work success had contributed in some large part to his "crappy life choices," as Christine in Oregon had described them.

Rich had seemed a bit overeager, but I was sympathetic when he told me he'd been single for a while. I knew, though I wasn't telling, that my own motives were utterly impure. I was a disaster area. All I cared about was getting laid, in a safe manner, perhaps just so that I could tell myself I was really moving beyond Tomas. Imperfect as that situation had been, I had felt connected to Tomas on a level that I knew would take time to find again. Tomas and I had been friends before we became lovers; we had always liked each other as people, and I had loved him genuinely.

A few weeks before meeting Rich, I began a frank talk with Liza one afternoon after school. I told her that I was lonely and that I wanted to find a boyfriend.

"It's okay," she said. "Do I get to choose?"

"Well, if I meet anyone I like enough, I'll bring him home and you can decide if you like him. I'll be going out a bit more than I used to, but I'll make sure you get to go someplace fun. Also, I've found you a nice babysitter. I think you'll like her. She goes to college. She says she likes to play games."

"Will she play Attack? How come Tomas doesn't come here anymore? He's good at that."

"I don't know if this babysitter will play Attack, sweetie, but maybe I'll meet someone who likes that game."

Rich lived in a town south of mine. When he contacted me from my online profile, the convenience was undeniably appealing, as child care was always my predicament, even with the new babysitter. Rich and I went for a walk one evening after our initial meeting at a local bar. He drove to and parked his car at a town park area I'd never seen before, and knew I'd never in a million years find again. He took my hand as we walked up a hillside path. I wasn't ready to be holding his hand, and as we approached a steep area, I withdrew my hand to leverage the incline. He remarked that his birthday was coming soon. I took his hand. It is not so great to be anticipating spending your birthday alone.

"What are your plans, then?" I asked pleasantly.

"I never plan anything, because terrible things always happen on my birthday." *Oh, for chrissake. Now we'll have a sob story.* I had, actually, tried to minimize my own sob story at dinner.

"Such as?" I continued, trying for an upbeat tone, now feeling very wretched about having to hold his hand, some creeping anxiety growing about being alone in this nighttime park with a man who was potentially troubled about the upcoming birthday.

Women always chose this day to leave him, he said.

Shit. This was some big, bad baggage—almost as heavy as my baggage. Naïvely, I had hoped to meet someone with much less baggage than I had. I was pretty sure that whatever happened between us wasn't going to work out the way he hoped and that in fact it might all go down quickly, ending before dawn on the dreaded birthday.

There wasn't a long courtship. While I would have liked to have had more time to consider what I wanted from him, we reached a "Ma'am, this ain't a library, are you gonna buy that magazine?" situation within a week's time. I felt nothing much for him physically apart from a kind of curiosity. But I let him stay one night, after feeding him a good roast chicken dinner.

And now I was trapped in bed with a yeller. I'd heard about these types, though I had never met one till now. I might as well have stepped out of my body and gone to the kitchen for a drink of water, as my actual presence did not seem to be required at all. It had devolved into a theatrical performance, one that had stupefied me into embarrassed silence.

I believe he very much hoped to please me. I muffled a snigger, thinking how I would describe this night for Anna—offering her a good girlie guffaw being perhaps the only way to salvage anything positive from this evening. Anticipating her explosive laughter brought me back to a self that could endure the mess I'd made. He had five orgasms without ever going soft, which was certainly impressive, but numbing.

I had to gratify him, if only to make him stop by faking it, a depressing but effective skulduggery. But at last he moaned, "I have to sleep now . . . ," and snapped off, unconscious in an instant. I watched him as he slept for a few minutes, then tiptoed out of bed to the bathroom, where I sat quietly on the toilet. I was going to dump him—soon—on or just before his birthday. Which was too bad, really, because he was a nice guy, and if I hadn't been idiotic enough to have sex with him, he might have become a friend. I could have used a friend who was a guy, in addition to an actual boyfriend. Now he'd just have more baggage. And I would feel like shit, being too much of a coward to tell him just why I was dumping him. I hoped he'd find a woman who, unlike me, would be happy to be with a guy who could come five times in a row.

He said he was leaving for a business trip to Los Angeles the next day and promised he'd call me. He did call me, and I chatted friendly-like. And then I did the slimy deed via e-mail.

I promised myself that the next time I would offer myself more time to make a decision I would not regret in the morning.

Who can resist the promise of that English accent? Eliot was Oxford educated, with a stylish scruffy Vandyke. His Match.com profile said he was six foot three, too tall for me. Five foot one and a half, the measurement on my driver's license, was possibly over-stating the case. I had never liked feeling so dwarfed by a man. And he lived in Connecticut, about two hours away.

When we talked on the phone, Eliot had a self-deprecating, saucy, and irreverent sense of humor. Lying on my red velvet couch, cordless phone cradled on a cushion against my ear, I laughed and laughed. He was a big, naughty flirt, and that was a tonic. While it was hard for me to speak about Henry's betrayal to a man who was still a stranger, when I did tell him the con-densed version of what had happened, he was comforting and kind. Another tonic.

We made a plan for dinner in a week's time, having chosen a spot in the middle—Danbury, Connecticut, a small city I knew only as a string of highway exits featuring malls and gas stations on I-84, the route I took to visit my parents at their weekend house in Litchfield County.

I liked Eliot. Right away he seemed like a truly okay guy. I enjoyed his raunchy humor, which might have offended me in an earlier time but now was a relief. *So this is what men really think about.* I could tell he knew all about dating. Maybe he would teach me.

I couldn't see myself dating or living in Connecticut—subur-ban New York State was already such a definitive personal disas-ter. Driving to Connecticut for dinner dates was not going to work in the universe where I lived. If things proceeded further, I might find myself waking up startled in a bedroom two hours away from my child. I wasn't ready for that kind of separation at all. I knew this as I hung up the phone and climbed the stairs to get ready for bed.

Liza was already asleep in what we now referred to as "our"

bed, clutching a ragged stuffed lion, one that had belonged to my brother and had somehow been entrusted to me. Eliot might be horrified to discover these not very grown-up facts of my domestic life—that I cherished the stuffed lion, and that my daughter still spent most nights in my bed, because she and I, ignoring my therapist's well-intentioned advice, both wanted it that way.

Eliot called me the next day. Not to give me driving directions but to cancel dinner.

"I'm pretty sure you aren't ready for anything serious yet," he said sincerely. "I am ready. I don't want to be your, you know, 'transitional man.'" Eliot had it so right. A smart fellow he was. Relief flooded my chest. I liked him even more.

Could we still be friends? I wrote back the next day. Why yes, he would like that. We agreed to stay in touch. And I thought that would be the end of that.

Several weeks later, missing his lighthearted humor, I sent him an e-mail. By then I'd met another man—Daniel—and Eliot had met another woman.

Daniel was smart and funny, in a quiet, mordant sort of way—a quiet way I hoped would not become boring. His profile indicated that he was divorced with a son. I thought that he'd understand the parenting issues in my life.

In any event, I was dating. Dating meant going out with someone, getting to know him, eating some meals together, yakking, not having sex right away. I'd settled on that much. No commitment, nothing I couldn't walk away from in a hurry.

On my third date with Daniel—an autumn hike up a nearby mountain trail—he told me that he thought he was falling in love with me. I cast an eye over his long, placid face, dad-looking red plaid shirt and jeans, sensible and sturdy brown leather walking shoes—garb Tomas never wore, of course, or Henry. I hadn't expected such impulsive behavior from this man. I was completely bewildered, once again feeling blank and nonpresent, an observer watching myself act in a film. I was sitting in his lap when he told me this (and was regretting the kissing that had been good fun a moment earlier), and now I wanted to charge down the trail for home immediately. I had absolutely no idea what I thought about this man. I didn't love him. I was still working on just liking him.

And there was also Tim, another man with whom I'd corresponded online, who was divorced with no children. We'd talked, but I'd thought maybe it was best to try out men one at a time. Plus, my amateur theorizing held that it would be better to date a man who had kids. But fuck if I knew anything about men.

And there was still Eliot, who was turning out to be a great pal. I called him on the phone to tell him that Daniel had confessed love on the third date. Did this mean I couldn't wait for a few weeks before having sex?

"Are you joking, Jools?" Eliot snorted. "No real man will put up with that kind of nonsense, waiting a month to have sex."

"Really, you're sure about that? You'd never wait if a woman you really liked wanted you to?"

"Nope," Eliot replied. "I'd figure she just had some weird sex hang-ups or wasn't that into me. Doesn't sound like you're really that into this guy."

And of course I didn't know either.

"But, Jools, apart from the sex, the really important thing to remember is the three-month rule," Eliot reminded me gently. His repeated advice did have the ring of truth and common sense about it. The idea was to wait three months before bringing some-one home to meet your kid. The reasoning was that it was diffi-cult to mask the darker aspects of one's real personality (ax murderer, run-of-the-mill cad, or control freak) for longer than three months. "Once you bring this guy home, your daughter will either get attached or maybe hate the guy. Then it's going to be harder the next time to introduce a new person into her life."

"Okay, yeah."

"You didn't listen to me, did you?"

"So don't be mad at me, Eliot. I already let Daniel meet Liza last weekend. He doesn't seem like a nut job, he seems nice enough. He might be a bit too old for me. Not his actual age. I think he's just four years older than me." Than I am, I remembered too late for Mr. Oxford-educated (who I hoped was used to American bastardized English). "But he seems older, maybe kind of quiet, but very kind. He brought his dog. Lizzie loved his dog—it's a big friendly black Lab."

I paused, waiting for Eliot to say something nice. "Eliot, you're going to tell me that I screwed up. Did I screw up?"

"Yeah, Jools, I do think this is a mistake, it's too soon. Do you care about this man?"

"I don't know." I laughed nervously. "I thought I'd let my kid decide."

"I'm serious, Jools. You have to feel something. That's not go-ing to work."

"Okay, okay. Shit. You're right. I fucked it up."

I did fuck it up, quite royally in fact.

Daniel was quiet and steady, a man of habits. He seemed to live nearly a hermit's life, which saddened me—I'd hoped to have a bit of silly fun during this time of my life. Daniel had a proper office job, just what I'd thought I wanted in a man. He owned the sensible-dad red plaid shirt, and a few more like that one. Sometimes khakis. No ragged T-shirts of any sort. Running shoes, and the sturdy leather walking shoes. I began to suspect that his politics might be more conservative than mine. As time passed, I worried that he might be an actual Republican but was too afraid to ask, as this would be an instant deal-killer.

But this man had told me he loved me with a quiet intensity that I believed and was curious to understand. What could he love about me, since he couldn't know me yet, since I didn't even know me? I wanted to know what was lovable about me. I wanted to feel loved.

We made plans to see each other on Saturdays, and I quickly felt trapped, unable to see other friends. Of course, it wasn't like I'd been whooping it up on Saturday nights before meeting him. Plenty of weekend nights had been spent at home with Liza watching TV or a movie we'd both seen twenty times. It was the routine of it that speedily wore on me. Routine was already too much a part of my life. He was forty-eight and I was forty-four, but I felt and began to behave like a twenty-year-old having an affair with her English professor, who always remembered the correct use of the object pronoun in his letters.

It was Daniel's daily e-mail letters that initially won me over and revealed a great and dark wit. I read them and laughed out loud—there was humor and the heady delight of being wooed by such a fearless and natural writer.

I wanted to be with someone younger at heart, more spontaneous, though not as spontaneous as Tomas or Henry. The Daniel who wrote me letters was someone I liked a lot, even if the actual physical man wasn't "my type." But "my type" had gotten me into a marriage of big trouble. "My type" was The Crush, and I sensed nothing but big trouble there. I thought I might do well to avoid "my type."

One night Daniel brought over photos. I took out my albums, and we looked through our lives together. He showed me his life as a young father, embracing his then wife and young child, bundled against the cold on a skiing trip. I cried. His losses saddened me.

I decided—it felt like a good and rational decision—to be with him.

Daniel took a personal day one Friday. I followed his directions to his house: "Driveway on right, house with weeds," he'd e-mailed. I smiled as I pulled into the driveway. He had not exaggerated. Presented with a bland split-level house fronted by a mangy lawn, I walked up the cracked concrete stairs and opened the screen door. I called to him, but he did not answer. In the hall was an old upright piano, clearly unused, since the seat was covered with boxes of sporting equipment and dirty clothes that might belong to a boy his son's age. More sports shoes littered the hallway floor. I might have yelled at my own child for leaving such a mess, but in this case I welcomed the familiar signs of life lived with untidy children. Through a doorway I could see a living room with the underfurnished look of a just-moved-in space. There were no photographs hanging on the walls and no other sort of artwork, just two quite hideous tan couches, and a large TV placed in front of the fireplace. Farther on, a simply laid out dining room, the table strewn with a few magazines and yesterday's paper. From the hallway I was able to peer beyond into the kitchen. There, it seemed, a renovation had been considered, but the project appeared to have been abandoned, given the evidence of everyday life's debris. The light wood cabinets were from some decades earlier. I imagined for a moment the time when they were new and this house set the standard for convenient modern family living. Now the plywood was peeling apart.

I understood that Daniel saw this as a temporary place, for which he had little love. Not like the wonderful Vermont house he often spoke about wistfully, the family home of many summers. This house I stood in now was more like a storage place for his life, postdivorce, until he decided what to do next. In profound ways I admired his lack of attachment. I felt overattached to my house and my stuff in a way that plagued me, especially when I allowed myself to think about leaving it behind. When he came to my house for the first time, Daniel remarked that I should charge admission, because it was like a museum of curiosities.

I called out again, and this time he answered. He was downstairs. I walked carefully down the narrow, carpeted stairs.

There, splendidly, was the oasis of his bedroom, the one room that had been decorated to his taste. It was a wonder of peacefulness, in muted natural colors of earth and sand, with the hushed feeling of an elegant retreat. Perhaps a retreat in Japan, I thought, noting the row of Asian ceramic pots arranged elegantly across a low wooden dresser. A painted screen of swooping calligraphy hung on one wall. He had told me that his parents had spent some years overseas.

Across the room was a low bed, where Daniel lay watching me, with the covers pulled up, looking boyishly expectant. I sat down next to him on the bed and started to undress, since it seemed the right thing to do. The sheets were perfect and white and clean. I noticed that there was music playing. A woman's voice, achingly sad, accompanied by a solo guitar.

"Who is that singing?" I asked.

"It's Patty Griffin." It was just the woman and her guitar. The words reminded me of Joni Mitchell lyrics, poetic yet never obscure. I knew just the kind of sadness she was talking about. There was loneliness, men she couldn't hold on to, bars she spent too much time in, children growing up poor. One song, titled "Forgiveness," was so apt that I decided to buy the CD as soon as I got back home.

He pulled back the sheets and welcomed me into the bed. We made love quietly, accompanied by the sad songs. He was incredibly attentive and affectionate. I was nervous but wanting to enjoy myself for whatever this was. I cried when I came. I still felt confused about my feelings for this man, but at least I felt engaged and present and had no urge to run away. After, we spoke about our lives and marriages, and I observed that he was a good listener, even when I rambled on a bit. I slept for a time in his arms, then woke up with a start, in time to get dressed quickly and rush off to pick Liza up at her bus stop. As I stood chatting with the other moms, the time with Daniel had already become one of those strange, disconnected experiences where you feel like everyone must know where you have been all afternoon. But of course they had been busy with their own days and noticed nothing different.

I worried that Daniel's steadiness would incite me to behave badly, like the moderately rebellious teenager I had been but absolutely was not anymore. At forty-four, I was a responsible working mother, who shopped, cooked, did laundry, paid bills. Mostly, I wanted to integrate my life as a mother with my time with him. After his visit to meet Liza with his dog, there had been no more meetings. I wondered if he already knew what I suspected—our lives were not well suited to each other, and there was no use pretending otherwise.

Yet every night when we spoke on the phone, he told me he loved me. I began to say the same, though I still wasn't sure exactly how I felt. It was not the love I had once felt for Henry, or even Tomas. It was a sincere respect and affection.

Friends in town were heartened to hear of my new relationship and responded with dinner invitations. But Daniel didn't seem interested in becoming more engaged in my social world. He seemed interested only in being with me, writing to me, or calling me up in the evenings to have one of our long conversations— I lay on the red velvet couch in my darkened living room. I knew that he was lying on his bed in his beautiful bedroom.

In December, we talked about going away together for a week-end. I found an inn in the Catskills and made reservations for us in early February. My brother kindly offered to take care of Liza. The prospect of the weekend away seemed like a positive step forward in our relationship of three months.

My college friend Sara had invited Liza and me to join her fam-ily for the Christmas holidays in England. We left as soon as Liza's school term ended. While I was away in England, Daniel sent me daily and loving e-mails, but although I enjoyed reading them, I saw that I did not miss him the way I had hoped. This just wasn't right, though it had seemed like such a well-conceived idea.

Unable to imagine a complete deviation from my married life, and in part to distract myself from the upcoming anniversary of Henry's death, I decided to host a small gathering for New Year's Eve after our return from England. Though Daniel seemed less than enthusiastic when I told him of my plans, he braved a snow-storm to attend. But as the evening wore on, I saw that my urge to bring him into my world of friends and family life was not likely to succeed.

I had been busy in the kitchen preparing food. I noticed Daniel's absence and heard childish laughter and squeals that suggested that he had been recruited for Attack. I found him in the hallway looking beleaguered and possibly miserable, with a bunch of kids, including mine, hanging off him. He was, I concluded, done raising small children. He had parented with love and care, had made his sacrifices. My adorable seven-year-old would not be inducement enough for another go-round. I did not blame him—he was entitled. Eliot had been right. I'd have discovered this in time if I had been more patient. Now, unfortunately, Liza actually liked Daniel. I could tell from the way she was hugging his leg.

Shortly after this evening, he sent me an e-mail that would have been devastating had I been in love with him. He said that he anticipated a busy work period and that he would have less time to see me, though he was looking forward to our February weekend. I was too distracted to see what he was after—a gracious exit. If I had, I might have canceled the trip right then and still recouped my hotel deposit.

———

The January 8 anniversary of Henry's death was peaceful, though the lead-up was tense and sleepless. I invited Tomas and a few friends over to dinner. We raised a somber glass to Henry's memory. Tomas didn't stay long after the meal, but I was happy he'd come.

After the guests left, I e-mailed my brother to tell him that I thought I might, after all, consider a move back to Brooklyn. I felt guilty about all the money I'd spent on the attic renovation, but he didn't seem troubled by that. He reminded me that my house would now sell for a better price. Take your time, David wrote, no need to rush, just let things work themselves out. Some part of me was getting ready to move on.

Maybe both of us were ready. One evening Liza looked up from her dinner and announced, "I'm sad that Daddy died, but I think I can have a happy life."

....

I had allowed the flirtation with Tim, my other online correspondent, to continue intermittently. He had shown me discomfiting moments of drama that would have pleased, even thrilled me, as a younger woman but now felt oddly invasive. The most alarming was the winter afternoon when I found a note and bouquet tucked under the wiper on the windshield of my car as I prepared to pick Liza up from her bus stop. I had not been alone in my house that day when he drove up to leave me this gift. Daniel's car had been parked near mine.

But after I received Daniel's cryptic letter, I felt cooped up and ornery. Perhaps it was that hemmed-in feeling that explained why I visited Tim one January afternoon, and why I let him stay over another night when I knew full well that doing so was unkind and wrong. Daniel wasn't for me, but he was a good person and did not deserve my childishness. In retrospect, I wish he had just dumped me cold. Then only I would have been hurt, and just a bit.

I told Daniel about Tim. I canceled our weekend trip, forfeiting the deposit. Daniel and I officially broke up. He wrote that he had concluded weeks earlier that things were not meant to last, and of course, he was correct. His letters, as we unraveled, became surprisingly mean-spirited, but I figured he was fully justified. I had screwed up.

In an effort to salvage something from my latest bungle, I

broke Eliot's three-month rule once more and invited Tim over for a meal. The following weekend I dragged Liza off to meet Tim at local skating rink. He took her hand to make a turn around the rink, but Liza did not seem pleased. In fact, Tim told me that Liza had kicked him in the shin, which alarmed me—she was not an aggressive child. I apologized to him and spoke sharply to her as we drove home. Perhaps, I reasoned, she would come to like him better as time went on.

I invited Tim for another dinner. He arrived eagerly, perhaps too eagerly. After dawdling with him for some months, I had now abruptly offered him a chance to win me over. He brought Liza a present. She mumbled thanks, continued to survey him silently, and remained curiously withdrawn. Observing her, I knew that I had screwed up yet again. It had been too soon to present her with someone new. As Eliot had predicted, I was running out of chances.

After Tim left, Liza said, "Mama, I don't really like him."

"What don't you like about him?"

"It's like"—she looked upward in her characteristic way, plucking the kindest phrase from the ceiling light fixture, then returning my gaze—"he's trying too hard."

"Okay," I said. I felt tears come and quickly wiped them away before she could see me fall apart. I had been reckless with two entirely decent men who had liked me. I felt like a spoiled brat who needed a time-out, or maybe a good old-fashioned spanking. A few weeks later, when I had gathered up the energy, I ended things with Tim.

After the activity of the fall and winter, I finally took a longer look through the paintings I had made in Maine. Tomas had been enthusiastic about them. Sara had always encouraged me to pursue my artwork, long relegated to the few summer weeks I spent in Maine. "They will be appreciated," she said of my paintings in an e-mail. I took a few pictures to the local frame shop, so that they would feel more official and presentable.

Meanwhile, Henry's book notes and research lived on, now unwanted relatives overstaying their welcome. Occasionally I'd go into his office and open the file drawers, rifling through the impenetrable documents. I struggled to read his longhand notes, kept in several small Moleskine notebooks, the ones Bruce Chatwin supposedly used. After the events of the summer, I had no interest in finishing Henry's book for him. In fact, it required great discipline to resist hurling the contents of his file drawers into a large black plastic trash bag.

Irena had been right. I had been drawn to self-absorbed, creative men, and they had sucked all the air out of the room. I felt ready to try a life that wouldn't be the death of me but would still involve some adventure and risk taking. Nothing as physically bold as climbing Mount Everest, or crossing the Sahara, but for me, who had played by the rules to a fault, a bit of daring nonetheless. Henry had wasted the gift of time I had given him. Eliana reminded me in all her e-mails that I had been given a gift of time and that it was important not to waste that opportunity.

I read the man's profile. Here is Derek, and he is a bad boy. Let me imagine the contents of his closet. Black jeans. Black T-shirts. A few pairs of black boots. A motorcycle, probably black, unless it's red. A black leather jacket to go with the motorcycle. He lived in the city. It seemed like a good idea to start dating men there, to get used to the idea of urban living. I figured that this man would usefully determine the outer edge of what I could tolerate; he'd be a research project.

One photo showed him with a naked, wiry torso. And was that a tattoo on his upper arm? It was, he replied, in his first e-mail to me, and there were more elsewhere on his body. I wondered where they were. I had one tattoo (a hummingbird on my right calf, a birthday present to myself when I turned forty), but I wasn't a tough motorcycle girl, just a girl who had wanted a tattoo. This guy was definitely a bad boy, who rode his black or red motorcycle above the speed limit and could drink Boris Yeltsin under the table. I was counting on it.

I arrived on time at the restaurant he'd picked, a Mexican place in the East Twenties. Despite the festive atmosphere, I was feeling prim and guarded that evening. *Don't drink too much, just observe*. I sat at the bar to wait, looking up nervously as unattached men entered. Derek, unmistakable, strolled in a few minutes later in black jeans, black T-shirt, black boots, and a well-worn black leather motorcycle jacket slung over his shoulder.

Derek ordered both of us tequila, fancy stuff. Then he ordered a second round for himself. Derek was an effusive man, and I was happy to let him do most of the talking. The waiter arrived with our food. I was suddenly very hungry and ate the unmemorable meal with gusto, grateful to have something purposeful to do with my hands. He told me a bit about his work, then moved on to the topic of his marriage, which had ended several years earlier. Talking about one's checkered past was First Date No-No Number 1 (I'd read that recently in a women's magazine at the hair salon), but I didn't mind, since I'd asked, and since this was a research project. His tale seemed somewhat rehearsed.

"My wife calls me on my cell phone, while I'm out of town on a work trip, to tell me she wants a divorce."

He continued to speak about the dissolution of his married life with sorrow. He had lost a house and custody of a beloved dog. I wouldn't have picked him for a homeowner somehow. I tried to imagine him mowing a lawn in black leather boots and black jeans. Then I imagined, as I had frequently, how bitterly Henry and I would have fought over our house and Liza's custody.

Derek, now looking a bit woozy after a couple more tequilas, seemed intelligent, capable of love, but still genuinely broken-hearted. And not someone I would ever present to Liza. Not someone I'd have sex with even once. Just a quick kiss would feel dangerous.

The waiter brought the check. I promptly pulled out my wallet and asked Derek if we could split the bill. He blew off my offer with a mumbled comment: "Chicks don't pay."

Whoaa, there. The last time I'd been called a "chick" (sometime in the seventies?), whoever it was had gotten a mouthful from me. Tonight, it didn't seem worth the effort to complain. With some guilt I gazed across the table toward the bill. It wasn't cheap, especially for a first date, a one-off at that. But then, I consoled myself, a good part of the bill was the liquor.

We left. He held the door. Outside, he put his arm around my shoulder. *Is this affection or lust, or does he need some propping up?*

"I's early," he slurred. "How 'bout I buy us a bottle of champagne? Would ya come back to my place? We could have a drink?"

Anna, Chloe, and any other friend who loved me would have told me to hail a cab right there and get on home. But I really wanted to see how he lived. Looking at his glassy eyes, I didn't feel in any danger. He was sloppy drunk. I was stone sober. Given his present state, I was pretty sure that I could take care of myself.

I felt a great clearheaded pleasure in allowing my curiosity to run wild. I wanted to open my eyes wide, see everything I could see, and then I wanted to hail a taxi and go home.

We walked down Third Avenue to the nearest liquor store. Derek removed his arm from around my shoulder and strolled, a bit wobbly, to the refrigerated case. He took out a bottle of Veuve-Cliquot. I didn't even offer to pay. I waited quietly by the register while he fumbled with his credit card and clumsily signed the receipt.

I followed him up the wooden stairs in his drab lobby, which were sinking in places and rickety where they were not sinking. *I can still turn around, and take a forever rain check.*

As he stumbled across the second-floor landing, he wheeled around, as if caught in a strong gust of wind, and pointed to the door of a neighbor's apartment.

"Cuckoo," he mouthed, twirling his pointer finger around his ear. He whirled around again, and smashed his head into the support beam along the landing. He staggered, looking dazed, then stopped and staggered again, his hand reaching up to his forehead. He was bleeding profusely, blood dripping onto the floor.

"I've cut. Cut myself. Badly," he said.

The laceration was at least an inch long and literally gushing blood. The blood made me queasy and frightened. *Shit. Only in New York.*

"Maybe we should go to an emergency room," I said. "You might need stitches. You might have a concussion."

"No, no, I don't wanna to do that. I feel stupid. I was, I was showing off for you and it was all . . . going so well."

I felt sorry for him, really and truly. He had wanted me to like him. He didn't know me at all. He didn't know that this evening had been just a research project.

"Okay," I said. "Let's get this cleaned up."

He managed the last flight up to his apartment, fumbled with the key, opened the door, and flopped down onto a futon couch— black—just inside the door.

While he slumped on the couch, I walked quickly through the apartment. The tiny kitchen area was an unabashed bachelor's mess. After some cautious rummaging, I discovered what appeared to be a clean enough dishcloth, acceptable in the absence of a roll of paper towels. I brought the cloth over to Derek, whose gaze had followed me dizzily around the room. He seemed more focused now, and began mopping up the blood on his forehead.

On the back of his apartment door, still ajar, I noticed a collage of pictures of his family and one of a very cool-looking woman, standing in a windswept landscape. She looked like just the sort of woman he ought to go out with next. She looked like she would be very comfortable on the back of a motorcycle.

The bleeding subsided and he let me look at the cut.

"Derek, you really need to go to an emergency room. It's a deep cut. I think you need stitches."

"But I really don't wanna do this. What a pain. I'm leaving town day after tomorrow, and then I'll have to get the stitches taken out somewhere."

"We have to go to a hospital and get stitches. It'll be okay, I'll go with you."

On the street, I realized that I had not been to a hospital since Henry died. I thought about that and felt afraid. I started to cry. Derek stopped in the street.

"Wha's wrong? S'okay. Just a cut."

I couldn't really explain, not then. He took my hand. It felt good to connect on some level, any level. So many private feelings we would never share: my own pain that he could not understand, his shame and disappointment about whatever he had anticipated from this evening.

We sat in the ER waiting room on the brightly colored plastic chairs. I asked him about his work, and he seemed to relax a bit.

He sat forward, looking at me. It made me uncomfortable—he was looking at me so directly and he was still unsteady from the tequila.

"Sit back, relax," I said, "we're going to be here a while."

"Don't you want me to look at you?"

"You can look at me." I sensed his regret that he had lost an opportunity to try to win me over that evening. I understood that he was as lonely as I was. And he didn't have a lovely child to return to as I did. In that moment, I couldn't wait to get back to my brother's house in Brooklyn, where Liza would be sweetly sleeping. I couldn't wait to kiss her cheek. Derek admired the hummingbird tattoo on my lower calf. I felt he might have liked to touch it, but he did not.

Finally a nurse called Derek's name, and he went off to get patched up. I arranged my coat across a chair and lay against it. Some time later I felt his hand touching my shoulder—I had dozed off. He seemed surprised that I hadn't already disappeared into the night. The cut had been patched up with a new kind of skin glue—no stitches.

"I'm tired," I said with the peacefulness that follows the happy resolution of a medical crisis. "I'd like to go home now."

Back outside, a welcome streak of yellow flashed by, and Derek charged chivalrously down the street after the taxi. I was winded by the time I caught up, looking forward to the warmth and quiet of the trip home. As I tugged the door handle, Derek grabbed me and kissed me on the mouth firmly and with some passion. I turned away and got into my taxi, relieved and exhausted.

But I thought, as the cab pulled away from the curb, this was not a bad person, not at all, just a muddled person, still trying to understand how his marriage had ended and what to do about the rest of his life. That felt a lot like me.

Eliot said maybe we should have dinner after all. And I was curious to meet him after so much entertaining dialogue. The level of stupid flirting, a delightful distraction from my considerable failures in Boyland, required some action one way or the other. I only hoped that I was suitably chastened after my encounters with Daniel and Tim. A date with Eliot, who I was quite sure actually liked me, in spite of my obvious unreliability, seemed like a safe adventure.

"Okay, Eliot, let's do it. I'll be visiting my parents this weekend. I think they'll watch Lizzie for a night."

"I'll be back tomorrow morning. I am just going to have dinner with a friend." I said this with a quick glance at road directions, trying to act casual. My parents looked at me curiously as I laid out my evening plans while preparing dinner for Liza. We were in the kitchen of their Connecticut weekend home, which was about forty-five minutes from Eliot's house.

"It's late already," my father said, checking the time. "Are you all right driving back late tonight?" Since Henry's death, my parents had become quite protective, which I mostly appreciated.

"Oh, he has a guest room. He's got a big house." I felt like a conniving teenager, my regression depressingly complete. No wonder Daniel had grown fed up with me.

My father shrugged as I continued to arrange Liza's meal. I was grateful for his concern and the way he knew me well enough to just let some things go, without asking too many questions. As I set Liza's plate before her, I figured this might be a good skill to cultivate in time for her adolescence.

Eliot's house was larger than I had expected. He took care of the garden himself, he told me with pride. Even in late winter the borders were carefully tended, the perennials clipped and mulched. I had entirely abandoned my own garden. But seeing his effort sparked an urge to take advantage of the coming spring's spirit of renewal. I would make an attempt to reclaim my flowers, if they hadn't already been overwhelmed by my neglect and winter's frosts.

While Eliot prepared an elegant first course of grilled shrimp, I hopped up onto his counter so as not to feel completely dwarfed by his height. After dinner and several glasses of wine, consumed while lounging and snogging on his couch (on a couch, everyone is the same size), he persuaded me—it wasn't that hard—not to stay in the guest room.

Eliot was an affectionate lover, showering me with attention and compliments that felt genuine. But after he fell asleep, with his arm around me, I lay awake in the unfamiliar setting, listening to the dripping of the bathroom faucet, fretting about Liza and my fate.

In the morning, however, I woke exhilarated, as if purged and absolved. I twirled a few pirouettes in his expansive living room, while Eliot made me coffee and chuckled. I didn't care if he thought I was a loon. He fed me an ample breakfast, and I warmed under a delicious shower. As I walked toward my mud-splashed station wagon, I took a last, fond look at his adorable silver BMW M roadster parked in the driveway. A nice life he had, but it was not going to be my life. Every day I was edging further toward the idea of moving back to Brooklyn.

We'd stay friends, I thought, I hoped. Mindful of my recent failures, I didn't trust myself not to mess up a real relationship. And he was still too tall.

Soon afterward he met another woman—also tall. They seemed to hit it off right away. She wanted to get married. He wanted to get married. And I felt lucky still to have Eliot for a pal, someone who wished me well, whom I could count on to make me laugh at my weaknesses, who would tell me I was pretty even when I felt like a cranky crone. It was my first date that qualified as a resounding success. We had some fun, and no one got hurt.

My foray into dating had been instructive, but I often felt depressed and lonely. I cried at night and punched pillows. Liza watched me with concern that in turn made me worried for her. I continued to flee with her to the city on weekends. While we stayed with my brother and his wife, life was comfortable for at least a few days.

Liza and I roamed around my old neighborhood. One day I took her to see the brownstone where Henry and I had lived when she was born. The owners had painted it a shade of salmon pink that pleased her. I was too afraid to ask her directly how she would feel about a move, so I tried to fill our weekends with the kind of fun we couldn't find in our small town. We went to movies, strolled in the botanic garden, ate lunch in cafés on Seventh Avenue. Sometimes I wandered over to the store run by The Crush. I managed to create a conversation that allowed me to leave behind a business card. But I'd heard that he had a girlfriend, or at any rate was dating someone. Dating. Whatever that was.

I had a short affair with a friend.

I'd called him up, and we met in Brooklyn for a drink on one of my city weekends. Perhaps the margarita was to blame. Because I didn't drink them often, they induced immediate euphoria.

I looked up at him, enjoying his familiar, handsome face and said, "Sometimes I wish we could be together," because I liked him and I knew he liked me.

He looked at me with surprise. I felt myself flush immediately like a royal idiot. What had I said? He was ten years younger than I was. For as long as I had known this man, he'd told me that he was earnestly interested in marrying and having his own children, two things that he was entitled to want but that I did not think I would ever be doing again.

It was late after the drink, so I asked him to walk me to my brother's house. I fumbled in the dark with the keys at the brownstone gate while he stood a few steps back, waiting. He said that he wanted to kiss me. Without thinking enough about the consequences, I watched him approach me. We kissed in the doorway.

I had forgotten how kissing could make me feel completely cherished, but he reminded me. I pulled him into the little area just inside the gate and we kissed some more and there was some urgent groping.

We saw each other a few times after that. He came to visit

(with Liza safely away), and one weekend I went to his apartment, where he fed me a good chicken dinner and we watched a movie. Later, we had blissful sex and then slept close in his bed. I tried hard—very hard—to imagine any universe in which this thing might work for all of us. And failed.

———————

On a warm Sunday in late March 2004, I left Liza with my brother and sister-in-law to take a yoga class in Manhattan before heading back to the train that evening. We'd spent the weekend together eating meals, playing Connect Four, and endless games of Crazy Eights and rummy. When she was small, I used to let Liza win games, until I noticed that she was beating me easily. By now I was used to losing despite my best efforts.

After the yoga class, I felt good changing back into my street clothes in the small curtained dressing room. The air outside was warm and fresh, the sky blue and unsmogged. I was happy to be in the city, to hear the sounds of cars and snorting buses, the snippets of cell phone chatter. I loved feeling part of this strange urban organism, which allowed me to belong to something while still experiencing anonymity. In spite of the noise all around, I felt quiet inside. I took out my phone and dialed Anna's home number.

"I'll do it, Anna. Let's move back to the city. I think we can do it."

"Oooh," she yelped. "I'm so glad!"

"Let's promise to help each other through this. It'll take a lot of planning." I considered the ordeal waiting for both of us— dismantling our lives in large houses to move back to the city, where inevitably we would each live in something like a shoe box by comparison.

"We'll have to keep this to ourselves for a while," Anna said.

I thought about Emily, who would not be happy to find out that I was leaving town. She might even feel betrayed if I kept my plans secret. "I think you're right about that. But we'll be okay, right?" I had a vision of my house full of moving boxes, and a sudden realization that at least half my furniture needed to disappear. Not to mention finding a school for Liza.

"Yeah, we'll be fine," Anna said, perhaps imagining her own moving ordeal. "I feel like we need wives, though, not husbands."

"You might be right about that."

"Hey," Anna proposed with mock coyness, "will you be my wife?"

"Of course"—I laughed—"if you'll be mine."

I continued walking up Lafayette Street, over to University, where, filled with sudden optimism, I impulsively allowed myself to enter my favorite (and expensive) dress shop. I left half an hour later wearing a newly purchased frilly black and patterned dress, urban and flattering, just right for the city girl I wanted to re-become.

part four

daylight

fourteen

April–September 2004

My storehouse having
Burnt down
Nothing obscures the view
Of the bright moon

—MASAHIDE

After much internal preparation, I went to see Emily one afternoon after school let out. I thought that I had planned for the worst possible outcome and that choosing an everyday moment would help me deliver the news. In retrospect, I see that I chose a terrible time to tell her I was moving. We were both tired after a long day, and we were alone in her kitchen, without Justin, her husband, who would have provided some levity and comfort during a difficult moment.

I took a deep breath, began unfolding my news, and realized quickly, as her eyes filled up with tears, that I had completely miscalculated. She told me she was devastated, took my hand, and began to weep. I felt wretched and resentful at the same time. I wasn't doing this to her on purpose, it was just that I couldn't stand my life and had to get out. I couldn't live so close to Cathy, who had caused me so much harm. Thinking about her still sent me into waves of misery and fury. But now Emily felt abandoned in a way that could not be fixed.

The fallout from this event came swiftly. What had always separated Emily and me was the difference between my working life and her life as a mostly stay-at-home mother and artist. Occasionally we had clashed over this issue—when I cautiously suggested possible work opportunities, when she wanted to have a leisurely lunch during a deadline week. Within a month, what began as a momentary squabble, which at any other time might have been resolved with a few days of phone silence, escalated into a larger conflict, from which we couldn't engineer a gracious recovery.

Now, like spiteful middle school girls, we were no longer speaking. The catastrophe of Henry's death had dogged us since she had taken me to the hospital after his collapse. From that day, she had been waiting for her former friend to return, but the woman I'd been then, who now felt like someone I'd once known but could no longer visualize, was long gone. I had no idea to where and still no clear idea of who I would become. I wanted to feel like something I could genuinely call myself. Now I was lost en route—temporarily, I hoped—desperate to get to somewhere. The first step was getting out of town. The second step was accepting that this long rebuilding process would be all about what the poet Elizabeth Bishop called the "art of losing"—people as well as objects—and that much of it would not be pretty. By this point, I had already lost many people and judged (correctly, as it turned out), that I was not done yet.

After the fiasco with Emily, I felt I had to tell Liza about the plans to move, before she heard about it from others. It was difficult to explain my reasons for relocating, without telling her about Cathy. I tried to frame the move as my need to start over, but she had no wish to start over, and I felt selfish, taking her away from a school she loved, her friends, and the house. She hated the idea, and we spent many tearful evenings together. Always she asked, "But why?"

By late May, after a few more springtime dating mismatches, I was thoroughly exhausted by men. This was worse than high school, the feeling that as a forty-four-year-old woman I knew no more than an overeager teenage girl. I decided to take a break. Perhaps after the summer, I'd have better luck.

Then, on the day I decided to shut down my online profile, a new man appeared. Will's wry letters made me laugh again, and he had a cool-sounding job. He lived in the city. Better yet, he lived in Brooklyn, just a few streets from my brother's house.

After a half dozen e-mails back and forth, Will called me one evening. He had a friendly voice, with an accent I couldn't place, Canadian perhaps? Nope, he was from Wisconsin. He'd grown up in a big family in a rural area, number six of seven kids. He sent me a photo of all the children squashed into a group, everyone looking like they'd been playing in the woods five minutes earlier. Though he had never been married, he seemed to welcome the idea of a seven-year-old.

"I can't wait to meet her," he said. "It'll be a blast."

Liza walked by and asked who I was talking to. "I want to say hi to him," she insisted when I offered the vague answer that I was talking to "a friend."

I passed Liza the phone, and to my surprise she and Will

talked for twenty minutes about her school and friends while I passed in and out of the room, taking advantage of their conversation to ferry laundry upstairs and garbage to the curb. I wondered what he'd done right to engage for so long a child he'd never met. Whatever that thing was seemed like just what we needed.

And then The Crush called me. The crush feeling had never passed. I still felt the unnamable physical yearning for something about him, a something that was all kinds of trouble. But of course when I heard his voice on the phone, I was thrilled.

"I wanted to see if you'd go out with me this Saturday," he began a bit hesitantly. "Have dinner, see a movie?"

"I have to say," I remarked, noting, a moment too late, that my tone was a bit harsher that I would have wished, "the timing here seems kind of weird. Why're you calling me now? And aren't you dating someone?"

"Well."

"So that's over now?" I wanted to smack myself. I was starting to sound like an inquisitor or a stern high school principal, though another little devil was whispering in my ear, *Go, go, go out with him. It's only dinner.*

"Come on," The Crush said warmly, "just go out with me. It's only dinner."

"Let me think about it. I'll call you back."

The next day I called The Crush back. "Okay, I'll have dinner with you. But let's not bother with the movie this time." I had visions of him taking advantage of the darkened theater and of me happily letting him take advantage of the darkened theater.

I wanted to go out with him, but I had my doubts about this guy. When I'd jokingly mentioned my crush to one female acquaintance in the neighborhood, she'd bluntly remarked that she thought The Crush was "bad news." I didn't need more bad news.

The crush part was a force I could rely on to mess me up completely. I'd go out with him, we'd kiss, we'd have sex. I'd be a goner. I'd try to figure this guy out for months or maybe a year, till he got tired of my frequently unexciting, schedule-bound life with child and took up with someone else. I would begin to make this guy a priority, the way I had done with Tomas, even Daniel for a short time. But unlike Tomas, who had been happy to draw pictures with Liza at the kitchen table and play Attack, I couldn't quite imagine The Crush outside his shop, engaging in my domestic life. I needed someone who could do that, who wanted to do that, who wanted nothing more than to do that.

But one dinner wouldn't be so terrible. Maybe I can just get it all out of my system and then get on with life.

I called Will that evening. "Look. There's this man. I've had a big crush on him. And now he's asked me out to dinner. I think maybe I should just go do that. You know, get it out of my system." I felt like a moron, hearing and then actually believing the words I was saying.

After a pause, Will said, "Um, I don't want you to go out to dinner with this guy. Please don't do that."

Here was a choice. Will was telling me how he felt in clear, straightforward language. There was something savory, as in protein-based, nourishing, and healthful, about what he was offering and asking. Things might not work out between us for ten thousand reasons, but they might just work out as delightfully as a carefully simmered stew, one that tastes better the next day, full of rich and complicated flavors, one that would embody that idea of *umami* Henry had been struggling to understand.

The Crush, on the other hand, would likely—no, about this I

could be entirely certain—turn out to be like the bag of peanut M&M's that I always buy at a movie theater concession stand, rip open, enjoy completely, and regret later, when the sugar rush and nausea kick in. After a bag of peanut M&M's, nothing else tastes any good. Not even homemade raspberry pie.

Savory or sweet? Sweet or savory?

"Okay, I won't. I'll have dinner with you instead."

Our first date was not very promising. A week earlier, Will had suffered a minor fall from his bicycle and ignored the resulting scrape on his elbow. It's difficult to see one's own elbow, so he also ignored the soreness that persisted for a few days. By the time he realized it was infected, he had to go to an emergency room, then ended up staying in the hospital for a few days hooked up to an IV antibiotic drip. As Will and I sat across from each other a day after his hospital discharge, I thought he didn't look too healthy; in fact, I worried that he might fall face-first into his dinner plate. All the talk of hospital visits made me nervous. Nevertheless, I decided that our weeks of writing and phone conversations merited a second meeting.

This time I met him in the city. We ate sushi; I got a bit tipsy on sake. I was so terrified, because he was kind, funny, and attentive without being pushy, that I practically ran away from him on the street after our meal, under the pretense that I had to catch a cab, quickly, immediately, so I wouldn't miss my train back home.

A week later, Will came up on the train and I picked him up at the station for a picnic by the river. I'd made a roast chicken with a fresh salad, bread, and cheese. He'd brought a bottle of wine. After some of the wine, we kissed, sitting on the picnic blanket under the trees. Having made a choice, I felt like a fifties girl, a bit shy and cautious, nervous and uncomfortable, wishing I'd brought Liza along for support instead of leaving her behind with her excellent babysitter. But this time I was really going to listen to Eliot's advice.

Will said, "We shouldn't rush things. Let's just talk and get to know each other." This guy seemed to have read my mind. Or maybe he just wasn't that into me. But we continued to talk and exchange e-mails every day. We called our decision to get to know each other slowly The Plan.

A few weeks later, I traveled down to Brooklyn again. I arrived at his apartment and peered cautiously through the doorway into his tidy and modern bachelor pad. Milky aqua walls, comb glazed, a large trophy fish hanging on one wall, a gorgeous curved blood red sofa positioned on an entirely impractical but inviting rug fashioned in long noodles of cream-colored wool. Small white boxes arranged on a wall in evenly spaced rows of three held tiny glass vases, each with one brightly colored gerbera daisy. I stood enjoying the view, thinking that the last guy I'd known with such cool taste in home decor had been gay. But as I crossed the threshold, Will scooped me up, carried me into his bedroom, and threw me onto the bed.

After that weekend, and a few weeks sooner than Eliot would have liked, I invited Will up for a visit to meet Liza. She crushed him at checkers on the blue-painted kitchen floor, where fortunately I no longer saw an image of Henry's body.

Will laughed after being beaten. Observing their easy interaction, I thought that maybe letting Liza pick my boyfriend wasn't a bad idea after all. I wondered what she'd seen so quickly, why she was so immediately comfortable. I wasn't comfortable yet, but then I had accepted that hardly anything made me comfortable. I'd be patient and wait for comfort. As long as Liza liked him, I'd wade forward a bit further into the stream.

. . .

I wrote to Eliana about Will, and she expressed happiness for me.

"The more you begin to blossom," she wrote back, "the more healing, love, compassion which enters your being, the more you will begin to find others who not only admire, but who also want to care for and nourish you deeply."

By now, we corresponded less frequently. I did not value Eliana's e-mails less but was happy to see that we were both moving onward and forward with new plans. We wrote to each other about our work lives, and she shared with me the beginnings of a relationship that sounded entirely different from those in her past. Her new man sounded calm and loving, and their connection was a true partnership.

Will came up on Fridays after work and stayed till Monday morning. I drove him down to the train station, just like the other women with commuting husbands. But I was happy this was a boyfriend, not a husband. I was glad to have my own space during the week, and glad to see him again when he returned.

Will said, jokingly, that I was a fancy French girl (perhaps because of my fondness for frilly-edged skirts) and began addressing me in the French manner. So now I was Jzhooleee. In the mornings he sang me quirky songs of his own invention, which made me laugh in a fierce, goofy way that felt entirely new. As after rigorous exercise, muscles in my chest and throat ached and then expanded. It seemed like a miracle to rediscover my sense of humor. Bravely, after a few months together, Will even ventured a few dead husband jokes that made me spit out my morning coffee.

Mostly, I appreciated how he was able to listen to the full, sad story of my previous year without running away at high speed. I found I needed to talk a lot, to be sure he knew everything, so that he could be patient with me while I worked through all that baggage. He said he understood my skittishness but did not shy away from expressing his own interest in pursuing what we'd begun.

The journey of these long talks revealed strange coincidences. It turned out that while Henry and I had lived in Brooklyn with our newborn Liza, Will, then a graduate student, was living just around the corner. I'd walked up his street countless times, pushing Liza in her stroller, trying to get her to nap.

"Didn't you ever see me," I joked, "pushing a blue and green plaid Maclaren, with a bunch of grocery bags hanging off the handles? I used to sing her Gershwin songs to get her to sleep." Here I launched into a verse of "Our Love Is Here to Stay." Well, maybe he'd seen me, he said, laughing, perhaps mostly at my singing. We had shopped in the same markets and eaten at the same restaurants, but in those days he would have been trying to dodge the onslaught of Park Slope strollers on the way back to his apartment to study, while I was elbow deep in Earth's Best puréed peas and diapers.

Will might not have been interested in parenting in 1996, but he was very motivated now. I came to see quickly that raising a child with this man would be an entirely different experience than what I'd lived with Henry. Will didn't try to compete with me; he did want to begin a real relationship with Liza. After the "honeymoon" phase, Will graciously endured a few weeks as Liza withdrew a bit, but she emerged from that with enthusiasm. She couldn't have her "real" father back, but this guy might do after all. He was fun, he was a good listener, and he was happy to play games, all sorts, even Attack.

In contrast to the blistering and damaging fights Henry and I had over the years, the occasional conflicts Will and I had seemed to propel us forward. We discovered that we were both solitary by nature. While his work required meetings and engagement with many people, he could hang out with Liza and me on weekends without too much other excitement. At night he held me tenderly and I felt appreciated.

One sweltering July weekend, Anna came over with Leo for a swim and, of course, to check out the new boyfriend. She took a little stroll with me, supposedly to inspect my flowers, and whispered the words every woman wants her close friend to say.

"He's cute! Nice butt! A real mensch . . . and clearly, he completely adores you."

The annual August trip to Maine was approaching. Anna planned to come up for two weeks of the month with her son, and once again she and I began packing up foodstuffs and linens. I decided, after consultation with Liza, to invite Will to visit us for part of the time on the island.

From that time there is a photograph of Will and Liza standing by their bicycles. She is tiny next to him. They are hugging. She looks relaxed and content, perhaps a bit shy. One knee displays a large white bandage, a souvenir from a bike fall earlier that week.

Will, it turned out, was a serious cyclist. At twenty-seven, he had cycled alone from Seattle, through the Canadian Rockies, across the Plains and the Midwest till he reached New York City, sleeping in a tent while living on cheese and bread, Alberta peaches, sardines, and the occasional beer, an odyssey that suggested much about his self-reliance. He was eager to help Liza embrace her inner athlete. She proudly showed off her healing wound to her island friends, displaying some of Henry's story-telling flair.

Will accompanied us on our shore trail hikes, where I painted and he and Liza hunted for more interesting rocks to add to our exploding collection. We drove down the dusty road to the sand beach, where to Liza's delight he swam in the frigid water without complaint, while I huddled on a beach towel.

He drove down to the city for a week of meetings, but he was back with us the following weekend—ten-hour drives didn't seem to bother him at all, and we were glad to see him. We hit a foggy patch of days. Stuck indoors, remembering past years on the island with Henry, I became gloomy and sullen. Will had a knack for finding humor in my dark moments, a talent he'd need and use during our early time together. In this case, the mood changed with a Monopoly game, one of those three-day ordeals where alliances are formed, all the official rules are bent, sweet deals are made, and properties are swapped and mortgaged to the hilt.

On the day of Will's final departure, Liza and I followed him in our car to the ferry landing. I watched him drive onto the ferry with a sense of genuine loss that pleased me. This was how it was supposed to feel. Once on the ferry, he got out of his car and waved to us. He was wearing a white shirt that flapped in the breeze like a ship's flag. I remembered an entry from my child-hood encyclopedia that had particularly fascinated me, diagrams of sailor's semaphore hand signals. As the ferry sailed away, I raised my arms in a V shape, and from the deck Will responded. Liza joined the game, and we continued sending made-up signals until the boat picked up speed, his white shirt just barely visible in the distance.

. . .

Fall arrived, and we each returned to our separate homes. Will continued to travel up for weekends.

"So," I asked him one night as we lay in bed, "I have lived through one man's truly horrible midlife crisis. What's yours going to be?"

"You are my midlife crisis," he said, giving me a playful squeeze. "This is what I always wanted. To have a partner and a family."

"Okay then," I said, stunned. "I think I can handle that."

Though we were still a new couple, Will and I began talking about living together once I moved back to Brooklyn. I was more eager than ever to start searching for a place to live, and once our kids were back to school, Anna and I began real estate shopping. Miraculously, a conversation with a friend I hadn't spoken to since Henry's funeral produced a buyer for my house. I packed my first box—the elegant wedding dishes I knew I wouldn't need again for a long time. I was surprised how few dishes fit into such a tall box. I concluded that I'd need a shocking heap of boxes to move my life. A trip to Wal-Mart was in order.

As I approached the exit lane on my way to buy more boxes, I recalled another otherwise forgettable October lunch hour, like many during that last autumn of Henry's life, when he and I were still going about the business of being married, parenting, and stocking a house. On that day in 2002, Henry was driving us toward the same Wal-Mart, where we stocked up on paper towels, spray cleaner, jumbo cans of crushed tomatoes, and the like—life, purchased in bulk.

From his command post behind the wheel, and without looking at me, Henry said, "Julie, I just want to say that I am sorry about the Caines' dog. I don't know why I behaved like that. I would never do that again."

In movies, when The Important Scene is set in a moving car, a character often turns his or her attention away from the road to communicate the big bombshell to the driving companion. A nervous moviegoer, I can never pay attention to the big news—I am more worried about the car accident that would occur if this were not being shot on a soundstage. In this case, however, the big news was delivered with no interruption in Henry's driving flow, so it took me a moment to process the importance of his apology. As if sensing that he needed to reinforce the message, Henry looked over, and our gaze connected for just a flash. I looked away, stunned and inexplicably heartbroken, as he said, earnestly, "And I hope you can forgive me."

"I accept your apology," I answered, bewildered, feeling ambushed. We continued on, silent. *What happened to change his mind?* A sad and vacant feeling grew inside me—too little, too late—that diminished his apology, though I didn't have the heart to tell him so. He might be genuinely sorry now, but I couldn't quite believe him when he said he'd never behave like that again. I didn't trust him anymore, to care for me and support me through a hard situation. I knew he'd do something else like this, maybe bigger, and he'd apologize too late and again ask for my forgiveness. Really, I was on my own. I had lost the important faith one needs to be with a partner. I had lost love. Yet paper towels had to be purchased, and life had to go on. Marriage was for keeps.

"Julie, I just want to say that I am sorry about the Caines' dog. I don't know why I behaved like that. I would never do that again. And I hope you can forgive me."

I changed the words "the Caines' dog" to "Cathy." That's

how he would have apologized to me later, about Cathy and the other women: "And I hope you can forgive me."

Now I opened the car door and stepped onto the asphalt, fixing my gaze on the large Wal-Mart logo above the store entryway in order to memorize my position in the parking lot. I paused, wondering how I would have answered. There was so much at stake: our life as an intact family, the big house, the car, and the other trappings of our comfortable world.

I suddenly had a sad image of Henry as a lonely terrier abandoned in a backyard, racing around and around in circles, barking, trying desperately to get my attention, everyone's attention, anyone's attention.

"Do you still love me? Do you really love me? I don't think you still love me," he had said to me repeatedly during his last few years, during which he had most flagrantly betrayed my trust. I had always answered yes.

fifteen

September 2004

Your body is the life force power of some fifty million
molecular geniuses. You and you alone choose moment by moment
who and how you want to be in the world.

—JILL BOLTE TAYLOR,
My Stroke of Insight

The shelves of Henry's office library were packed past ca-
pacity. I needed smaller, sturdier boxes for the books. I stopped
by the local liquor store to ask Henry's redheaded eulogizer when
their next wine shipment would arrive.

Even with thirty wine boxes, this was to be a survival-of-the-
fittest selection process. The titles, organized by subject matter,
included works on philosophy, food, and science, books I wished
I had time to read but knew I never would. I began sorting, a process that felt uncomfortably like performing a vivisection, because in this room Henry always felt very present. The larger
pile, the books I would not keep, I planned to donate to the local
library.

A black-spined paperback with white lettering stood out from the chunkier and more colorfully jacketed titles on the shelves. A battalion of Post-it notes caught my eye, a parade of flags above the book's spine. When I slipped it from its position between Steven Pinker's *How the Mind Works* and *Consilience* by Edward O. Wilson (a new display of Post-its now visible along the long right side of the book), I recognized *The Evolution of Human Sexuality*, published by Donald Symons in 1979. Henry had spoken about this work frequently during the writing of his first book. Almost every page of Symons's well-thumbed book was marked with notes in Henry's script. The sheer quantity of Post-its signified that somewhere in its pages I might find clues about Henry's understanding of human nature and relationships. And sex. Because it always comes down to sex. Without having read the book, I nevertheless sensed that I had stumbled upon Henry's bible.

My attempts to read a few pages were discouraging. It seemed that Don Symons had written mostly for his peers in the scientific community, at any rate, not for a lay reader such as myself. The book assumed knowledge about biology and Darwin's theory of evolution by natural selection that I had not retained. Unfortunately, the dissection of formaldehyde-preserved frogs in ninth grade had turned me off science for the remainder of my high school and college years.

Nevertheless, I was intrigued, and stopped my packing to look through the book. After perusing the table of contents, I bypassed niceties such as the introduction and early chapters and opened straight to "The Female Orgasm: Adaptation or Artifact?" The conclusion of the chapter offered a not altogether encouraging view that our interest in pleasure-seeking in sexual behavior was part of the larger human "ability to transact favorable compromises in the economy of the emotions" (p. 95). I had

hoped for something more poetic than "economy" when it came
to sex.

And this passage from a chapter titled "Pair-Bonds, Marriage,
and the Loss of Estrus," described my life as a wife-mother all too
precisely:

> Wifely virtues—overlapping only partially with indices of sex-
> ual attractiveness—might have included evidence of sexual
> fidelity, youth, health, industry in gathering, and skill in moth-
> ering. As discussed above, marriage is not in essence a sexually
> based behavioral association between a male and female, but
> rather an economic and child-rearing partnership, embedded in
> networks of kin, and entailing sexual rights and duties. (p. 131)

Henry had highlighted these lines with a yellow marker pen and
flagged the page with one of those hundreds of Post-its.

I mailed a letter to Don Symons at the University of California, Santa Barbara. I briefly detailed the discoveries I had made
about Henry's affairs and asked if I could speak to him about
male and female sexual behavior in a professional way. I recalled
Henry's glowing account of meeting Professor Symons and the
photos he'd shown me of the two of them on a beach, their tanned
skin glowing in the late afternoon sunshine, Don the handsome
older man, with close-cropped gray hair and an open smile. To
my delight, Professor Symons replied by e-mail within two
weeks, apologizing for the delay. He had since retired and didn't
check his university mailbox regularly.

After an exchange of e-mails, in which I further explained
events since Henry's death, we spoke on the phone. Don (we were
now past the need for the formal "Professor Symons") recalled
his conversations with Henry but said he'd had no idea about his
"secret life." We ended our call, agreeing that I would contact

Don once I was resettled. Meanwhile, I wrestled with the last cardboard boxes of my old married life, carefully packing away Professor Symons's book.

I e-mailed Don again and asked if he had written any other texts that might be friendlier for a reader such as myself. A few days later a package arrived with a dainty-size hardcover titled *Warrior Lovers: Erotic Fiction, Evolution, and Female Sexuality.* The first half of the book, coauthored with Catherine Salmon, provided just what I was looking for: Darwin 101.

During this time I had noted with interest several mainstream magazine and newspaper articles on relationships and fidelity. Genes were the hot topic. They made you fat, they made you depressed, and it might be, these authors suggested, that they explained our sexual habits, specifically, why men seemed to be "hardwired" for infidelity and women ended up raising the children.

Don Symons offered himself as my "go-to guy" in my attempt to understand these issues. My central concern: if men and women were so seemingly incompatible in their mating goals, were we in some ways prisoners of our genes, or were we responsible creatures, capable of free will? In other words, was Henry a lying, cheating, no-good spouse because he couldn't help himself? And if our genes incline us toward certain likes and dislikes, can we still make choices? My initial impression, based on passages like the following from *Warrior Lovers,* was not entirely optimistic.

> Humans evolved a taste for sugar, fat and salt because these substances were both nutritious and relatively difficult to obtain during the overwhelming majority of human evolutionary history. In recent, evolutionarily novel environments, however, in which technology and capitalism have rendered these

tasty substances abundant and cheap, most of us consume far more of them than is good for us. . . . Our gustatory adaptations—like all our complex adaptations, psychological and nonpsychological—are designed to function in the conditions and circumstances of the evolutionary past. (p. 27)

The food analogy was easy to follow. Any trip to a neighborhood grocery store or a fast-food restaurant at the nearby mall would confirm what I already knew—left to our own devices, most of us head straight for the snacks. Only self-restraint, strong cultural habits, and knowledge of nutrition help us refrain from living on French fries, burgers, and Häagen-Dazs. The problem of modern life is that we now have easier access to many things—fatty, sugary foods, fast cars, and willing sex partners—than we ever would have had as members of hunter-gatherer bands on the prehistoric plains.

At Don's recommendation, I bought *The Blind Watchmaker* and *The Selfish Gene* by Richard Dawkins, the eminent Darwinian scientist. I read—and, because of those abovementioned lapses in science education—misread texts. Don kindly redirected me. I tackled the texts again. Our dialogue continued as Don gave me a crash course in evolutionary science.

Charles Darwin didn't discover evolution. Many scientists had been exploring this idea before Darwin published *On the Origin of Species*, in 1859. Darwin's revolutionary contribution was an explanation of the process that drives evolution and produces adaptations. Unlike the vague and sometimes mystical explanations during his own time, Darwin's theory of evolution by natural selection was based on his observations in nature. His theory depends upon the existence of inherited variation within populations. He saw that the variations exist and that, as generations go by, these variations continue to exist. He couldn't fully explain how this happens, and it wasn't really explained until well into the twentieth century, with the new field of genetics.

Even a small child can observe how the different parts of living creatures indicate functions. Wings promote flight, eyes promote sight, and hearts promote the circulation of blood. In organisms, these components with particular functions are called adaptations.

The goal of evolutionary psychology is to study brain adaptations. As Don explained, the human brain, like the rest of the body, is a collection of adaptations, evolved over immense periods of time to solve the particular adaptive problems encountered by our ancestors. Our brain mechanisms and our behavior are, like our ability to see, hear, and breathe, the products of evolution by natural selection.

Human culture has changed dramatically since the dawn of what we call civilized society, moving from Pleistocene nomadic hunter-gatherers (1.8 million to 11,000 years ago) to early settlements, from the great cultures of the Mayans and the Egyptians to our own modern, high-tech society. But this massive leap has happened in a mere blip of evolutionary time. Our biological makeup has not changed. As Don succinctly put it, "In short, it's a mistake to think of ourselves as somehow containing remnants of our primitive ancestors; in every basic adaptation, we ARE our primitive ancestors."

Don further clarified the concepts of mutations and natural selection: from the many random mutations that occur in nature, the individuals of any species who survive well enough to reproduce in a given environment are able to pass their traits, desirable or undesirable, to the next generation. Thus, natural selection is nonrandom, but it is not some long-term "improvement" plan.

We only have to look around us and at ourselves to see that survival and reproduction do not require perfection.

Don described the world of early man, our ancestors, whom we resemble more than we might like to admit. In that time, people lived in hunter-gatherer groups, which varied in size according to the availability of resources. Support by the group was essential to survival—and being expelled from the group might be fatal. Within the group, almost all fertile women were married, and access to multiple partners was limited and full of risks.

By contrast, present-day nuclear families live in larger, less structured communities. Individuals can meet many people in all sorts of contexts. We can travel in our cars, and most recently, we can hide behind the anonymity of the Internet. Sexual mores have changed dramatically in a very short time. So, it's a bit like McDonald's—lots of easy access to food and behavior that can get us into trouble.

Don put it this way: "The glacial slowness of natural selection compared with the rapidity of environmental change humans can manufacture pretty much guarantees that we don't have any complex adaptations to recent environmental novelties."

Don and I continued our e-mail discussion:

ME
So, men and women, evolutionarily speaking, are really operating at cross-purposes in mate seeking. Women are "wired" to seek a reliable partner with healthy genes, and men are "wired" to seek as many partners as they can attract, at the least cost.

So to what degree can we make choices and think of ourselves as creatures with free will?

DON

On the free will question, I can confidently say that our brains are, for all intents and purposes, the same as those of our late Pleistocene hunter-gatherer ancestors, so whatever the free will situation was with them, so it is with us.

Twenty-five years ago I mentioned to George Williams, one of the great evolutionary biologists of the 20th century, that many people make the argument that you suspect Henry was making, that womanizing wasn't his fault; his genes made him do it. George seemed genuinely surprised to hear this, and said that he would have supposed that people would have the opposite reaction: "those impulses are just my genes talking, and I don't have to obey them."

Evolutionary psychology can provide some insight into why we have the impulses we do, but it doesn't tell us anything about how free we are to act on them or not. The impulses that we're primarily talking about—sexual desire for new women, especially young pretty women—are impulses everyone knows exist, if they're paying attention. All laws and rules and ethical injunctions exist to curb impulses that many or most or all people have; there are laws or rules against murder and theft, but there are no laws against eating rocks.

I wouldn't be surprised if some of the Post-its in Henry's copy of *The Evolution of Human Sexuality* were there because he believed that an adaptationist account of the human male's taste for sexual variety somehow meant that he was absolved of exercising choice; but it does no such thing.

I asked Don if he felt that infidelity was a near inevitability in our modern culture of increased opportunity, restrained only by conscious, mindful effort. It seemed that Henry's misadventures were a kind of primitive hunt. Especially after reading—and possibly misreading—Don's book, he might have concluded that he was simply being a man, acting on healthy and in any event irresistible impulses. In our culture, the nature of risk has changed. What would have been an unacceptable risk in family-based hunter-gatherer bands is now quite acceptable in a community where small family groups function autonomously, and even anonymously, with fewer nosy, nagging elders and fewer societal restraints. Although our town turned out to be much like those ancient tightly bound communities.

DON

It's important to keep in mind that the vast majority of living foragers (and other peoples as well) are polygynous, in the sense that some men have more than one wife and that polygyny is "permitted." There can't be any question that over the course of human evolutionary history some men sired offspring with women they weren't married to, but a much more reliable way to increase reproduction was by being successful enough to acquire multiple wives. What I'm getting at is that the male psychology that often leads to affairs perhaps should be thought of more as a polygynous than an adulterous psychology. Where polygyny is normal and sanctioned and a sign as well as a perquisite of high status, things are different.

Legitimate polygyny would have suited Henry very well. But, along with all the other fast changes in modern life, women's expectations and options have shifted radically, in a flash, evolutionarily speaking. Reclusive Mormon cults aside, most modern women would not be content to live as one of a number of partners rearing one man's children. Polyamory, the more hip approach to multipartnering, seems problematic as well. My conversations with a few practicing polyamorists suggest that we are hardwired for jealousy—and overcoming that jealousy so we can have more partners can bring misery along with pleasure. Perhaps future generations will find a solution.

What did I take away from my exchanges with Don Symons? I learned that we humans are unplanned and therefore imperfect. In our physical and psychological adaptations, we are more suited to that ancient time when we roamed the plains in family-based bands, hunting and gathering, moving with the seasons.

We are not well adapted to this age of speed, technology, anonymity, and easy availability. Even the concepts of the monogamous couple and the nuclear family are new for us. Without the established rules of culture, religion, a nagging mom, or whatever we individually call moral grounding, we will likely succumb to our ancient impulses. We cannot easily restrain ourselves now that our urges can be so easily gratified. After my exchanges with Don, I felt a new appreciation for traditions like Buddhism, where the goal is to calm the body and, thus, calm the mind. Without understanding the physical mechanics of how the mind and body work, those monks did come to understand so much about how to cope with what we are and what we cannot change.

Men and women can't live with each other easily, but we must live together, otherwise we'll all die out. So we must muddle along, not quite understanding each other. Couples fall in love and out of love, and in many cases it might be best to end unions. Whatever happens to couples, children must be cared for, and obligations fulfilled. There are honorable ways to end unions and honorable ways to live.

Perhaps the project of conducting a relationship can remain a work in progress, an ever-changing, amoeba-like creature that must be fed and nurtured, occasionally tamed, but not overtamed. The trick, of course, is finding the balance between what we are in our essential nature—late Pleistocene men and women with cell phones, laptops, and fast cars—and what we can be when we live our lives with thoughtful and honest effort.

sixteen

October 2004

When you are fully in your emotions, when they are simple and appealing enough to be in, and the distance is closed between what you feel and what you might also feel, then your instincts can be trusted.

—RICHARD FORD,
The Sportswriter

Once I had made the decision to move, there were a few days of startling clarity, when I had a sense of the infinite possibilities of truly accepting change. One day, an "ordinary" day, still shines in my memory as one that gave me hope that other days like it would follow.

On this weekday morning in October 2004, I wake up at 6:30 to get Liza ready for school. Sometimes, most times, we still sleep together. Before waking her, I enjoy looking at her resting hands, which more and more resemble my own, as they might have looked had I not bitten my nails when I was young. I am most pleased to see her peacefulness and the absence of the nervous habits that plagued me as a child. This reassures me as I begin my day. I have struggled to preserve her childhood. Wedged between a cat or two, I reach for the clock to turn off the alarm, disturbing a stuffed animal, one of the several that, along with the live cats, make the bed feel like a small petting zoo.

We dress, and Liza spends some time brushing her hair, fussing over the part and the stray strands that pop up disobediently. I remember that age when you imagine that the waves in your hair are going to rise up like so many unruly elves and embarrass you at the lunch table. After she beats them into submission with hair goo and brush, we trot down to feed our cats, who circle and whine hopefully when they see me rummaging in the cupboard. I know my place in their world. I am the designated can opener.

Once the cats are guzzling at their dishes, I cook some eggs, and Liza and I eat while discussing any of the topics of these days—the complex and ever-changing social dramas at school, why we are even on the earth anyway, how do batteries work? (Dunno, we'll have to look that one up), how are snowflakes formed? (Ditto). What is gravity? (I forgot that physics lesson). And that old favorite, why is the sky blue? And what's a rainbow? I have finally looked up those last two and can now discuss light refraction and absorption competently. We ponder daily the eternal question of why our cats' poop is so smelly and why one in particular has a knack for dumping a big one just as we are ready to begin eating.

Some mornings we edge into a discussion of the day Henry died, as Liza has an eidetic memory of the events of that afternoon and evening, which altered her life so completely. Over and over she asks me to explain why he died. My medical descriptions never vary, though more and more I feel, but cannot yet tell her, that the physical events that caused his death were part of a much larger picture. A spiritual and emotional collapse came first. Just at the end of his life, he might have tried to crawl out from under, but he lost his grip and slipped away.

I keep an eye on the kitchen wall clock, which is set seven minutes fast, just confusing enough so that I will follow the time indicated without second-guessing. At 7:25 by the clock, we are pulling on our shoes and jackets and then skittering across the gravel drive to our wine-red station wagon for the short drive to her school van.

I have spent much time in the parking lot where the van picks up the children in the mornings and drops them off in the afternoons. The site is the cracked asphalt lot behind the village health clinic. I like to park in the particular spot that offers a view of a bit of meadowy lawn straight ahead and an enormous and wonderfully ovoid purple beech tree to the left that is beautiful in every season. In the mornings, all activity is rushed and practical, but in the afternoons, when the bus is late (often), I have knitted sweaters or dozed in its shade on a spring or still warm autumn afternoon. We have enjoyed throwing snowballs well into spring, as the last March snow is preserved in the shade of the tree's branches. Mountains in the near distance fade backward into layers of softer and cloudier blue-gray. Sometimes flocks of hawks or turkey buzzards cascade down from the hills after an unseen prey in a burst that always startles me. The afternoon sunsets are dramatic in winter, with fast-moving clusters of watery gray clouds.

The passing seasons here are a movie I have watched like a time-lapse photography sequence: at the beginning of the school year, the purple leaves cascade into a ring at the foot of the beech tree; the leaves turn brown and blow away in blusters of wind rushing up from the river, leaving behind the bare skeleton that reminds me of the baobab trees I saw in Africa on my honeymoon. I feel lonely in this place, but it is a good kind of loneliness—I am spending time with myself, a person I am coming to know clearly and fully appreciate.

I am rushed this morning. I need to leave for the city in a few hours, so I settle Liza into her van seat quickly. I kiss her good-bye, as always, delighting in the soft press of her mouth on mine. She extends her rosy lips with intention. I enjoy the kiss, wish her a good day, and remind her that Tanya will pick her up this afternoon. I walk off to my car as the van pulls away.

The aisles of the grocery store are still empty at 7:30 A.M. The fruit and vegetable manager knows me by name, and I like talking with him. He is a man with a calling, who has absolutely improved my life, often giving me some exotic green or fruit to taste. I will genuinely miss him.

I stand in the checkout line, just long enough to make me feel agitated, with my half gallons of milk and Tropicana, and a chocolate bar for later. I have confused and anxious feelings about the pile of documents waiting for me in the city, which represent the end of my life here. I am officially selling my house today, though Liza and I will stay on, as tenants, till the end of her school year. The clerk at the cash register looks tired and harassed, as hers is the only register open at this early hour. *Things to do, train to catch.* I tap my fingers on the black conveyor belt as the woman in front of me pays for her groceries, counting out loose change, while the clerk slowly bags her purchases.

I remember a scene in a book I read recently, *Long Quiet Highway*. Natalie Goldberg watches her Zen teacher, Katagiri Roshi, standing on the street outside the Zen center in Minneapolis. Another student is due to arrive to take Roshi to the airport for a scheduled conference. The student is late, and Natalie is getting worried and anxious that Roshi will miss his flight, as we all might do if we were late and impatient and normal humans. She describes the experience of watching him: he is standing but not waiting. He is experiencing the present moment, not feeling anxious about the future, over which he has no control.

Standing, not waiting. I need something to focus on to keep me present. My eyes are drawn to two cobweb strands swaying gently from their attached points on a corner of the cash register. I look at them, enjoying the movement of their strangely beautiful forms. The breeze from the air-conditioning system gathers and releases the strands, and I marvel at their resilience. I note the light coating of dust on the strands. The cash register hasn't been dusted in weeks, long enough for a spider to create an architectural wonder and then pack up and leave his home to move on to another, more fruitful location.

I see that, having been through a year of loss and change, I will change still more in this next time of my life. I will need to get comfortable with that idea and struggle to find a way to move through all this with some calm, though calm is not especially my nature. At least now my life feels like my own, after a marriage filled with noise and conflict.

Fear of change is the crippling thing. Because of this fear of change and death, we create fortresses we hope will protect us. I am about to let the last of my fortress go for a life that offers uncertainty, though I am also returning to a place where I have family and the prospect of a new life with Will. He tells me that he sees his life connected to Liza and me: that we can head forward as a trio. We will not be at sea in an unworthy boat.

I want to live life unafraid of failure and success, though it will always be in my nature to worry and fret. I want to teach my daughter at least one thing I have learned with so much pain: Be prepared as best you can, make effort, but be prepared to not be prepared. In fact, it's best not to get too attached to the idea of always being prepared. While still being prepared. Perhaps "being prepared" could be redefined as "paying attention."

At last, I pay my bill and gather up my purchases in their plastic sack, while I continue to contemplate the threads of cobweb on the cash register.

At home I settle on an aqua blue velvet dress, one of my widow splurges, appropriate not for the meeting with my lawyer but for the PR event at Irena's showroom that will follow in the early evening.

I have just time enough to make some phone calls, read and respond to the morning e-mails, flip through my bills, and grab a book and a bag of knitting for the train. I drive to the train station and park my car. I fumble for a few dollars for the parking meter, choosing the meter on the left—the one on the right ate five dollars the last time I used it and I haven't forgiven it yet.

A few minutes later I am seated on the train, happily pulling out my knitting. One stitch at a time, I work, then doze until the train hits the tunnel at 125th Street, when I startle awake and, still bleary, collect my belongings.

After the midtown real estate transaction, I begin my walk to Irena's jewelry showroom. Snippets of conversation along Thirty-fourth Street, a singsong of world accents, blend into the modulated tones of a familiar melody that is my birthright. I feel at home again in my city.

Irena's showroom is lushly arranged with her beautiful jewelry, food and drink, and the women from fashion magazines in their This Moment's Uniform of pointy spiked heels peeking out from under tight, low-slung jeans and trousers. I take a glass of Veuve-Clicquot from a waiter's tray. I nibble a little chocolate cookie treat and wonder if I can negotiate a chocolate-dipped strawberry without dribbling on my velvet dress. I chat with Irena, friends, and colleagues and take a moment to enjoy the splendid view of the rooftop city from her high-up windows. The aroma of chocolate and strawberry mingling with the scents of women's perfume diffuses in the heat of the overhead spotlights. In the midst of this moment of urban glamour, Will calls on my cell phone, and we arrange to meet back at Grand Central in an hour's time.

Back outside, on Seventh Avenue and Thirtieth Street, I pause after spotting a young guy with one of those new bicycle taxis. It is painted robin's egg blue, like a bag from Tiffany.

"How much to Grand Central?"

"Ten dollars," he replies. It seems extravagant to me for such a short trip, and I hesitate for a moment, admiring again the blue color of the carriage.

"It's really fun!" the young man adds exuberantly.

I decide that fun is required. I hop in. A smile plasters itself on my face as soon as he pedals into the street, as if I were my own eight-year-old daughter on a ride at the small-town carnival we went to a few months earlier. The driver careens with verve and confidence through the traffic. It is a still tender fall evening, not too cold. The city looks glorious, the last sunlight glittering in the skyscraper windows, gilding the top of the Chrysler Building, the sky the deep, rich blue of a Magritte painting. I can hear strains of Leonard Bernstein's dissonant ode to the city—*It's a hell of a town!* I begin crying in the happiest way as we speed by pedestrians waiting on the curb corners. Sometimes they look at me, and, because I am smiling, they smile back.

I arrive at Grand Central and wait for Will at the information booth. A black-tie event is about to begin in Vanderbilt Hall. The invitees stand milling in their fancy outfits: men in tuxedos, women in gowns. I feel a longing to be part of this other, glamorous New York City evening about to unfold, but I am also grateful just to observe it—to see and enjoy the details of my life again. This has been the real gift of everything I have experienced since Henry's death.

A tap on my shoulder. I turn away from the elegant scene to find Will looking at me. He has submitted to a radical haircut this very morning—shaving off most of the remains of his hair. He is wearing a black newsboy cap I gave him, and he takes it off to show me his clean-shaven head. I laugh because he looks so boyish. His blue eyes sparkle in the lights of the hall. He reports that his shaved head has gone over well at his office.

We eat some pasta hurriedly in one of the downstairs restaurants and board the 6:40 train, packed with commuters. Too late, Will realizes he has left the black newsboy cap at the restaurant.

A genius catnapper (a talent I envy), Will dozes for a while, his head resting on my shawl-draped handbag. I stroke the grayish velvet nap of his newly buzzed hair, play with his gently pointed ears, and pat his still brownish-reddish beard. Then we talk and kiss a bit. Some people stare, and I wonder if they find us tiresome. The woman just opposite us in the four-seat section near the doors moves after another space became available. So I guess we are tiresome.

From the parking lot in town, we drive to pick up Liza. We walk through Tanya's mural-covered house into the backyard garden, where she has arranged branches into fanciful fencing, topped with a plastic rocking horse she found discarded on the street. Her two cats and bunny roam the yard, dodging some of the neighborhood children. Liza and a half dozen other kids are squealing with delight on the trampoline, but Liza comes away cooperatively after a brief hunt for her shoes.

Liza does not like Will's new haircut. She pauses, screwing up her face before delivering her assessment of the situation: "It looks like a teenager haircut, but the face doesn't match!"

He laughs. "Thanks for your honesty, bub."

Back home, after dishes of fruit and ice cream, Liza asks if she can have a bath and if we will read to her. The full restoration of reading time in the evening is an unforeseen benefit of this new relationship. In the face of crisis, such niceties were discontinued for a time—there was laundry to do and work to catch up on.

Upstairs, I run the tub and Liza steps into the water in her cautious way, easing into the froth of bubbles with a grateful *ahhh*. Will and I take turns reading. After the bath and teeth brushing, we resume reading in Liza's bedroom, the three of us squashed on her narrow bed. Then I turn the lights out, Will heads for the bathroom, and Liza and I snuggle for a while. I feel tired after the day, afraid I will drop off, as I used to do when she was younger. But I want to have sex more than I want to sleep.

I rouse myself and find Will still in the bathroom brushing his teeth. I brush my teeth, change into my warm flannel robe, and hop under the bedcovers while Will does his stretching exercises, recommended for a back injury some years earlier. I remind him of the first time he stayed over. I observed him doing his exercises on that evening with great fascination, intrigued and pleased that he was disciplined enough about his exercises to do them even when another man might have had more pressing desires, like getting my clothes off. We didn't even have sex that night. It was part of the Plan to take things slowly. But now we are old hands, so to speak.

Liza comes in briefly to tell me that she has finished Book 18 of the Boxcar Children. I congratulate her and give her another bedtime kiss. Will wishes her good night and tells her he loves her. She offers a muffled response. She is still finding her way in this new situation. It will take time for her to find out what will be good for her.

I resettle Liza in her bed and return, closing the bedroom door, before climbing back into the warm bed. I am always cold, and Will's body is warm under the covers. He's a good size for me, trim but not overdone in the muscle department. The legs of a cyclist taper gently to sculpted knees, well-proportioned calves, slim ankles, and well-defined feet. His torso is slim but filled out nicely at the shoulders. He has a slender neck, a small chin cleft, a large and angular nose with a dent from his days as a junior boxer. And those very blue eyes. And his elfin (or are they Vulcan?) ears. And now, not much hair. His arms are surprisingly strong for his slim build. He lifts me up into a playful toss—the brief seconds in the air are thrilling. I am relieved to land solidly on the bed with a bounce.

Now we are facing each other with our legs overlapped under the covers. He is wearing a T-shirt and a pair of green Christmas boxer shorts, decorated with wee reindeer. I am still wearing my flannel bathrobe. He seems dreamy and tired, and I think maybe we'll just enjoy this and we won't make love. We embrace and draw each other tighter. His hands wander around under the covers, touching me on my waist and in the space between my lower back and the rise of my bum. We kiss and he sighs and I sigh. He says I am a sex bomb. This is a good thing for a woman to hear when she is forty-five. I am thinking *dayanu*—it would have sufficed—the refrain from the Jewish Passover prayer. If God had just brought us to the desert for forty years and not given us manna, it would have been enough. But he did give us manna. Life is good, even for a heathen Jewish girl, who can't remember any of the other words of this Hebrew prayer. Off with the flannel robe, off with the T-shirt, off with the Christmas boxer shorts.

Later, we drift off to sleep, pulling the warm covers back over and nestling in tight like furry, hibernating animals. Sleep is overtaking, my eyes are closing, and my final thought is *yes*. A big, bold word in bubble letters with outlines and drop shadows in shades of hot pink, red, and orange, and an animated John Lennon prancing in Pepperland, the people waking up from their paralyzed, gray sleep, and the Blue Meanies relenting at last with the opening trumpet blasts of the sampled Marseillaise, and then the music softens, the letters collapse softly, and the room is peaceful darkness.

seventeen

2005–2007

We don't have much truth to express unless we have gone
into those rooms and closets and woods and abysses
that we were told not to go into.

—ANNE LAMOTT,
Bird by Bird

Many days after that perfect one were full of difficulty. One evening during the spring of 2005, my mother called me. She'd felt unwell, and her physician had found fluid in her lungs. My dad had taken her to the hospital for a biopsy.

"It's cancer," she said with her trademark frankness. I was devastated. My parents, in the tenth year of a well-deserved retirement, were about to leave on a long-planned trip to France.

My mother didn't want to talk long that evening. After she said good-bye, I did the only thing that felt useful. I Googled "mesothelioma," carefully typing out the unfamiliar word, and arrived at a BBC website. In the course of thirty minutes, I learned that mesothelioma is an unyielding cancer. After exposure to asbestos, even a tiny amount, small tumors grow in the patient's lungs over many years. The disease is therefore usually diagnosed in a late, inoperable stage. While other lung cancers respond to chemotherapy, mesothelioma is unresponsive in most cases. Life expectancy from the time of diagnosis is twelve to eighteen months. After this brutal crash course, I felt like I had been kicked in the chest. My mother was going to die from this disease. The question was only how soon.

My mother, a refugee from Hitler's Austria, was a tough survivor, and she tackled her treatment options with determination, though she was already weakened from the growing tumors. My parents canceled the trip to France and consulted specialists. When surgery was ruled out as a possibility, my mother's oncologist urged her to try chemotherapy. He talked about life extension and quality of life. After my research, I wasn't convinced, but I accepted my mother's wish to try anything that might help. My father took her for months of chemotherapy treatments, which only depleted her further and had little effect on the tumors.

Meanwhile, I packed up my house slowly, waiting out the last of Liza's school year. Our family drew closer during this time, even as we watched my mother fade away. When my brother and I visited my parents for the July Fourth holiday weekend, our worst fears were realized. My mother was wasted and pale, her bald head wrapped in a scarf, her hands shaking. I had seen those advertisements for antinausea medications featuring Grandpa or Grandma chasing grandchild on a gorgeous soft lawn. In my mother's case, the antinausea drugs were mostly ineffective. On a good day she sat in a chair, got down a bit of food and tea without vomiting, stared into space, read a few pages, drifted in and out of sleep.

Her life during chemotherapy was like pressing the Pause

button during a disaster movie when you need to use the toilet. When you return and press Play, you are right back where you left off. The plane is still going to crash; you just froze the frame for a short while. None of us who witnessed her ordeal would have called this a good quality of life, and neither did she.

"What did I do in my life to deserve this?" she asked my father. He told me this later, when it was almost over.

Moving Day, June 30, 2005, arrived in the midst of this family crisis. The real estate transaction I'd attempted had gone seriously south, which meant we'd all be moving into Will's one-bedroom apartment till we could find something else. After the moving trucks left us behind in our empty home, a couple came over with their kids, which softened the hard edges of the morning. Liza took a last swim in the pool, where she'd attempted her first doggie paddles as a three-year-old. I took a photo of her, dripping wet, her swim goggles perched on her forehead like the flying goggles of a World War I flying ace. The image captured her brave cheerfulness as we prepared to head off to a new life that very afternoon. She was losing a lot—friends, belongings we'd had to pass on, a school where she had been nurtured, and now the home she loved. She had repeatedly made it clear that she was not happy about our move.

As the afternoon drew to a close, we piled our last luggage into Will's Honda CRV. We pressed our four complaining cats into their carriers. Loaded to the rooftop, we pulled out of the driveway for the last time and headed to Brooklyn.

It was not the glorious reentry I had hoped for. I wished we were moving to the new apartment I had tried to purchase, but New York City is always a wondrous creation on a clear summer evening. We crossed the Triborough Bridge, and I admired the sparkling sunset over Manhattan. Despite my disappointment, I was happy to be home, almost ready to kiss the grimy sidewalk on Seventh Avenue.

From that first night, as we unpacked at Will's apartment, I was relieved by the possibility that I would never have to see Cathy again. I hadn't realized how pervasive her presence had been, even though I rarely saw her in town after the Halloween parade.

I had forced myself to drive by her house a week before our move. Will sat next to me as I piloted onto her street. I saw her, reading a book in her hammock, just as she'd been the July morning I had confronted her. She looked up, our eyes met. She turned away.

"There she is," I remarked sullenly to Will. *And perhaps there she will stay. Maybe now I can leave the ugly thing they did together behind me. Perhaps one day it won't be the first thing I think about as I wake each morning.*

The rest of the summer passed in a blur.

While getting Liza settled in a new school that fall, I tried to juggle parenting, work, apartment hunting, and visits to my parents, but plans frequently deteriorated—sometimes just doing the minimum was too much. During that time, it was helpful to remember that life could offer flavors other than sour and bitter.

What I had was companionship. During the first and the subsequent move and my mother's illness, Will managed to find lightness on dark days while tirelessly schlepping our stuff to and from storage units in rented vans. He parented with pleasure, eagerly attended parent-teacher conferences, and helped Liza with her math homework. While feeling upended and homeless, I also felt supported.

By December, my mother had had enough of the chemotherapy. "I don't want to play this game anymore," she remarked with gallows humor. "I don't really want to leave, but I'm ready to leave."

Her last family Christmas dinner, at our new apartment, was a bittersweet meal. At least the chemo was over. She enjoyed the lamb stew I made, a glass of good red wine, and some chocolate truffles. I hadn't seen her eat with such pleasure in months.

During a brief respite before the inevitable final decline, her hair reappeared as short gray fuzz and the color of her skin refreshed. She could walk with effort to a local restaurant, or sit on the porch of their weekend house and enjoy a summer breeze. By the end of July, she had grown weaker again, and in early August she decided she wouldn't get out of bed anymore.

She died on October 22, 2006. At the end, she was just a ghost in the bed, cared for by two hospice nurses who traded shifts during her last three months. She left peacefully, and we were grateful for that. But I still wish I could rewind the movie. In my version, she would refuse the chemotherapy and head instead to the jetway for the night flight to Paris, to enjoy a last adventure with her partner of fifty-nine years.

In the days after she died, we began looking through her drawers. I found a well-used child's toothbrush, three metal diaper pins, and two pieces of enamel jewelry I had made for her at sleepaway camp. I found a bag containing my childhood hair ribbons and the white cotton gloves she made me wear when we went to concerts or to see *The Nutcracker* at Lincoln Center. My brother found a leather tube with straps, something like a finger

glove. He recognized it after a few puzzled moments as the protective covering he wore in 1965 after I squashed his left ring finger in our toy cupboard door, "accidentally on purpose." I
remembered getting in big trouble for that one. In one of her coat
pockets, I found a small black pebble, like the ones I have collected on Maine island shores. In a yellowed plastic bag, I found
what was possibly her wedding bouquet—the dried roses disinte-
grated on contact—and a small keepsake book filled with notes in
German from friends and family in Austria. The entries were
from 1938 to 1940, dark times in Vienna. My father and I wondered how many of the signers had made it out alive; my mother's
escape with her family in 1940 was already perilous and miracu-
lous. My father said he'd never seen the book before. My mother
had her secrets, though I wish I could ask her about that little
book and her childhood friends. As a mother, I know why she
kept the eclectic mementos of her childhood and ours. As Liza
once said, memories are good, even painful ones.

During the last months of my mother's illness, my father
and I ate a good number of meals in a restaurant near their apartment. He needed time away from the sickbed.

My father, vigorous at eighty-two, is well known for his fan-
tastic memory. He remembers the scrawny sandwiches he ate at a
picnic seventy-five years ago during the depths of the Great Depression, songs and jingles from the 1940s, baseball scores from
the World Series in 1956 or any other year. So I was not surprised
to discover during one of our dinners that he had a vivid memory
of a day I had completely forgotten.

Liza was about two and a half. We'd just moved away from

Brooklyn, so this was possibly one of our first trips back to visit family. My parents met us at Grand Central Station. My father recalled his delight as he spotted Liza on the platform, running up the ramp toward him. Then he looked beyond her and saw Henry and me walking slowly behind her.

"Liza's face was so full of joy, she was running up that ramp with her arms stretched out, but you two looked so miserable," he said. "We didn't know what was going on, but we were very upset to see that."

My father told me about his growing suspicions that Henry had lost his way and that something was wrong in our marriage. My parents never spoke directly to me about their fears. For a long and happily married couple like my parents, it must have been heartbreaking to see me unhappy. And in the end, I doubt that I'd have been able to listen to them, any more than I would have been able to hear Irena's more direct evidence.

I was glad that my father remembered. His memory was now mine again. After he told me the story, I was able to recall the day, though I could not remember the fight Henry and I must have had on the train as we traveled to the city.

I was ready to see other forgotten days. I had some home movies, films Henry shot on a long-gone Hi8 camera, transferred to DVD. I was curious to see those years again, through his eyes. Me feeding Liza strained beans, me giving her a bath, the scintillating material only new parents record and view again. One clip, a bit of film I'd never watched, showed a birthday party at Cathy's house, for her daughter, Amy, who was turning four. The cake is presented, the song is sung, and Amy blows out her candles.

Packages are unwrapped to the drone of too-cheerful oohs and aahs over gifts that will soon be forgotten. Cathy winks and sticks her tongue out at Henry behind the camera. Now I could understand the body language, the suggestive glances, and Henry's coy comments. I am occasionally on camera, distracted, focused on Liza.

I was able to watch the film with the curiosity of encountering my past self. When I saw Liza in her party dress, I smiled with pleasure. I was even able look at Cathy without feeling injured.

I don't keep much of Henry out in the open. One photograph of him looking at me fondly with a blurred two-year-old Liza in the foreground is positioned discreetly on my dresser, usually well concealed behind piles of clothes I have forgotten to put away. The gold claw ring clasping a piece of coral and our wedding rings rest in my jewelry box, objects for Liza to consider when she gets older. I do cherish the copy of *Macbeth* with illustrations by Salvador Dalí, though I wonder if I shouldn't donate it to a rare books library, where more people could appreciate such a unique work. The menu he wrote for my fortieth birthday party is tacked onto the side of our refrigerator. On days when I still wonder about the nature of the love he had for me, I consider that well-planned menu. Though Henry aimed to impress my friends who attended, though he flirted with all, though Cathy was present at that gathering, I believe that the effort he put into the preparation of this meal represented a genuine love I can now appreciate without anguish.

—————

During one of my long talks with Will, early in our relationship, he said something that I knew was difficult but correct: "You have to forgive him, for us to move on together."

Forgiveness is a wonderful thing, the only truth that saves us from eating ourselves alive and causing damage to everyone we love. I continue to work on forgiveness. I do not, however, wish to forget any of this.

I cannot forget what Henry did. Nor can I forget Cathy's part in such a layered deceit, though the pathetic absurdity of the fruit salad she left in my refrigerator now summons up something softer than outrage.

I have concluded, in the aftermath of everything, that I am a terrible judge of character. My friends laugh and assume I am joking when I declare this, but it is not a laughing matter for me. The problem is those brief fits of exuberant optimism that sometimes cloud my first impressions. I won't always see through the beautiful smile, the clever remark, or the practiced gesture. I find that I need to allow myself many meetings to take the right measure of a person.

Cathy and Henry remain in my mind toxic persons, the likes of whom I hope I will never encounter again at an intimate level. I believe that I have, at last, learned to identify other such persons. I see them now at parties, in shops and restaurants, at school gatherings. I try to observe their confusion, and connect it to my own confusion as another struggling human. I can engage such people in polite conversation if required, but I do not want them in my life.

When I think about Christine, Ellen, and especially Eliana, I experience different emotions. These women briefly crossed a terrible line. They never knew me until after Henry's death. They never ate in my home or pretended to be friends. Confronted, they did not run away from me. We struggled as best we could and learned something. We were able to make changes in our lives. I am proud of the effort we made together.

On a good day, I can tell myself that Cathy is another imperfect human, for whom I can have a good deal of sincere compassion. On such a day, I can remind myself of the bottomless tragedy of Henry's choices and feel a genuine sadness that he never had the chance I received to start over. On a great day, I do not think about Cathy or Henry at all. I am doing my best, living my life, in the present moment.

Henry's idea of a perfect day was an action-packed race from waking to sleeping. He was afraid of the tedium of everyday life, with its chores and routines. Every real day, however, includes a portion of boredom.

I have struggled to resolve my own boredom through frantic mental activity or shoe shopping. In rare, blessed moments, I have understood that, with patience, boredom can lead to stillness and calm. And in calm, I can experience a meditation where I connect with my true self. I can greet myself with kindness, before I return to my work, parenting, and chores. These uncharted moments, whenever they happen, are as close as I have come to heaven.

Henry fought off every meeting with his true self, with all its flaws, contradictions, and talents. For his own sake, for Liza's, though no longer for mine, I wish he had made the attempt to see himself.

One afternoon in Brooklyn, during a surge of home-office tidying, I reencountered one of Henry's small black notebooks, among the dozen I had saved and stored in a set of work drawers, all that remains from his *umami* project. I had never read through the notebooks, but now, with effort, I deciphered lines in his looped script.

Symbols arise from the instant and continuous deterioration of sensation in the memory since first experience.

One of the urges to lie or embellish is an attempt to re-create the original intensity of sensation.

There is nothing quite so seductive for a woman as a man who is apologizing and admitting wrong.

Everyone understands this level of obsession. As Wilt Chamberlain (from an article about how they couldn't sell his house because of the stigma of his sleeping with 25,000 women) said, "We tend to get addicted to our activities so you better make sure you love what you do."

All important activities are addictions, otherwise they wouldn't be important.

Henry had made his choice to go for the extremes, to try to re-capture first-time experience every day. But he might have lived a longer life if he had been able to take more pleasure from every-day activities, the scintillating thrills of real love, the heart-opening delights of parenthood, the occasional flashes of success in work life. I do not agree with Henry's view that "all important activities are addictions," not to mention that the rare occasions of his apologies were hardly turn-ons. We cannot experience *umami* in every moment—that would be like a heroin addict finding the magic potion for an ever more ecstatic high—but we can remain open to "perfect" moments and appreciate them when they appear, perhaps more so from a place of calm.

On an unseasonably mild day in early January 2006, Will and Liza decided to take a bike ride in Prospect Park with Molly, one of her new school friends, and Molly's father. I had just returned from a yoga class and was swallowing the first bites of a hastily made tuna sandwich when I received a call.

"Mama," Liza reported with admirable calm, "Will fell off his bike, the ambulance is coming."

Dropping my sandwich on the plate, I grabbed my coat and ran up to the park in time to find two EMS workers prepping Will for the waiting ambulance. He was strapped onto a stretcher, his neck in a plastic brace, his face smeared with blood and road dirt. Fresh blood oozed from a one-inch-long gash on his left cheek. My head felt light, my stomach queasy. I hoped it was because I hadn't finished lunch. I took Liza aside to comfort her and to ask her more about what she had seen.

"Is Liza okay?" Will kept asking.

"She's fine, don't worry," I reassured him. Liza did seem remarkably calm.

"Mama," Liza said, "Will didn't recognize me right away after he fell. He sat up and asked me who I was." This suggested that he'd had a concussion, though I comforted myself that at least he knew her name now.

Molly had been riding with her father a quarter mile ahead on the bike path. They'd stopped, waiting for Will and Liza to catch up. When no one appeared, they turned back and were now able to take Liza home with them while I boarded the ambulance. Molly's mom called on my cell, offering to meet me at the hospital later. I got into the ambulance.

Will was still rambling. "Is Liza okay?"

"She's fine, please don't worry."

"Is Liza okay?"

The siren whooped and wailed. The ambulance surged forward into Brooklyn traffic as I glanced at the wall clock. It was 2:00 P.M.

"Sir," I asked with a sudden shudder, "what's the date?"

"January eighth, ma'am, for the rest of the day," he replied, looking up from the forms attached to his clipboard. "You don't happen to know his social, do ya?"

Will rattled off his social security number.

"Hey," the EMS worker said with a chuckle, "you in the military or something?" He began asking Will questions—name, rank, and serial number. Will got through most of it, remembering his office telephone number but stumbling for a moment over our new apartment address. This was good news. He might have had a concussion, but it looked like he'd be fine. The bad news was, I'd forgotten the date. Will had fallen from his bike on the third anniversary of the hour and day of Henry's departure. Now I really felt light-headed.

After my earlier encounters with Henry following his death, I took a pragmatic approach to the afterlife. Spirits might not make sense, but I'd had experiences that had felt real enough. We'd forgotten his day. This time Henry wasn't a kitchen spirit encouraging me to salt a steak before cooking. He was pissed off.

After a night of hospital observation and more than twenty stitches around his left nostril, under his left cheekbone, and inside his lower lip, Will began a speedy recovery. He remained cheerful during the three days he took off from work, padding around the house, his wounds and road rash covered with a mask of newfangled bandages we bought to help heal without scarring—the

Phantom of the Opera. By week's end, Will was back at his office with just one bandage over his cheek. He looked like the feisty boxer he'd been as an adolescent—bruised but ready for another round.

When we returned to the site of the accident, there were no potholes. Will was an expert cyclist; he'd been riding the Prospect Park loop for years. When Liza described the accident again for me, she said his bike had just stopped and he'd flown straight forward. It could have been some mechanical failure, but I had my own opinion: Henry was jealous of Will's new dad status.

Will didn't think much of my haunting theory. He started singing the theme song from *Ghostbusters,* which made me laugh but didn't change my mind about what had happened. I knew the angry Henry better than he did.

I felt wary in our apartment, wondering what calamity would happen next. Would Henry drop a pot on my head from the overhead rack as I washed dishes at the sink? Would I trip and fall down the stairs? I needed a housecleaner, so to speak.

I wrote to Eliana. She didn't think I was crazy. She said there were people I could find to help with this kind of "energy" problem. I lived in Park Slope—not California but still a New Age mecca; there had to be someone here who wouldn't laugh at me.

When I sheepishly mentioned my predicament to a neighborhood friend, she told me, to my surprise, that she'd once hired a woman to visit her house for what was termed a "spiritual cleansing." She e-mailed me the contact information. A week later a sprite of a woman appeared at my door. She said that before she became a spiritual healer she'd been an attorney. With thoughtful, no-nonsense movements, she filled a spray bottle with kitchen tap water, chanted prayers, and then walked through the apartment spraying water here and there, whispering more quiet prayers. "He was here," she remarked calmly as she peered into the corners of the living room, as if confirming that Henry was no longer huddled behind the couch. "It's not good when they linger. He needed help moving on."

Yes, yes, move on, please move on.

"Now you will find that this home will feel refreshed and you will work well here," she said. We hugged. She thanked me as she accepted my check and left. I wasn't sure what had happened, but as I watched her walk down the stairs of my front stoop, I felt better already.

January 8, 2007, passed peacefully. I had found happiness and productivity in our new home. I purchased a Yahrzeit memorial candle from the grocery store; Liza and I had a quiet moment together. I hoped that if Henry dropped in for a visit from his astral plane, he would observe our family life and leave us in peace.

the present moment

"Do you not believe in heaven, Mr. Fielding, may I ask?"
she said, looking at him shyly.
"I do not. Yet I believe that honesty gets us there."

—E. M. FORSTER,
A Passage to India

Even at twenty-two, long before frantic motherhood and the onset of pre-senior moments, I worried about losing memories and the sensations that fix them in place. When it comes to pre-serving love's fragile, clear moments, sometimes the only thing we get to keep is an image, as fleeting as the splashes of light on curling waves.

I was with Paolo, a man I loved, in Italy, on a sailboat in the Mediterranean waters of the Cinque Terre. A friend had invited him for a week's sail, and he'd stopped back in the town where I was still staying, persuading me to join him for a few days, though it meant changing my return flight to New York.

We'd met two years earlier, at the beginning of my college junior year in France, and we formed an immediate, though not

easily nameable connection. I spent time with him during that
school year, wrote to him when I returned to campus for my senior year. A year after graduation, I traveled back to see him for
the few weeks that ended in this boat trip.

Once, while we walked the curved shore, lined with colorfully painted houses and swaying palm trees, he said, *"Ci sposi-
amo?"* I thought he was teasing me and didn't answer. I knew
what the words meant, though I had never heard anyone say
them. *Sposare,* to marry. *Ci,* the first-person plural reflexive pronoun. "Shall we marry?"

In the end we never spoke much about the nature of our relationship. He had a real girlfriend in Torino, where he wintered, a
popular arrangement for many of the men he knew. As the weeks
passed, I wished for the courage to fight for something more
nameable, but I was afraid that the fragile thing we had would
shatter like a wineglass hitting a terra-cotta-tiled floor.

I woke up early in the forward sleeping cabin to the sound of the
clanking halyard on the mast and the gentle sway of the boat.
Paolo was still sleeping next to me, his body curved into a half-
moon shape. I was going home that afternoon, returning to my
life in New York, whatever that would be. Paolo hadn't asked me
to stay in Italy. I knew he wouldn't do that. I also knew that staying in Italy would be more difficult than learning the language
well and finding work. The cultural divide was huge and might
overwhelm me completely. Life in the Italy I knew always looked
romantic, but I'd seen plenty of unhappy young American women
that summer with their Italian men and thought, *That could be me,
too far from home.* I didn't think Paolo's hovering mother would
want an American daughter-in-law. I was what some people

of my parents' generation referred to as a "goddamn women's libber."

Paolo was not the kind of man that most women would call beautiful. He was thin and wiry, with ropy muscles, the kind of guy who has to drink high-calorie protein shakes to keep on weight. His hair was already receding at thirty, leaving a prominent forehead patched here and there with a few short, tumbleweed curls on an otherwise barren, tawny desert. His face had a carved quality, with the angular cheeks and down-curved nose of a much older man. He wore a short, dark beard and mustache that tickled when we kissed. When we walked hand in hand, I could feel the bony knuckles of his muscled hands and the bitten fingernails he worried when a cigarette wasn't handy. His best friend called him *"bruttino,"* an affectionate form of the adjective "ugly."

I looked at his sleeping self with tenderness. This was the man I wanted, this man. I could not have explained why. At twenty-two, I couldn't truly explain why I did anything. I was old enough, however, to imagine the immediate future.

Later, in the afternoon, Paolo would take me to the station in Monterosso, where I would purchase the cardboard train ticket I have kept all these years. I would travel back alone to Santa Margherita, pack my bags, take the overnight train to Paris, and fly home to New York. *We will never be in bed together again.* He would return to Torino, to his teaching job. I would find a job, and we would proceed through our separate lives. One day he would marry his girlfriend in Torino, and maybe I'd meet somebody I loved as much as this man and marry him. I did not want to forget this morning, the last of its kind.

The sun rose. A shaft of yellow light pierced though the porthole, forming an elongated triangle of yellow on his back. *I will remember this triangle of light. I will save this moment in the triangle of light.*

Paolo walked me from the harbor to the train station. We stood on the platform quietly. I saw the train approaching, on time, this one accursed day. He turned toward me, hugged and kissed me.

I clung to his neck, then released him, unable to speak.

"Allora, ci sentiamo," he said, as if we'd be chatting the next day.

I told him I loved him.

"Anch'io ti amo," he said with a smile. His lips pressed against mine, his beard tickled my mouth and cheek.

Then I was gone on the train.

Twenty-six years later, the memory remains vivid and well formed.

There are, in the end, moments from my life with Henry I want to keep, moments, like that triangle of light, that were true. A morning walking to work, a few months after we'd met, when I understood that I loved him and that he loved me. Our walk together across the great Nyika Plateau in Malawi, when all things still seemed magnificently possible. The exhausted morning of Liza's birth, his blissed face as he held her tiny, perfect body.

But more and more days pass now when I forget Henry. I find that I think almost every day about other people I have lost through death or parting: my mother, Henry's aunt Rose, a man I knew in the 1980s—not even a close friend—who died of AIDS, my friend Jim from the island in Maine, and Emily, with whom I have not spoken in several years. In living too much for himself, Henry missed the point of living for others. I am sorry that Henry cannot live through me in an everyday way, that his daughter alone bears that quiet burden. Though for the duration of this writing, Henry has been my frequent companion, watching me, even as I type.

I never forget to salt the meat. But I am ready to let him go.

I took a big chance and told Liza about her father's affairs while we were in Maine this past summer. She listened quietly.

"Are you happy he died?" she asked. What a question for an eleven-year-old child to ask, but of course it was the obvious question, one that deserved an answer.

"What happened to your father was a tragedy. He made some big mistakes in his life, and he died without having a chance to do better, to apologize. He did great harm to you and to me, though he loved us."

"Do you think you would've gotten a divorce?"

"I don't think we would've been able to stay married. So, I'm happy to have a chance to make a new life for us, but it's terrible that he died the way he did." I hoped I didn't sound like a politician at a televised debate, artfully dodging. "I hope that answers your question."

Liza nodded thoughtfully.

I recently received a letter from a woman named Avery, who met Henry in February 2002, during his traveling research year. I'd made contact with Avery through the friend he'd stayed with during that week in Northern California, who told me that Avery had something important to share with me. Avery and I talked on the phone, and then she sent me an e-mail describing her brief and unusual encounter with Henry at a dinner party:

The party was delightful, filled with family, friends, laughter and music. I sang "My Romance" and then I sat in the living room to take in the rest of the evening. I sat next to Henry who did not occupy a large space and wore his black jacket zipped all the way to his chin. I remember thinking that this was odd as it was quite warm in the house. Funny, the things we remember when we study our memories for answers.

We exchanged names and handshakes and listened to the music for a while. He said that he was an author and deeply passionate about food, here to visit with his friend while also visiting restaurants in San Francisco to interview famous chefs.

I politely smiled and asked questions about his family. I like to know more about a person's life and family since it is the center of my life. I was at the time and continue to be happy in a loving and fulfilling marriage, a mother of two daughters. He said that he had a beautiful and successful wife and an adorable little girl who was the light of his life, then showed me photographs. We continued our conversation and walked outside, as I was planning to head home early. Henry asked if there was a good place to run in the area. I said that I was planning to run in the morning at the reservoir and invited him to join me. We met at 10 A.M. the next day for a 5 miler. I could not keep pace with him, so he ran around once to catch me on the second lap. It was time for me to slow down a bit, so we walked.

That is when his story began to trickle out. He asked if he could tell me something and wanted my opinion. He said that he loved his wife, then he added something about not being sure he was a good partner but he knew he was a good father.

I remember thinking, "Wow, what am I going to do with this?"

Then he mentioned this other woman/friend in town who had made herself available, who'd never put any pressure on him, with whom he had been having an affair for a quite a while.

I asked him if he loved her.

He said, "No."

I said something like, "What about a life code . . . how do people do that and sleep at night?"

He said that he had trouble sleeping and was trying to leave this woman but, recently it had turned very sour and he had discovered that she was violent, unstable and had even threatened to harm him and/or his family if he stopped seeing her.

"I feel trapped," he said. "I am afraid of what might happen if I stop seeing this other woman."

I asked if you knew about the affair. He said that he didn't think so. I told him that no matter what is truth, it was important that he was brave enough to make a decision to change and preserve what was most important in his life, his family. Perhaps he was not brave enough to choose.

We stopped for a sandwich and I told him that I thought he should tell you everything if he believed that the two of you had something special and strong enough to overcome this challenge. I also suggested that he talk to a lawyer and if necessary, face this woman with legal counsel to protect himself and his family.

His phone rang a couple of times while we were having lunch. He said it was "her."

I suggested that he just come right out and tell her that he didn't have the energy to be what she needed right now, that it was a mistake and he regretted any pain that he caused, but that he needed to go back to his family.

Henry said that he was afraid you would not understand and might refuse to take him back.

I encouraged him to believe in you and that he would not know if he didn't try.

He said, "I'm like a spider caught in its own web."

He asked if there were any shops nearby, he wanted to pick up something for his daughter. I suggested that if he had time we could drive into town where there are some cute shops for kids. So, off we drove, in two cars. We found something sweet for your daughter and then walked into the Indian Artisan shop next door. Henry handed me a thin silver bracelet with instructions to try it on. I balked but he insisted, thanking me for being an honest friend. Although the clasp broke, I felt that I should not throw it away. I will be honored to send it to you, if you like.

So, we hugged and went our separate ways. I wished him good luck and asked him to stay in touch. I did not hear from him at all. I suppose we won't ever really know what happened and I am sorry for your loss. But, if Henry was so torn and tortured in his heart and mind, perhaps his spirit knew that he could not exist that way.

How sad . . . to have known him and have been chosen to "see" him like this. Although, I have learned to be a better friend to my friends by asking more questions and demanding truth when they are struggling . . .

Please feel free to ask me any more questions. I would like to have been a friend and known you then as well, so that I could have called you, for I felt that I did not want to mind my own business. Perhaps then it might have been a story with a different ending. I often wonder why we are chosen to share pieces of other lives. Thank you for trusting me to share this with you.

Fondly,

A.

––––––––––

Will and I went down to City Hall one Friday morning to become domestic partners. Our reasons were entirely practical.

He had good health insurance, while mine was costing me an arm and a leg, and involved monthly arguments with the friendly folks in the Claims Department. Needless to say, the Bush administration was not going to help me out here. However, Will convinced his employer to expand coverage to opposite-sex domestically partnered couples.

We were directed to the dingy, fluorescent-lit waiting room on the second floor. We filled out our forms, looking up from our task to watch other couples, who unlike us (we'd shown up in our jeans) were preparing for their big moment in wedding attire— white dresses, bouquets, tuxedos, corsages, the whole nine yards. When the clerk summoned us to his little window, we handed over our paperwork. The clerk asked a few questions, looked over our drivers' licenses and utility bills. He asked us the required question: "Do you have any other domestic partners?" We laughed over that one, signed the forms, and the clerk stamped the forms and handed us an official document announcing our new status.

"We're done?" I asked, expecting something a bit more dramatic. "That's it?"

"That's it," the clerk replied with a smile.

And yet, I felt surprisingly changed as Will and I walked away from City Hall in search of a quick lunch on Court Street. After a lot of mess and misfortune, I felt lucky. Though it might be, as Will remarked between gooey bites of hot pizza, that we make our own luck and that he himself felt just as lucky. In any event, we'd made a commitment. Now we were a for-real family.

I heard the subway train singing one morning. As the brakes released on the Number 2 train at Atlantic Avenue, I distinctly registered the first three notes of "Somewhere" from *West Side Story*, drawn out, longingly.

Transfixed, I wondered if this performance was just for me, a one-time fluke. None of the other travelers seemed to notice. The next time I rode the train, I heard the song again. I had to smile because that melody could not be more appropriate for me, the prodigal daughter, returned home to the city I tried to leave.

It's true that the Big Apple doesn't exactly roll out the welcome-home mat. I had to develop my urban body shield and reawaken the third eye. Not the one you hear about in yoga class, the one in the center of your forehead. I'm talking about the one in the back of your head. For a few months, I was constantly bumping into people and lampposts until I relearned the refined Manhattan pedestrian ballet. I had to teach Liza some serious street smarts so she could deal with crazy Brooklyn traffic on Union Street.

But the city and I, we are good friends again now. At the last minute, she threw me a life preserver and reeled me back home. Gowanus might not be as gorgeous as the Hudson River view I left behind, but on a springtime walk home from downtown Brooklyn, the late afternoon sun hits the warehouse windows on Union and Bond, and the Kentile Floors sign shimmers and flares in the distance. Liza and I hold hands as we cross the Union Street Bridge, admiring the improbably lush princess trees in full flower perched over the canal. A lone seagull floats high above us on a salty breeze, squawking and kibitzing. On days like this, I think to myself, *this is the place for us.*

It's Saturday night at Hope & Anchor, a vaguely sailor-themed restaurant-nightspot on Red Hook's main drag. We are out for a family-friendly night on the town with Liza's friends and their parents. The kids are finishing plates of macaroni and cheese; we grown-ups are polishing off a jumble of Asian noodle salad and pierogi. I am anticipating an ample wedge of truly evil chocolate cake. I squish the lime down the neck of my Corona, where it bobs like a buoy on a fisherman's line (as the late, great comic Mitch Hedberg liked to say, I have been "saved by the buoyancy of citrus"). My child is no longer wide-eyed shocked, merely intrigued and delighted by our MC, a cocoa-skinned drag queen named Dropsy, nearly seven feet tall (including the blond Afro wig), busting out of a black spangled minidress, who strides to the microphone in black platform boots to lead us in karaoke. She opens the set crooning "Sitting on the Dock of the Bay" in a breathy falsetto. Our kids—Dropsy calls them the "Hope & Anchor Children's Choir"—are waiting to sing their recent favorite: Queen's "Bohemian Rhapsody." The audience claps and whoops its approval. The waiter arrives with my slice of chocolate cake. I don't think it gets much better than this, at least not with a PG-13 rating.

――――――

After years apart, Irena and I live just five blocks from each other. Despite Henry's earlier attempts to undermine our friendship, it's almost like the good old days. There was a time, years earlier, when we all lived in adjoining brownstone buildings, our backyard gardens separated by a fence we vaulted using an old kitchen stepladder. In those days, we'd hang out in our gardens after a freelance workday indoors, form spontaneous dinner plans depending on what either of our refrigerators contained. Our cats wandered back and forth under the fence while we organized the menu. Irena's eight-year-old daughter (now in college) would entertain Liza, who was just an infant. Finally, Henry might grill a steak and rummage for a bottle of wine, Irena might make an expert pasta dish and discover another bottle. A salad might get tossed with the mingled contents of our crisper drawers. Other friends and family might appear. We'd eat here or there, we'd sit around the table till Liza fell asleep on my lap.

That era when we were young with nothing but time is certainly over. But once in a while, we have idle afternoon hours together. When our new apartment proved too small for four cats, Irena and her partner graciously adopted my old cat Katie, who spent her golden years in the paradise of their elegant apartment, napping on refinished Danish midcentury modern. When I visit Irena, we muse on survival—old Katie cat's and ours, and the many twists and turns that have brought us back together.

"No, Mr. Smarty-Pants," I retort, directing a nicely crisped *frite* at Eliot's grinning face, "I am not going to write up the nitty-gritty of our one and only date. And don't be looking so hurt."

Every few months, on a day when my friend Eliot, now happily married, travels to the city for work, we eat lunch together. At a bistro table, everyone is the same size.

Today, I get to hear about the time he met Patrick Stewart (one of my celebrity crushes), who had finished a voice-over for a company sales presentation. Following the recording session, Stewart invited him for afternoon refreshments—tea, Earl Grey, hot—just like he did on *Star Trek: The Next Generation*.

Eliot listens while I yammer on about the latest book I've read. I've been rereading my favorite E. M. Forster novels—most recently, *A Passage to India*. The Marabar caves will always be a mystery for me, though after this reading, I can imagine the darkness in which Adela Quested experiences her flash of terrifying self-awareness.

Over the last mouthfuls of strawberries and cream, Eliot and I compare notes on our respective partnerships. He tells me about his rose garden, and we share weird pet stories (the time his dog impaled his chin on a bone tops all).

"So, Jools, can I be in your next book?" he asks.

The bill arrives, and we split the check with our business cards. I am pretty sure this lunch qualifies as a legit tax deduction.

Anna and I live just a few streets from each other in Brooklyn. We still share many things, including our handsome dentist (if you have to sit in the wretched chair, at least you should have something pleasant to look at). We call on each other when we have troubles—professional, personal, or, as it sometimes turns out, imagined. Her forceful "I hear ya, sister!" always snaps me out of my gloominess. On in-sync days, we find ourselves in the same yoga class, sipping a coffee together on the bench outside a local food shop, or eating takeout together with our kids at her kitchen table.

Her red hair has never looked more vibrant than at her recent birthday party, a gathering of eight women at a large round table in a downtown Manhattan restaurant, where we ordered extravagantly, right through dessert, "one of everything" being the guiding principle.

Living in the city is never easy, but for both of us it makes sense, at least for now. While we pursue our separate work and

love lives, there is an abiding comfort in talking about our children's difficulties and successes, and making future plans.

––––––––––––

I still correspond with Eliana. Her interest in my life feels authentic, and I often find myself thinking about her in idle moments.
I consider her a most unusual sort of friend, mostly unknown and
unknowable to me, but feel strongly that we wish each other well.

In the most recent photo she sent me, I couldn't help thinking
how much we have both changed. Her black clothing is long
gone, replaced with more colorful choices. Her light eyes engage
and sparkle without heavy makeup, and her hair, shorter and
lighter now, blows about in a breeze. She looks relaxed and open.
I wonder if I'll ever meet her again; I'd like to be able to thank her
in person for her openness with me.

Eliana and her partner married in June 2007. I am glad that at
least one of us has that kind of optimistic faith in traditional ritu-
als, though I imagine her wedding was anything but staid.

Liza says she doesn't care if Will and I get married. "That'd
be okay, I guess. But I get to pick out your wedding dress and go
on the honeymoon with you." She's too old now to be a flower
girl. She'll probably insist on being a bridesmaid, and I can't imagine a better choice.

––––––––––––

Will, Liza, and I go on a spring break vacation in Tulum,
Mexico, where we are sleeping in a platform tent in a national
park. A steady wind has brought us a week of brilliant blue skies.

As dusk approaches, a bank of low-hanging, dark clouds hovers on the horizon, still a safe distance away.

We have made friends during this week with a man named Doug and his daughter, Savanna, who both seemed relieved to discover that we are not the perfect nuclear family we first appear to be.

"Do y'all live together then?" seven-year-old Savanna asked in her Southern lilt, after hearing me refer to Will as my "boyfriend."

"Yes," I replied cheerfully, "we're a funny little family, we none of us have the same last name."

Doug nodded with the wisdom of one who has already been entangled in some of life's complicated unhappiness and has emerged bruised but intact. "Whatever works," he said.

"Indeed," I replied.

Doug, Savanna, Will, and Liza play in the surf, two dads helping two daughters out to the curling waves, to catch the sweet spot for the big boogie board ride in—big in kid terms, of course, and too big for me. I am fully dressed in a top and skirt, with a sweater even, against the breeze, watching from the safety of the sand with delight as my brave girl and Savanna return again and again, riding waves that would intimidate me.

The dark clouds edge closer, the wind bends the palm trees. I have seen that curved form of trees and these saturated colors of whipped sea and sky. In a painting—*The Coming Storm* by Winslow Homer.

I wave my arms vigorously in the universal maternal sign of distress. Will looks toward me and smiles, graciously acknowledging another of my many frantic mom moments.

Within half an hour, our children washed and changed, big lightning flashes as bright as noon over the sea and the nearby lagoon, and the first large drops patter on windows and the concrete terrace of the restaurant where we are seated. By then we adults are happily downing fresh margaritas, wondering if our bungalow-size tent will be dry when we return (we forgot to close the flaps) but not worrying enough to dilute any joy in the fresh fish tacos our waiter brings to the table. The local tawny-colored lizards have joined us in the safety of the restaurant, arrayed across the walls and ceiling. It is good to feel safe and cared for.

My relationship with Will continues to evolve. It is nothing like the love affairs of my younger life, which featured longing and desperation. It is nothing like my marriage with Henry. What we strive for is the kind and loving embrace that allows each of us to feel cherished, think clearly, and possibly make some decent choices. Amid the thousand moments that keep the machinery of daily life moving forward, I welcome the bursts of love and lust that overtake me, like the first sip of a rich red wine, while walking through a subway corridor, inspecting oranges at the grocery store, or waking up to see his blue eyes looking into mine. This is my idea of *umami*.

Liza told me sheepishly that when she was "little" (because of course she is not that anymore) she thought whenever you put a disc in a CD player, the musicians were playing live, just for you. She confessed that this understanding changed one day when she was four, when I told her, while we listened to the Beatles' *Sgt. Pepper's Lonely Hearts Club Band*, how sorry I was that John Lennon was dead.

This was a useful moment in understanding the magical thinking and self-centeredness of children, as well as a good number of adults. And yet, sometimes we all need to feel that we are the live performance. There are times when we must take the stage to make choices, the best ones we can. We must make an effort, whether the audience is twenty thousand screaming fans at Madison Square Garden, the smaller world of our family, or just our solitary observant self.

I have seen that wisdom can come from unexpected sources. I have learned from my daughter's honesty and insight. I've appreciated the guidance of my family, my old friends, and new ones I've made during this journey. I've also found that the surreal, comic, erotic, and even terrifying moving images of my sleeping hours can reveal the concerns of my life with startling clarity. This recent dream seems to express my strong desire to embrace change and my fear about doing just that.

I am in my old neighborhood on Manhattan's Upper West Side. I know this even though the streets do not look the same and there are no street signs. I am walking on what feels like West End Avenue, stone-cobbled, as it was during my childhood, heading off to meet my mother somewhere. I have dressed with care, in a grown-up uniform: trim brown skirt, brown jacket, and brown leather pumps. I am carrying what I hope is a ladylike brown handbag. Everything matches.

Suddenly, an open, stone-paved plaza appears, filled with rows and rows of large corrugated boxes, an array that seems endless and expanding. The boxes are heaped high with shoes.

My hands shake, my palms are sweating. I want the shoes. The temptation is too great, despite worry about keeping my mother waiting. There are hundreds of choices to make—so many shoes in countless colors. I reach for the scent of the warm, tanned leathers. I throw off my plain brown leather pumps, step bravely away from the security of my handbag, and rush up and down the rows of boxes. Eagerly, I start trying on shoes, first in matched pairs; then, in my haste, I carelessly seize lefts and rights from different pairs.

When I remember, with a startle, to look for my handbag, all the boxes of shoes vanish just as suddenly as they appeared. My handbag and my original pair of brown shoes have also vanished. I am standing alone in the empty plaza with just the mismatched shoes on my feet—two unsuccessful experiments of entirely different heel heights, one a high sandal in peacock blue, the other a too-pointy pump in saffron orange. I feel a pang of filial anxiety—this isn't how I planned it. I have no cell phone to call my mom. I'm late and I look ridiculous and now my mom will be worried or mad or both. I tell myself that I will have to go meet her just as I am, arriving late, looking like a lopsided clown. Later, there will be time to cancel credit cards and buy a new wallet. I try to reassure myself with words Will says to me when I feel overwhelmed by daily life's frustrations (computer problems, work deadlines, disputes with our landlord): "What's the worst that could happen?" Typically, the short answer is, nothing life threatening, financially ruinous, or even scary.

Still considering the absurdity of my situation, I watch, amazed, as the blue and orange shoes begin to transform. They shimmer and whirl through colors till they are both the green shade of fresh-picked olives, ripe, juicy, and savory. One is still a sandal, and the other a closed shoe, but the heel heights are roughly the same. I hear footsteps—my own—as I make my first wobbly efforts across the paved stones of the open courtyard. The shoes continue to change as I take more confident steps. I can do this. I can go meet my mother now. It won't be so bad. I am beginning to embrace my awkwardness.

The sandal straps expand and stretch over my toes as my

eyelids flutter open and the dream slips away, my sleepy eyes taking in the ceiling of my bedroom, a familiar cool and placid white. Will stirs next to me with a sigh, rearranging his pillow. Liza appears in the doorway. She comes closer for a hug, then rushes off, ready for morning cartoons, pancakes, and the rest of our Saturday. I linger in bed for another moment, enjoying the warmth as Will drapes his arm around me. Maybe these new shoes, mismatched but magically changing, will turn out to be a perfect fit.

Acknowledgments

I would like to thank:

—My family and all the friends old and new, near and far, who have watched over me while I rebuilt my life.

—Anna, for sharing the journey; Sara and Irena, for our many years; Tomas, for being there; Eliot, for making me laugh; Eliana and Avery, for their trust.

—My amazing agent, Elaine Markson, for embracing me from the beginning with unwavering affection and confidence.

—Everyone I have worked with at Voice/Hyperion: Ellen Archer, Pamela Dorman, Barbara Jones, Sarah Landis, Laura Klynstra, Susan M.S. Brown, Claire McKean, Christine Ragasa, and interior designer Sue Walsh. Your enthusiasm and hard work on my behalf have been an inspiration.

—Jeffrey Davis, for getting me organized.

—Jill Herzig at *Glamour*, for putting me to work (nothing like learning to write on deadline . . .).

—Don Symons, Ph.D., for our conversations, correspondence, and his evolved sense of humor.

—Jofie Ferrari-Adler, for his support.

—Cynthia, for our talks about *Jane Eyre*.

—Elizabeth Gilbert, for her generous help and advice.

—Scott Adkins, and my other colleagues at The Brooklyn Writer's Space.

—Clark, for bravely deploying his Number Two pencil on every draft; Leah, Leigh, and Suzanne, for reading the many re-writes; my other wonderful readers, for taking time to share their ideas.

—Monica, for helping me to keep all the balls in the air while I wrote this book.

—Sarah T., for keeping my feet on the ground.

—My yoga teachers, for leading me through this time of change. *Namaste.*

—My wise and patient daughter, for teaching me something new every day.

—Clark (again), for becoming, on short notice, a great father and true companion. I love our excellent new family.

Finally, I would like to thank The MacDowell Colony for an invaluable fellowship. At Wood Studio I truly found a room of my own.